When Alan Bond won the America's Cup in 1983, Australia celebrated and welcomed him as a hero. Now, eight years later, the nation's most famous entrepreneur has become almost a villain. His empire is in ruins, he faces the threat of bankruptcy, and a special investigation is about to pass judgement on his business dealings.

The Rise and Fall of Alan Bond is the story of how we made this man a hero and why he fell from grace.

It is also the story of an era—when Greed was Good; when banks blindly lent billions of dollars to Australia's high-flying entrepreneurs to build their paper empires.

Smiling, loud-mouthed, uncomplicated, almost always cheerful, Alan Bond was a rags-to-riches success, a role model for young Australians. The poor immigrant-turned-signwriter who became a multi-millionaire was living proof that, for those who worked hard and believed in themselves, Australia was the land of opportunity.

But there was another Alan Bond—the one who didn't care a damn for the rules, the one who manufactured profits, the one who paid himself massive fees for services of doubtful value.

Award-winning ABC-TV *Four Corners* reporter Paul Barry made headlines in 1989 with his dramatic revelations about Bond Corporation's business deals and its Cook Islands tax schemes. Now he traces Alan Bond's scramble to the top of the pile, how he plundered his public companies and how the banks and corporate regulators let him do it.

But *The Rise and Fall of Alan Bond* is not just about a business empire; it is about the man and what drives him on. It is about a boy who longed to see his name in lights, who was desperate to be accepted by the establishment, who wanted to be Sir Alan.

A lot of myths have evolved around Alan Bond—about his background, his education, his early business career. Now, after extensive research in Australia, the United Kingdom and America, Paul Barry has sorted the fact from the fiction. By talking to Bond's schoolmates, teachers, relatives, and early business partners, he reveals the man whose father used to say: "Alan will either become the richest man in Australia or end up in Fremantle jail."

WHAT THE
PAPERS SAID

"It's more than just a look at the man, the America's Cup winner, and the corporate raider. It looks at an era of arrogant paper giants—those chosen few who borrowed billions and are now called to account. Barry's book is excellent..."

Sunday Mail

"**The Rise and Fall of Alan Bond** tells you most of the things you always wanted to know about big business but didn't really want to find out."

City Independent

"Paul Barry... has written this very readable, and illuminating, account of the rags-to-riches immigrant signwriter who became a multi-millionaire."

Saturday Mercury

"This book is the best thing that has ever been written about Alan Bond. It is a lively, well-researched and authoritative account of the public and private lives of the man who is the quintessential Aussie entrepreneur."

West Australian

"It is difficult to read **The Rise and Fall of Alan Bond** without feelings of disgust and outrage... The Bond saga doesn't suggest there was too much morality at work among the people who helped him to do the deals."

Sun, Melbourne

"The intriguing aspect is that Alan Bond comes across as a super-salesman, a man so confident and aggressive that he could persuade banks and governments to help him without apparently inquiring into the validity of his claims. The disturbing aspect is that a personality like his should wield such power in corporate Australia."

Canberra Times

"...Paul Barry tackles many of the myths and exposes them as lies or at least half truths...

The picture that emerges instead is that of a master salesman living on the edge, taking risks that only occasionally paid off but also possessing an almost uncanny ability to pass off his failures."

The Herald, Melbourne

"This book is about excrescences. Excrescences on the corporate skin of Australia, the good the bad and the unspeakable."

The News

"Barry...packs 292 pages with details of Bond's business deals and lifestyle."

Daily News

About the Author

Paul Barry was born in England and educated at Sevenoaks School and Oxford University where he took a First in Politics, Philosophy and Economics. He worked as economics editor for a British financial magazine before moving to BBC TV as a reporter for *Newsnight* and *Panorama*. In 1987 he came to Sydney to work for ABC TV's *Four Corners* where his films have won several prizes including a prestigious Penguin Award for his 1989 investigation of Alan Bond's business affairs, "Bondy's Bounty". He is married with three children. *The Rise and Fall of Alan Bond* is his first book.

The Rise and Fall of Alan Bond

Paul Barry

BANTAM BOOKS
SYDNEY • AUCKLAND • TORONTO • NEW YORK • LONDON

ABC
BOOK

THE RISE AND FALL OF ALAN BOND
A BANTAM BOOK

Printing History

First published in Australia by Transworld Publishers in
association with the Australian Broadcasting Corporation in 1990,
reprinted 1990, 1991
This revised edition printed 1991, reprinted 1992, 1993, 1994, 1995

National Library of Australia
Cataloguing-in-Publication entry
Barry, Paul, 1952–

    The rise and fall of Alan Bond.

    Rev. ed.
    ISBN 1 86359 037 4.

    1. Bond, Alan, 1938 –   . 2. Businessmen – Australia –
    Biography. 3. Millionaires – Australia – Biography. I. Title.

338.61092

Published in Australia by Transworld Publishers (Australia) Pty
Limited, 15–25 Helles Ave, Moorebank NSW 2170 in association
with the Australian Broadcasting Corporation, 150 William Street,
Sydney, NSW, 2001, and in New Zealand by Transworld Publishers
(NZ) Limited, 3 William Pickering Drive, Albany, New Zealand and
in the United Kingdom by Transworld Publishers (UK) Limited,
61–63 Uxbridge Road, Ealing London W5 5SA.

Cover design by Denese Cunningham
Text designed by Trevor Hood
Cover illustration by Peter Bollinger from a
photograph by Evan Collis
Picture research by Joanna Collard
Computer setting by Global Graphics, NSW
Printed in Australia by McPhersons Printing Group, Maryborough,
Victoria
10 9 8 7 6 5

Contents

Prologue

It was 7.55 on a November evening in 1987, barely three weeks after the October stockmarket crash had wiped billions of dollars off share prices around the world and sent the rich running for cover. Outside, on the streets of Manhattan, it was dark and cold, but in the warmth of Sotheby's New York saleroom the lights were ablaze, as the largest crowd the auction house had ever seen awaited the sale of Lot 25, *Irises*, by Van Gogh. There were 2300 people, and more than a hundred members of the press, hoping to see the records broken, but some were afraid the sale would be a disaster. Plenty of preliminary work had been done: *Irises* had even been sent on a world tour to drum up interest from potential bidders. But there could hardly have been a worse time to sell such a valuable painting. There was fear of a 1930s-style Depression in the air, talk of the rich being wiped out in the crash. Surely no one in their right mind would spend many millions of dollars on a piece of art at a time like this.

Upstairs in Sotheby's boardroom, looking down on the hubbub in the saleroom below, one man was too nervous even to watch. For years *Irises* had hung above the mantelpiece in the sitting room of John Whitney Payson's Fifth Avenue apartment. Now, come 1987, with Van Gogh's *Sunflowers* selling earlier in the year for US$40 million, the painting had begun to look like a too-expensive piece of wall decoration. Payson, whose grandmother Joan had endowed New York's famous Whitney Museum, had decided to free the money and put it to good use. He planned to give bequests to various art schools and colleges, and to set up a charitable foundation that would fund research into AIDS. But it all depended on the painting selling well. John Payson, surrounded by his wife, his daughter, three sisters and thirty-five assorted nephews, nieces and friends who had come along to watch, was afraid that it would not.

Down below him in the saleroom, the canvas was now wheeled round to take the spotlight. "Lot number twenty five," announced the auctioneer, John Marion, "*Irises*, by Van Gogh." His delivery was matter of fact, as though this were any other day, and any other painting. "What shall we say to start? Who'll say fifteen million dollars to start? A bid of fifteen million dollars to start it?" But now the moment of truth had arrived. For a few seconds, there was silence and tension round the room. Nobody moved, nobody spoke.

On each side of the auctioneer's rostrum, seven Sotheby's bid-takers were whispering quietly into telephones, or scanning the room for gestures from the people they expected to enter the fray. And suddenly, the chase was on. There was a bid of fifteen million, and then another. "Fifteen-five, sixteen million, seventeen, eighteen, nineteen million dollars, nineteen, I have nineteen million dollars now." It was a fast and furious pace: each five seconds the price was rising by more than most people earn in a lifetime. "Twenty-eight million by two of you now. Twenty-nine million. At twenty-nine million dollars now." On and up it went, and still the hectic pace didn't slow: past thirty million dollars, past thirty-five, in easy million-dollar chunks, to gasps and applause, past the previous world record price for a painting.

There were two left in the race now, both bidding by phone from outside the saleroom. One was an agent from Europe, acting for an unnamed buyer, the other an American, buying for the Japanese. But even that was unknown to onlookers. They had passed forty million dollars now, but the race was only just starting in earnest. Up on the podium, the auctioneer John Marion felt that they had only now found their stride, they were running for the line, like horses stretching to the finish. Forty-three million dollars, forty-four million dollars, forty-five, forty-six, and still there was no hesitation. Upstairs, the Whitneys and the Paysons were almost hysterical. It was way above what they had hoped for, even further ahead of what they had feared. The reserve had been set at twenty.

Now they were at forty-seven million dollars, forty-eight million dollars, forty-nine. "I have forty-nine million dollars against you. Forty-nine million dollars on the far phone." There was at last a pause in the action: Geraldine Nager, a Sotheby's bid taker, handling the agent for the Japanese buyer, was speaking down the line to her bidder. The bid-takers were scanning the audience for anyone else with a fortune to spare. Geraldine was silent now, waiting for her bidder to decide, and then she looked up—a quick sign to the auctioneer, discreet but clear: "That's it, we're through." The hammer came down. At US$49 million, plus 15 per cent commission on top, *Irises* had just set a new world record for a painting, US$14 million more than the previous mark had been, and four times what anyone had ever paid until that year began.

As the hammer came down, few people, even at Sotheby's, knew for certain the name of the buyer. The previous record had fallen to the Japanese, who were sweeping all before them in the auction rooms, as they were doing on the world property markets. But there were strong rumours this time that Australian entrepreneur Alan Bond had beaten them to it—that he had been determined to get the painting, whatever the price. Some were doubtful that he had the money, others surprised that he would risk it now, so soon after the stockmarket crash. But Bond it was who had bought it. He had paid a fortune for a piece of canvas less than a metre square, and had parted with the money in less time than it takes to boil an egg.

In buying the painting, though, Alan Bond was hardly the only one being reckless. As with the rest of his acquisitions, it was other people's money that he was throwing around so freely. He had persuaded Sotheby's to lend him half the purchase price for the picture, and some of the rest, if not all, had been provided by a bank. And by comparison with some of his other purchases, also financed on borrowed money, *Irises* cost nothing. Barely a month before, Bond Corporation had shelled out $1700 million to buy an ailing US brewery called Heileman. Within another twelve months Bond would be planning to pay double that for Allied Lyons in the UK. This, after all, was barely a spadeful on his huge pile of debts: ten thousand million dollars high. And besides, it was a good picture: the best.

It was not until a year after that November evening that Alan Bond announced publicly that the painting was his. How he had kept quiet about it in the meantime was a mystery to anyone who knew him. But when the smiling plutocrat from Ealing finally opened his doors to the world's press and invited them in for a look, the pent-up excitement of a year flooded through. Alan Bond was ecstatic: this was not only the most expensive painting in the world, it was also the best, the most beautiful—just look at that brushwork, said the former signwriter. And for him, Bond revealed, the painting had a special meaning: Van Gogh could see the big picture, he could see what others couldn't; he had been mocked and undervalued in his lifetime, yet he had persevered because he believed in what he was doing. The judgement of history had proved him right. The same, Bond felt, was true of himself. He understood, he sympathised, he identified with that neglected genius, that one-eared lunatic by the name of Vincent Van Gogh. Van Gogh's story—or at least the story as Bond understood it—offered comfort. Like Vincent, Alan was a kind of prophet in his own country; and like Vincent, Alan too was unappreciated and unloved.

Some months later, *Irises* was sent on a tour of Australia. After much publicity about both the purchase price and the travelling exhibition itself, thousands of people queued to see the painting, but in each city hundreds also turned up to protest. At the launch of the tour at the National Art Gallery in Canberra, one of the quietest and dullest places in Australia, Alan Bond could hardly make himself heard above the barracking. He was allowing them to see his painting, yet he was being met by an angry riot. The art world had seen nothing like it before. Politics were involved, it was true—some of the protests were about Chile and Bond Corporation's presence there. But the real target was Bond himself and what he stood for. Alan Bond was puzzled and hurt. The trouble with Australia, he said, was that it was being seized by a "vocal and critical minority which knocks success and resents excellence".

The next day there were full page advertisements in the newspapers: "An Open letter to all Australians from Mr Alan Bond AO". Ostensibly, it was a response to the Australian Broadcasting Tribunal's verdict that he was not a "fit and proper person" to hold a television licence. But it seemed Bond's attack went wider. Why, he asked, had he been subjected to "the most searing process of public scrutiny ever endured by a public figure" in Australia; why had be been penalised and pilloried? Why, when he had done so much for Australia, was his reputation being stained? Why, in a nutshell, did nobody appreciate him? In 1983, Alan Bond had won the America's Cup for Australia. He had become a national hero. So what had he done to fall so far out of favour, to throw it all away?

One might well have answered: everything. He had plundered his public companies, crushed those little people who happened to get in his way, avoided paying taxes on a massive scale, and bent the rules at every opportunity. He also stood for excess, for the idea that greed is good, for magic ways of making money, for borrowing and buying on a gargantuan scale. In short, he personified some 1980s values that people wanted to leave behind.

The purchase of *Irises* had not in itself brought Bond down, although ultimately it would cost him money. But it stood as an analogy for his life story. It illustrated so well his need to buy the best, to be the best; his urge to be loved; his inability to understand why others did not love him. And it showed, too, his relentless drive to acquire. Both in his personal life and his billion-dollar business deals, Bond never could restrain himself. While the stockmarket crash stopped other entrepreneurs in their tracks, Bond would go on borrowing and buying, borrowing and buying, until the banks finally called time.

CHAPTER 1

Young Tearaway

At the age of seven, young Alan Bond was taken by his father down a coal mine in the South Wales village of Cwmtillery. Half a mile below the surface it was pitch black, dusty, damp and claustrophobic—a seven-year-old's nightmare. And what the young boy saw is still burned into his memory: pit ponies straining to heave truckloads of coal; dark tunnels disappearing into the bowels of the earth; and men stripped to the waist, with sweat pouring off their backs. It was then, says Alan Bond, that he took a vow never to be poor. He had already seen his uncles sitting in tubs of water in the backyard, trying in vain to scrub the ingrained black coal dust out of their skin. He had already observed their hard and hungry lives, and he swore at that moment never to become like them. Come hell or high water, Alan Bond would escape, he would make something of himself. He would be rich.

Or so the story goes.

Related more than once over the years, this epiphany in a South Wales coal mine might well have occurred; it may even have represented a genuinely formative moment in the life of Alan Bond. Less charitably, it may also have been a myth manufactured for posterity, the sort of apocryphal story often told about the great and famous. As we will see, much has been said about Alan Bond over the years that might be called into question. Sorting fact from fiction in Alan Bond's case is not always easy, but in the episode of the coal mine, there is at least some connection with reality.

Alan's father, Frank Bond, had grown up in the same village of Cwmtillery, and had lived in a tiny terraced cottage, just fifty paces from the pithead. All eight members of the Bond family, Frank's parents and their six children, had been crammed together into a two-up, two-down stone house, with little in the way of mod cons. There was cold water, an outside tap, and a lean-to lavatory out the back. And if life was hard in the material sense, it was no doubt austere in other respects, for Frank's father, Alan Bond's grandfather, was a devout chapelgoer, with a forbidding disposition and a set of strict moral values. A regimental sergeant major during the First World War, Alan's grandfather Edwin was forever addressed as "Mister Bond" by the people of Cwmtillery, and seems to have inspired, even in those who didn't have him as a parent, a mixture of fear and respect. Edwin Bond was a miner for more than fifty years, but he got precious little for it. When he was compulsorily retired at the age of seventy-five after a lifetime working underground, he was given a pension of just one shilling and sixpence a week. Not surprisingly, old Edwin hoped that his four sons would do better out of life, and not follow him down the mine. But in the South Welsh valleys there was no other work on offer, so miners they had all become, with the exception of Frank. Like his son Alan, twenty-odd years later, he had no desire to spend his life in poverty, digging coal.

Frank had decided as soon as he left school that he did not want to go down the pit, and he found an ally to help him escape. At the age of fourteen, he ran away on the train to London with his eldest sister Gladys, turning his back on Cwmtillery for good. According to Bond family lore, Gladys took pity on the boy and saved five shillings for his fare, and when they got to London, she also found him work. Gladys, who was eight years his senior, was in service with Lord Chelmsford, and she fixed her brother up with a job as a footman. Frank would come back later to Cwmtillery, putting on his new airs and graces, learned from dealing with his Lordship, to tell his brothers that they were crazy to dig coal for a living. And they, in turn, would tell him what they thought of him.

By contrast, Alan Bond's mother Kathleen Smith was from the ranks of the comfortable middle class, and was brought up in considerably more style than Frank ever enjoyed—the daughter of a Yorkshire chemist, she belonged to an altogether different social stratum. But like Frank Bond, she had strong views about what she wanted to do with her life— or, more precisely, what she did not want to do with it. Young women in those days were normally expected to learn how to cook, sew and find a husband, and this certainly looked like being

Kathleen's fate. But she wanted none of it. While still at school, in her early teens, her mother fell ill, and Kathleen looked set to abandon her schooling so that she might look after her. But like Frank Bond in rather different circumstances, Kathleen decided she would not play the allotted part. She, too, caught the train to London to seek her fortune instead. It was brave for a young woman to do such a thing—in those days most would have accepted their fate without question, or suffered in silence—but it was typical of Kathleen to defy convention. She had a passion to make something of herself, and she was not prepared to sacrifice her life for others.

It was at a Christmas party in London in the early 1930s that the paths of Frank and Kathleen eventually crossed, and it was love at first sight. By this time Frank was a private in the 2nd Middlesex Regiment, based down in Aldershot, and Kathleen living in a bedsit in Portland Place, so it must have been hard for them to carry on their courtship. Clearly they met often enough, for in October 1934 they were married in Marylebone Registry Office. It wasn't much of an occasion. Kathleen didn't bother to invite her parents, or even to tell them she was getting hitched. Nor in later years would she introduce them to her Frank's relatives. But perhaps they thought she was marrying beneath her. Perhaps, indeed, she felt the same.

After their marriage the newlyweds, who were still in their early twenties, moved into a house in Abbey Terrace, Ealing, now part of London's North Circular Road. Today, with four lanes of traffic roaring past the front door, it is not a glamorous address. In the 1930s, though hardly a romantic place in which to start one's married life, it might not have been so bad; it wasn't long in any case before the Bonds moved up in the world, buying a home in Federal Road, Perivale, which is where young Alan would grow up.

The house in Perivale was of a very familiar London kind. There are tens of thousands of them in the outer suburbs of that city, standing in their neat and endless rows of middle-class conformity. Whether you are in Croydon or Chigwell, Purley or Perivale, they all look the same. They are built of brick, covered in grey pebble dash, with dinky little wooden porchlets, and their bay windows sport little red-tiled roofs with scalloped wood around the eaves. The Bonds' house, at number 22 Federal Road, was no exception. The end one in a terrace of four, it had a privet hedge to cut it off from the street and two modest bedrooms upstairs, with a further two rooms downstairs.

In the late 1930s when the Bonds moved into Perivale, the houses were new, the green fields were still not far away, and the aspidistra flew proudly. On Empire Day in 1946, at Perivale First School, just out the back of the Bonds' house, the children carried flags in a procession around the newly-planted Victory Oak Tree, singing patriotic songs as they went. Quite likely young Alan was among them. For the residents of Federal Road in those days were proud to be British, and the Bonds, in the heart of middle-class suburbia, were as British as the best of them.

Alan was the second of the Bonds' two children. His elder sister, Geraldine Kathleen, was born in December 1936, just two days before Christmas, in Queen Charlotte's Hospital in Hammersmith. Alan, plain Alan, followed sixteen months later, on

22 April 1938, through the same delivery room.

According to Geraldine, who now lives in one of Perth's less fashionable suburbs, where it is hardly known that she is Alan Bond's sister, the two children were neither particularly close nor much alike. While she was like her father Frank, quiet, gentle and almost painfully shy, Alan was quite the opposite. He was independent, outward-going, confident and the apple of his mother's eye. Geraldine recalls him as conker champion, marble wheeler-dealer, and a boy who liked to get his way. Nobody, she says, ever pushed him into doing anything that he didn't want to do. Both in build and in character, Alan took after his mother, a stout and immovable Yorkshirewoman who never seems to have accepted that there was anything in life that couldn't be changed. According to Geraldine, she was "very energetic, very determined, such a fighter".

In the Bond family, Kathleen was the dominant figure. She apparently thought of herself as somewhat superior to her neighbours, and people remember her as someone who both stood out and stood apart. She went out to work, where most women did not; she always dressed smartly while others wore old rags; and to some she appeared stand-offish. Few people appear to have been close to her or to have known her well. But in her family she was a driving force. She seems to have been committed to getting on, and to Alan doing so if she could not. Even in his early business career Alan would often take her advice, or at least seek her opinion before doing things. And Kathleen, by all accounts, constantly pushed him towards the distinction she had always craved for herself. Despite her interrupted education, Kathleen always longed to be a teacher and was forever taking courses at night school in an attempt to improve herself.

Kathleen, however, was not the easiest of people to get along with. To this day, Frank's younger brother William remembers Kathleen, almost with a shiver, as "a hard woman, always arguing and quarrelling about anything and everything. We used to fight every time she came here." And William's wife is no kinder in her verdict. When asked whether Kathleen was a difficult woman, she says with great relish: "You're telling me she was. How she got on with anyone I don't know." Frank, she says: "was like a little baby under her. He had to do what he was told." Frank apparently got on with his wife by simply giving in.

Kathleen decided that Frank should come out of the forces, and saw the decision carried through. "She didn't fancy herself as an army wife," says daughter Geraldine, "and she wrote letter after letter until they discharged him." Work in London then would certainly have been hard to find, but that didn't seem to deter Kathleen. Nor was it allowed to deter Frank. He came out of the army and into a series of jobs, none of which lasted very long. One month he was a painter, the next a butcher, and then he would be back to being a builder's decorator again. By the time the war ended, he was working as the local milkman. Geraldine recalls times when she and Alan would cycle with their father down to the dairy, a twenty-minute bike ride away, where they would load up the horse-drawn cart with the milk and the cream doughnuts, before heading off on the regular run around Ealing.

Of the war years themselves Geraldine remembers little. Some moments remain vivid for her, like the thrill of a case of lemons arriving from North Africa, where their father was fighting with the RAF, or seeing him standing in the doorway with his kit bag, back from the war after years away. But equally there were times so horrible that both she and Alan have blotted them out. Perhaps the worst was that the two Bond children had found themselves suddenly without a father at a crucial stage in their development. Young Alan was less than two years old when Frank went off to fight, and Geraldine only three. By the time the war ended and their father came home again, Alan was seven, and Kathleen, the only parent on the scene for five long years, had become an even more crucial figure in the young boy's life.

The Bonds' house in Perivale was too far out of London to experience the full horror of the Blitz, but there was enough action in the locality for a thousand people in the borough to be killed in the five-and-a-half years of war. And while there weren't any direct hits on Federal Road, they did get a few nearby. In the summer of 1944, just a couple of hundred metres from the Bonds' home, four houses in nearby Devon Close were flattened by a direct hit from a doodlebug. For three months that summer there were air raid warnings virtually every day, as V1 flying bombs came over in a steady stream. On those frightening days Geraldine and Alan would sit in their local air raid shelter, singing "Ten Green Bottles" over and over again as the bombs fell around them. But that was the only time when the war came to their doorstep, because when the first wave of bombs fell in 1940, the two children had been evacuated to Cwmtillery, to the safety of the Welsh countryside.

The village of Cwmtillery sits high at the head of one of those narrow South Welsh valleys that spear their way to the edge of the Brecon Beacons. From the flat valley floor the hills rise steeply above rows of grey-roofed stone cottages. Today, on the upper slopes, far above the now-closed coal mine, there are sheep tearing away at the turf. But underneath their feet are millions of tons of black slag that once towered above the village. In the heyday of Cwmtillery, in the 1940s, when the pit was going strong, fifteen hundred men bent their backs down the mine and almost four thousand people lived there. It was a thriving community, and certainly a God-fearing one: there were no fewer than four chapels to keep the local population on the straight and narrow. And here, as a very young boy, Alan seems to have spent the first three years of the war, living with his uncle William (who, aged seventy-six, still lives in the village, in a house not a hundred metres from where the old pithead used to be). Then, after the war ended and the two children were back living in London with their mother, they would return to Wales for their school holidays.

Every summer, Geraldine and Alan would be despatched on the train with their dog. They would be met at the station in Newport and driven up through the valleys to their grandparents' terraced cottage in Cwmtillery, to a village where, according to Geraldine, "the houses seemed to grow out of the side of the mountain". There they would spend the days tobogganing down vast slagheaps on bits of cardboard; they would have baths in the evenings in a tin tub in front of a roaring coal fire, and wake up in the morning together in a large iron bed from which they could see the big turning wheels of the colliery.

Alan spent much of his time on these long summer holidays with his young cousin Eric, one of Uncle William's three sons, who is almost the same age. Between them, they seem to have given the neighbourhood something to talk about. They would climb on the colliery equipment, which was absolutely out of bounds, and be chased by the local bobby, then they would go down to Abertillery and terrorise the town. "Alan used to get us chucked out of the swimming baths," says Eric. "They had a balcony near the diving board where people could watch from. Alan and I used to jump off it, which was banned, and get thrown out by the attendants."

But there were vast tracts of country round the village where you couldn't get into trouble. Only a mile or so outside Cwmtillery, where man and mining haven't scarred the landscape, the valley is beautiful. There are heather-and bracken-covered hillsides, clumps of low-growing oak trees, and cold, clear fast-running streams tumbling down between the rocky outcrops. In the summer in particular, when Alan and Geraldine were there, when the hills weren't hidden in clouds of cold damp fog, it must have been a marvellous place for children to grow up. There were trees to climb, whinberries to pick, birds' nests to raid. And no one to bother them. The boys would roam free all day, arguing, fighting, having fun. Up there, cut into the side of the hill, way above the valley floor, was an old drift mine, which was still being worked. Here Alan and Eric were allowed to lead the pit ponies in and out, taking them off to a stream to drink, or to the pile where the coal was dumped.

With the possible exceptions of having to go to chapel on Sundays to be harangued by a fierce Welsh preacher, and having to put up with Grandfather Edwin's strictures and beatings, Cwmtillery offered far more joy than life back in London. Perhaps it was inevitable, given the disruption of the war years, or perhaps it was a result of Kathleen's desire that the family should better itself, but Geraldine and Alan's life in Federal Road was hardly overflowing with joy. Both during and after the war, Kathleen worked full-time, and the two children were often left to fend for themselves. From an early age, they were latchkey kids. While their father was doing his duty in the African deserts, Kathleen disappeared at the crack of dawn every morning to catch a train into central London, to work as a clerk in the Air Ministry. Geraldine, aged eight or nine at the most, was left in charge of getting herself and Alan off to school in the morning, and of making tea when they both got home. Geraldine, by all accounts, was very protective of her younger brother and looked after him well. Neighbours from that time, who still live in Federal Road, say rather disapprovingly that the children were left to roam the streets, and that Alan was forever making mischief. In their memory he was "a little devil", a dog-chasing little boy who, when he came to birthday parties, "used to wreck them".

One school chum of Alan's at Perivale First School, though unclear as to whether the boy's mother and father got on or otherwise, is sure things in the Bond household were not as they should have been. In Pat Dolphin's memory of the Bond family, even after the war, Frank seemed always to be away, Kathleen always working. "You got the feeling that Dad was never around." According to Dolphin, they were something of a rough-and-ready family, with Alan and Geraldine being shunted around from person to person to be looked after: she remembers feeling rather sorry for Alan, because he clearly wasn't a very happy child.

Apparently Alan often played hookey from school. He would nip over the fence that separated the playground from the Bond back garden and then he would be off to the park or the shops for the afternoon. Teachers were forever sending someone round to his house to see whether he was there, and then hauling him up in front of the headmaster to do something about it. You "got the feeling that he had a bit of an upset life", Pat remembers. The police were called a couple of times to look for him, and Alan was brought back in a police car. Everyone at school talked about it and thought how brave he was. Another schoolmate also remembers him being brought back by the police a couple of times: she was told he had run off to the seaside for the day.

On one occasion, young Alan seems to have run away from home in rather more serious fashion than usual. Mrs Parker and Miss Turner, who lived near the Bonds in Federal Road, remember quite a hoo-ha. The police were called, a full-scale search was started, and Bond, they believe, was discovered on the ferry to Ireland. There's no one now to vouch for the truth of that, and it seems an extraordinary story, given that Alan was only eight or nine at the time. But it tallies with later accounts of his running away in Australia. If true, it would be a remarkable illustration of young Alan's character, for if he really did get halfway to Ireland, he must have been an extremely determined child.

At school, it seems, Alan was admired because of all the awful things he used to do, but had few if any close friends. Children of his own age saw him as "a bit of a leader but also a bit of a loner". This is the view of Joe Kingston, who was possibly Alan Bond's closest school friend and who went with him from infants' through to Secondary Modern. According to him, Alan always yearned for more and used to try to buy friends by giving away sweets in the playground. "He used to have a lot of friends when he had sweets," says Joe. "He always seemed to have some in his desk; he always seemed to have money. I suppose his Mum and Dad were both working, so they were relatively well off. But I used to think he was a bit spoilt."

The general view is that young Alan was also a bit wild, and certainly not academically inclined. Those who remember his days at Perivale First School, which was a few doors up from the Bond home in Federal Road, have an almost unanimous verdict. He was a terror, a tearaway, a monkey, who did what he pleased. Another classmate for several years remembers as an example how they had coal delivered to the school to fire the boilers. It was left in a heap in the playground, and playing on it was forbidden, yet Alan always slid down it. Young Bond, according to Mrs Jessie Wood, the school's dinner lady at that time, "never took any notice of what the masters said to him. He just used to do what he wanted to do. And he'd always get his own way. The headmaster, Mr Neville, always said he'd go far."

From an early age, Alan seems to have been keen to make a living. He and Joe Kingston were always up to something to earn money for themselves: "a milk round, chopping firewood. Anything to earn a bob." And even in those early days, it seems, young Alan had a talent for business. His mother Kathleen used to delight in telling a story of how, shortly after the war in Britain, jam jars had been in short supply. One holiday Alan had started to collect them and sell them to a local shopkeeper. But he hadn't been able to make enough money doing it, so before long he had hit upon the idea of getting his mates to do the collecting for half what the shopkeeper would pay, and then pocketing the profit for himself. Alan's sister recalls that even as a youngster the boy was always dealing. Find a group of boys and, often as not, Alan would be in the middle, sorting out some scheme. "I don't know that he wanted to be rich," Geraldine says now, "but I think he liked the fun of wheeler-dealing. He also liked what money could buy, and he liked to outmanoeuvre people."

But it would have been perfectly understandable if Bond had been driven by a determination to be rich. He had spent much of his childhood taking lessons in going without, and making a fortune would have been the obvious way to fulfil his mother's ambitions for him. Indeed, to make money, back then, must have seemed almost a necessity, because for the Bond family, as for many others, those were hard times. Food was scarce, luxuries were incredibly expensive, and everything was in short supply. The Bond family might have had two incomes, but as well as working full-time, Kathleen made all the family's clothes, and even knitted their socks. Even then, funds were always tight, and Kathleen would scrimp and save dried fruit and nuts so that they could have a proper pudding at Christmas. One year, Geraldine's stocking held nothing but a new penny, an orange, a tin of mints, and an old doll wearing a new dress that her Mum had made.

Life should have become easier when Alan and Geraldine's father came home from the war in 1945, but, because he came back a sick man, this was not to be. Frank Bond had been on a boat torpedoed in the Mediterranean off the Italian coast, and had been lucky to survive. He had spent a fair amount of time in the water and might well have suffered from it. But whatever had exactly happened, he came back to England with tuberculosis, an infection that causes abscesses on the lungs. His illness led to surgery that cut half his ribcage and some of his lungs away, and his ability to earn a decent living must have been impaired. Yet, for some reason, he had been given no pension. Kathleen, in true style, set about fighting the authorities to get Frank some money, and through her persistence and bloody-mindedness succeeded. But even then, peace didn't bring plenty.

There were shortages and rationing to contend with, just as before. The only way to get oranges was with a child's green ration book, and then you had to queue for hours at the local corner shop. Frank grew vegetables in their little garden, and Red Cross food parcels from the Commonwealth were an occasional treat to which they all looked forward. Indeed, Geraldine and Alan got home from school on one particular day to find a parcel full of all sorts of delights, which they duly unwrapped and sampled—tins of butter and Milo and various other goodies wrapped up in calico. Then Kathleen arrived, and furious at what she saw, gave them a hiding. She was cross not because they had broken into the parcels but because they had lost the labels, which said who had sent them. Kathleen always wrote a personal thank-you letter to the senders, and this time she could not.

Most of the food parcels that pitched up on the Bonds' kitchen table had been despatched from Australia, and it was this, it seems, that caused the Bonds to wonder whether life might be easier there. But they would probably not have taken the decision to migrate Down Under if the decision to leave England had not been made for them. The winter of 1948 was one of the worst Britain had ever experienced, and not just because of the blizzards and record low temperatures. London's smog was at its thickest, blanketing the capital in impenetrable yellow soup for days on end. Poor Frank's health became so bad that his doctor told him he would be lucky to live another eighteen months. Unless he moved somewhere warmer and drier to live, the cold and damp would kill him. So, in early 1949, the Bonds took the decision to emigrate, with Frank Bond leaving his wife and two children behind, to set off for Australia. He was too ill to have any chance of getting an assisted passage—he wouldn't have passed the medical—but he was able to depart in style nevertheless. He, or more likely Kathleen, persuaded the Royal Order of Buffaloes and the Freemasons together to contribute the money for a ticket. And so, with his brother William and wife Kathleen waving goodbye, he stepped onto a plane at Northolt airport, did a turn over nearby Federal Road and bumped off on the long journey to a new life Down Under.

Some ten months later, Kathleen, Geraldine and

Alan followed by boat, having told officials at
Australia House that they could sail at seven days'
notice. The public servant who interviewed
Kathleen in London when she applied for her ten
pound Assisted Passage, scrawled on her application: "Home Duties. Excellent personal type with
two fine children. Husband in Australia." She had
been asked on the form to disclose how much capital she would be able to bring to Australia after she
had paid the fares. Kathleen had written "Fifty
Pounds". It was 5 November, Guy Fawkes Day in
England, when Kathleen applied. Exactly three
months later she and her two children would be
stepping onto Australian soil.

CHAPTER 2

Ten-Pound Pom

The ship that took young Alan Bond to Australia was the SS *Himalaya*, the flagship of the P&O fleet. Virtually brand new, she had been built specially for the Australian run, and was the height of luxury even for her tourist class passengers—at least by comparison with the austerity of postwar Britain. The SS *Himalaya* was the biggest and fastest ship commissioned anywhere in the world in 1949, and the pride of the country that launched her. On her maiden voyage in October she had set a new record for the London-to-Bombay run, knocking five days off the previous fastest time of twenty days, and had then made it to Melbourne in exactly four weeks, which was also a record. The *Himalaya* did not have air-conditioning or stabilisers, it was true, but nor did other great liners of the day. And if her funnels had a distressing tendency to deposit soot on the upper rear decks, that was also no cause for concern, since the fallout troubled only the passengers in tourist class. Having paid only ten pounds for the passage, most would have been slow to complain: after all, they were coming from food shortages, rationing books and a British winter into blue seas, sunshine, and parties every day. They would have been too excited to bother about a few specks of soot.

For the Bonds, and especially the two children, a cruise like this was wonderful. They had a whale of a time, eating glorious food, playing endless games, and going to fancy dress parties, with Alan looking dashing in an Indian turban and jacket. There was a swimming pool to dive-bomb people in and regular sports on deck, with egg-and-spoon races, sack races and all sorts of fun.

On the *Himalaya*, the sexes were strictly segregated below decks, so the Bonds, who were in tourist class with all the other ten-pound Poms, found themselves split up. Geraldine and Kathleen shared a cabin on one side of the corridor with two other women, while Alan was put into a cabin opposite, with a couple of younger boys who were travelling with their grandfather. Geraldine remembers one of her cabin mates as a rather shy and proper lady, who kept a safety pin in her knickers because she had once been "let down" by a bad attack of elastic failure. And Alan's companions certainly have not forgotten him. According to Mr Webb, the old gentleman who shared young Bond's cabin for the four-week voyage, the eleven-year-old Alan was pompous, full of himself, and a "spoiled little brat". He would still be telling his grandson three decades later, in his rich Lancashire accent: "D'you recall that bloke on t'boat? That were Alan

Bond, that were. I knew then he were going to be a right bugger." The grandson, who was only six at the time, says he remembers trying to drown young Bond in the swimming pool, but that may be an invention. A kinder verdict from another passenger is that Bond was: "very outward going, talked a lot, and never missed a trick". But she was in a cabin over the way—an altogether safer distance.

After four weeks at sea, having called at Bombay and crossed the Equator, the SS *Himalaya* finally arrived at Fremantle in Western Australia on 5 February 1950. It was a typical summer day, with the sun belting down, and the temperature above 35°C (over 100° Fahrenheit) yet Alan insisted on wearing a thick woollen coat over a thick knitted cricket jumper. In a picture taken of the three Bonds as they posed on the quay at the bottom of one of the *Himalaya*'s gangways, Geraldine is standing somewhat shyly in the background, while Alan is in front of her, looking very much the favourite son. He has a white handkerchief in his top pocket, his mother's coat folded importantly over his arm, and is looking the photographer straight in the eye. Alongside him is Kathleen, whose attention has been distracted momentarily. She is immaculately turned out in a white suit with navy piping. She stands proud, erect and prosperous-looking, not at all like someone with only fifty pounds to her name.

As they stood next to the *Himalaya*, all three of them must surely have wondered whether coming to Australia was a terrible mistake. They had travelled for a month, come halfway round the world and abandoned everything they had in England. And now, as they took in Fremantle, their hearts must have sunk. Alan would tell an interviewer in later life that it looked like a desert island, there was a feeling of desolation, he felt as if he had arrived on the moon. Most people who came to Western Australia in the early 1950s seem to have had a similar reaction: as they cruised slowly into Fremantle harbour they could see rows of tin sheds, a smattering of people on the quay, a few empty marshalling yards, and virtually nothing else. But the Bonds could hardly go back, because Alan's father Frank was waiting at the quay, ready to show them the way to their new home.

Frank Bond had come out some ten months earlier to get things fixed up, and it was just as well he had. There had been trouble getting a place to live, and trouble getting a job too. Eventually Frank had found work as a salesman and had set up home in a modest little house at the back of Fremantle High Street. Tiny, with four steep steps from the front door into the kitchen, it was no palace, but it still held wonders for the children because of what their father had to show them. Ushering them into the house, Frank proudly stood them in front of the fridge, and told Kathleen to open the door to reveal the contents. Inside, according to Geraldine, was the sort of food that people in England only dreamed about. There were "big fat peaches, ham, vegetables, and ice cream that he had made himself"—the fruits of a land of plenty. Alan's mother, Kathleen, was overcome. After almost a year of managing the family on her own, while ten thousand miles away a sick husband tried to build a new life for them, all the tension must suddenly have been released. She sat down and burst into floods of tears.

Looking at Fremantle in the 1990s it is hard to imagine what it was like when the Bond family was trying to find its feet there. Today the town is like the Rocks in Sydney or Covent Garden in London—full of brightly painted old buildings, and century-old architecture, an idealised version of what life must have been like in the Victorian era. Its streets teem with smartly dressed young people who drink real ale in stylishly-renovated pubs and eat in cafes that serve child-size portions of food at grown-up prices. In short, it is well-heeled and fashionable, a playground for the young (and not-so-young) things of Perth.

But back in the early 1950s when Alan Bond was a young Pommy immigrant, it was all rather different. The same buildings were there, the new coats of paint and the trendy tourists were not. It was a rougher, dirtier place than it is today, a working port that prospered when traffic was busy and went hungry when it was not. The economy of the west was supposedly booming, but jobs were in general hard to come by, and to make your way in the world you had to work hard. Bond's father, with two children to support, failing health and little in the way of capital, no doubt found life something of a struggle. As in England, he went through a variety of jobs, as milkman, painter and decorator, salesman and the like. But he did at least stay in work, and the Bond family made ends meet.

Young Alan, meanwhile, was packed off to school the day after the *Himalaya* docked, which must have been a shock after four weeks of fun at sea. Since he was not even twelve, he was promptly despatched to the nearby East Fremantle primary school, and there, as legend has it, he immediately made his mark. According to one of his schoolmates, Bond's form teacher Eric Hinchliffe had problems with

young Alan, who was constantly cheeky in class.
There was, for some time, a running battle between
the two of them, which ended with the budding
billionaire standing up in front of the class and
telling the unfortunate Mr Hinchliffe: "When I'm
older, I will buy and sell blokes like you." What
happened next the story does not relate, because
Bond's classmates reportedly ducked for cover.

Almost forty years later Mr Hinchliffe does not
recall the incident, but he does remember Bond,
even though he taught him for only ten months, and
he remembers him as a difficult charge. Bond, says
his former teacher, was "quite a withdrawn sort of a
boy. He didn't make friends easily. I found him, too,
a bit touchy, well, perhaps more than a bit touchy.
He had a chip on his shoulder. You had to be very
careful with him." Whether it was his temper, his
being from England, or the things that had set him
apart back home, young Alan didn't make too many
friends at East Fremantle and was something of an
outcast. Even he would later admit that he had a
hard time of it. He was teased because of his accent,
and he was unhappy enough to want to be back
home again. Some of Bond's classmates recall being
lectured by Mr Hinchliffe about the need to be nicer
to him. "I guess coming out from England he was a
square peg in a round hole," says Hinchliffe, "but he
found it difficult to fit into a new group of people."

The new boy did not greatly impress the girls
either. "'That Pommy Kid' was how we all used to
refer to him," says one of his classmates, who paints
a not particularly flattering portrait of the boy. "He
was one of those fat, tubby kids—you know, one of
those ones that would need all-elastic shorts round
the waist." And what did the girls think of him?

"There was no love for him, I can tell you that. You would have been belted for taking him home."

After a year at East Fremantle Primary, Bond moved on, aged twelve-and-a-half, to the Fremantle School for Boys, and sank back into relative obscurity. The Fremantle Boys' School no longer exists as a separate entity, having been swallowed up by John Curtin High in the late 1950s, but the Victorian Gothic stone buildings are still there in the middle of Fremantle, opposite St Patrick's Catholic Church. Back in the early 1950s they contained two schools side by side—one for the boys, and one for the girls, separated down the middle by a picket fence that the boys rapidly tore down. It was no small school—some five hundred children in all, drawn from mainly working-class families: hard-working, honest, likable people in the main.

Almost forty years later, the pupils who were particularly difficult are still remembered, as are those who were remarkably dim or exceptionally bright, and those who excelled in sport. But Alan Bond fits into none of these categories. From the sea of little boys who attended this school, his face does not now shine out to jog the memory of anyone who taught there. Alan was neither Bond the Brilliant, as he would later portray himself to one interviewer— nor Bond the Destroyer, terrifying teachers with his arrogant wit, as one of his schoolmates would maintain. He was merely Bond the ordinary. Like plenty of other remarkable people before him, he slouched through his Australian schooldays without winning any prizes, without getting expelled, without apparently leaving a trace.

Keith Bathgate, who taught at Fremantle Boys in the early 1950s, is pretty definite he would have

taught Bond, and thinks he was almost certainly
Bond's form master, but has no recollection of him.
The response is even dimmer from a dozen or so
other teachers still alive who were there at the time.
But a couple of teachers and a few schoolmates do
remember him well enough to know what his
passage through school was like—and they are
certain Alan was no scholar. Fremantle Boys, like all
schools at the time, was divided into Professional
and Technical streams, with roughly half the boys in
each. The Professionals did languages and the more
academic subjects, the Technicals did woodwork,
metalwork, and all the things that would train them
for a trade. Alan was in the latter, non-academic
stream, in a group which one of Bond's old teachers,
Tom Fuller, describes as "not the brightest lot". And
Alan himself, according to Fuller, was "not a very
bright boy".

This is not quite the impression that Alan Bond,
the successful businessman, has tried to present
over the years. Indeed, it is exactly the opposite. The
official Bond life story, told by Bond to Western
Australian journalist Hugh Schmitt in 1984 and
repeated since by *Bulletin* writer Bruce Stannard
among others, is that back in England the young
Alan Bond was a pretty exceptional pupil who
could speak four languages. To be precise, according
to Stannard, he was a "scholarship winner who, by
his own account, excelled at Mathematics, French,
Latin and German". Yet here he was in Australia in
the Technical stream, somewhere near the bottom of
a class of somewhat dull boys, and making no use of
the languages in which he was proficient. Perhaps
the staff of Fremantle's school had failed to notice his
great prowess, but the simpler explanation is that

Bond made it up. His first employer, Fred Parnell, was certainly not impressed by the boy's linguistic abilities: "Four languages?" says Parnell, "he could hardly speak English". Investigation of Bond's school record in England reveals that his last school there was Selbourne Secondary Modern School, which means that Bond failed to pass the 11-plus exam that everyone in Britain took in those days. It seems that the self-made Mr Bond has remade his past.

But by his own account Bond didn't have much time for school, anyway. And others back that up: according to a couple of his classmates in Australia, young Alan spent almost as much time running away from Fremantle school as he did attending class. Whereas in England he would slip off down to the shops or the park, in Fremantle he was forever playing truant and sloping off down to the wharves to spend the day there. But just as he did in England, he seems on one occasion to have run clean away from home.

The tale told by the Bonds' London neighbours of the eight or nine-year-old Alan being hauled off the ferry to Ireland seems to have had a sequel in Australia. Indeed, when Alan was just thirteen and living in Fremantle, he went missing for several months. Denis Sowden, the family's closest friend, claims that "Alan and a friend went on a trip to Kalgoorlie, and the next thing is that Kath and Frank found out they were in Queensland". Gordon Doohan, another of Bond's school friends, tells that Alan disappeared from his class at Fremantle for a while, and says everyone was impressed when they heard he had run away, but he adds: "He got into a bit of strife. He hadn't come to school for quite a few weeks. We went over and knocked on his door and asked if we could play with Alan. We were quietly told to go away because Alan wasn't there. We heard a rumour that he was in Kalgoorlie, but I never did find out where he had gone." The bare bones of the story are this: on 26 March 1952, Frank Bond notified Fremantle police that his thirteen-year-old son Alan was missing. Then, almost six months later, on 10 September 1952, the *Police Gazette* published another notice that the search for Alan Bond had been called off because the boy had been found. Where Alan had run away to, with whom and why, only Alan Bond could now tell us.

The episode must have been of great concern to his parents. But there wasn't just the running away for Frank and Kathleen to worry about. Alan was a problem even when he stayed at home. Gordon Doohan recalls the occasion when "Alan got his first ten shillings". After school one day, he and Alan were walking past a dry-cleaning shop in Phillimore Street, Fremantle, just near the wharf. The shop was empty, and the till was apparently just a drawer. The two of them walked past, whereupon Alan suddenly told his mate to hang on. "We stopped and he ducked back into the dry-cleaner's. Next he came running out. 'Come on!' he says, and then he took off down to the wharf with me after him. He left me for dead, actually, he was going like a bat out of hell. Anyway, I caught up with him and said: 'What's going on?' Then he pulled a ten shilling note out of his pocket. We bought cigarettes with it." There are other stories told by schoolmates, mostly of petty thievery—pinching oranges, nicking rowboats or stealing food and the like. Just as in later life, the teenage Alan Bond appears to have had little regard for rules.

Even Alan's father Frank, who is no longer alive, seems to have had a few doubts about the sort of person his son was. More than once, when Alan was a young man, he would confide to friends that he was worried what would become of the boy. "There's only two ways he can go," Frank would say. "Either he will end up in Fremantle jail, or he will become the richest man in Australia."

CHAPTER 3

———

Making a Quid

Aged fourteen, and with the permission of his
father, Bond left school to become an apprentice
signwriter with the Fremantle firm of Parnell Signs.
It was a natural course in a way—his father was a
painter by trade, and the young Bond had some
talent at drawing. But Alan's lack of academic
expertise almost stopped him getting even this
humble job, because Parnell Signs gave all its applicants a kind of exam, which Bond failed miserably.
Each year, Fred Parnell, whose business still thrives
in Fremantle today, would typically have half a
dozen would-be apprentices knocking on his door,
yet there was room for only a couple. So to sort the
good from the bad Fred would set them a spelling
test. Luckily for Bond, Fred Parnell was so
impressed with the young man's bright personality
that he took him on in spite of the exam result,
because Bond's spelling, according to Parnell, was

appalling, "just dreadful". Nor did it improve with practice. Some time later, when Bond was minding the shop, he took a message from a customer in Fremantle's "South Terris" who wanted "two moor signs". And still later, when Bond was wielding the brushes on his own behalf, the art of spelling caused problems again. His brief was to paint a sign to hang on the door of a barber's shop, with "Business Closed" on one side and "Business Open" on the other. Kay Zinnecker (whose father had commissioned the sign) remembers seeing the new sign and laughing out loud. "I said: 'Who wrote that?' and Dad said 'Why?' I said: 'Well, they've spelt business wrongly.' Dad did his block."

Bond's job at Parnell Signs, at least at the beginning, did not demand much skill—"the kind of thing he was doing was painting in the background on the signs, and sweeping out the shop," says Fred Parnell today with a chuckle. And young Alan was clearly bored by the whole business, just as he had been at school. The tradesmen he worked with thought he was "pretty average" and the boss had trouble with him. His workmates also came to regard him as a bit of an upstart, a big-mouth, and extremely cocky. To Bluey Pantall, three years his senior, Bond said one day: "When I grow up, you'll be working for me," which would turn out to be not far from the truth. But Pantall wouldn't have worked for the teenage Bond "for quids. He just wanted to make money and he didn't care if he trod on toes on the way up. He had no shame about anything. He used to say it's not what you know it's who you know. And if somebody suffered, as long as it wasn't Alan, it was okay." The young apprentice was continually boasting about how much money he was making, and how he had got the best of somebody. "He used to tell some tall stories," says Fred Parnell. "The men used to repeat some of them to me. I don't think they believed every word he said."

Alan was clearly not the model employee, just as he had not been the model pupil, and with Parnell there were eventually enough run-ins for the two to part company. The precise reasons are not entirely clear, but the "official" story, as told by Bond himself, that the young signwriter completed his five-year apprenticeship in three-and-a-half years because he worked so hard is well wide of the mark. According to Fred Parnell, Bond took too many days off for his employer's liking: he claimed to have trouble with arthritis, but Fred thought he was using it as an excuse. And there had been other disagreements along the way. So after three-and-a-half years, Bond's apprenticeship was terminated "by mutual consent". Without completing his five-year training, without having learned any of the real tricks of the trade, Bond struck out on his own. He and his father Frank formed a company called Nu-Signs, in more open rivalry with Parnell, and a business career was born. Almost certainly, there were no regrets on either side. Indeed, Fred Parnell was probably glad to see the back of him.

Setting up as a signwriter without proper training is not something many people would have contemplated doing in a place as small as Fremantle. But Bond was not one to allow ignorance to handicap him. And he had already been working up a bit of business on the side. Bond had been putting a team of painters together, and doing jobs at the weekend for a bit less than Parnell would charge. He had known what the going rate was for the work because he and the other apprentices delivered Parnell's bills around town. According to a workmate, Bond would stop off on his delivery runs at a cafe called Cully's in Fremantle and, while having his morning tea, would go through Fred's receipts: "He was checking out the prices. I know that for a fact. Seeing what Parnell was charging this bloke, what he was charging that bloke and so on. He would then know how much to charge for a job, how much he could get for it, how much he could undercut." And it wasn't just once or twice: "Every weekend he was doing jobs. Yes, he took every opportunity he could to make money. His aim in life wasn't to learn how to be a signwriter, it was to turn over a quid."

Whatever Alan lacked in signwriting skills he clearly made up for in business acumen and energy, because Nu-Signs was initially a success. One of Bond's first customers for the new company, or more likely for his earlier freelance work, was a local Fremantle butcher and family friend, Denis Sowden. Sowden got Bond to paint a new sign for the shopfront and was amazed at how quickly the job was done. "We figured it was going to take a couple of days, but Bondy knocked it over in an hour and a half. He was quick, dynamic, same as he is now. I don't think anyone expected him to work for someone else for long." Nor, on Sowden's account, did it take long for Nu-Signs to build up trade. "His Dad went into hospital at Wooroloo and left him with a couple of houses to paint, and when his Dad came home they had a business. Alan was just getting heaps and heaps of work, putting teams of blokes together and getting it done. He was a

bundle of dash in those days just like he is now."
And before long, Nu-Signs was thriving.

As young Alan went about establishing his own
business, there were also developments on the
personal front. In 1955, well before the property
deals and the millions, he married a Fremantle girl
called Eileen Hughes—the daughter of a distinguished local family. He met her one Friday night at
Wrightson's Dance Studios in Perth, at a ballroom
dancing class run by Eileen's sister. The red-haired
Eileen was at the time only sixteen and still at
convent school, but she was a girl who liked to
enjoy herself. And by her own account she was a
hot number in the jitterbug. Alan for his part, was
energetic, keen on the girls, and fancied himself as a
bit of a ladies' man. And if the ladies weren't too
keen on him, he didn't let that hold him back.
According to his companion of those years, John
Waters, "the girls didn't warm to Alan at all. He was
too much of an upstart." He was also a Pom, and a
short, somewhat tubby one at that. But what young
Bond lacked in looks he made up for in lip. And he
was never afraid to ask. Certainly, in making a play
for his future wife, he took the direct approach.
According to Eileen, hardly a shrinking violet
herself, Alan was "kind of forward, knew what he
wanted and came on pretty strong."

Eileen's father Bill Hughes was well known about
town. Described by some as the king of Fremantle,
he was a good Catholic, a man of substance and a
force in the community. He has been described as a
"crackerjack man, and a thorough gentleman". Bill
Hughes, or "Doozer", as he was always known, was
not fiercely rich or rolling in wealth, but he was
comfortably off, and he believed in sharing it with

his children, and even his sons-in-law. In time he would become chairman of the Harbour Board, a prominent local councillor, and president of South Fremantle football club, which was about as close to God as one could get in that town. His daughter was very definitely someone worth marrying.

Yet Eileen might have been quite a catch in her own right. Fremantle's Catholic priest, Father Hannah, who has known her for many years, says she was beautiful: "she was thin, and she had those beautiful eyes, and she was always a happy-go-lucky welcoming person. I think she could have done better than marrying Bondy." Bond's foreman at Nu-Signs, Lindsay McCreddin, thought she was wonderful, a terrific girl, a wag. "There was never anything snobbish about her," he says, "she was a real happy-go-lucky person." He remembers how she was a great gardener, and was always taking his bricks to build up her flowerbeds.

Alan's mother, however, never liked her. Even in later years there would be difficulty between them. And neither Kathleen nor Frank Bond approved of the marriage. It can't have been a good start that they were Protestants and the Hughes family devout Catholics. Nor can it have been helped by the fact that Frank was a member of the Freemasons, whose dislike of Catholicism is well known. But probably what irritated them most was that Alan had to adopt Eileen's religious faith to seal the deal. When Alan had first proposed to Eileen, she, or more likely her father, had turned him down because he wasn't a Catholic. So young Alan, whom Frank had been trying to ease into Freemasonry, promptly became one. It may be that the Hughes family put him under some pressure to do so, for young Eileen was pregnant at the time.

The wedding was a small affair, on a Sunday, at St Patrick's Catholic Church in Fremantle. Eileen wore white lace. A family friend remembers that there was a bit of tension between the two camps. At the reception the Catholics stood in one group, the Protestants in another. Since the guests were mainly family from both sides, it may well have been a rather frosty affair.

It is possible, of course, that the Hughes family was not entirely thrilled with the match their daughter was making. Young Bond was, after all, one of the town tearaways. And his prospects as a breadwinner might have looked somewhat uncertain. He had left school at fourteen, he was no more than an apprentice, and he had already had a few run-ins with his employer Fred Parnell. So Doozer might well have been a little disappointed in his daughter's choice. And the fact that Alan had put his good Catholic daughter in the family way before the marriage would hardly have helped matters. Years later, Bond's first employer Fred Parnell would find himself sitting next to Doozer on a plane, and would ask him whether Alan had caused him any grey hairs over the years. "Grey hairs?" said Doozer, "I lost the lot."

There were, indeed, a fair number of things in later years for Doozer to worry about—and one or two, fortunately, that he probably never heard of. But the first handful of thatch almost certainly came out less than a year after Alan and Eileen's marriage. For, at the age of eighteen, Alan's lack of respect for the law was exposed for the first time to public view—or at least to those who bothered to read the *West Australian*. On 12 June 1956, in the paper that Alan Bond would own some thirty years later, the brief but embarrassing tale was set down in black and white.

June 12, 1956

A woman answered a knock on the back door of her home in Barnett St, Fremantle, and a youth asked her whether a boy named Tony Brewer lived there. He later admitted that had nobody answered he would have robbed the house.

Detective A. Hurlstone told this to Mr K.J. Dougall, SM, in the Fremantle Police Court yesterday, when Alan Bond, 18, signwriter, of Quarry Street, Fremantle, appeared on two charges of having been unlawfully on premises.

Witness said that Bond then went to another house in the same street and, when nobody answered, tried to force open a window.

Bond was put on a £25 bond to be of good behaviour for six months on each of the two charges.

Arthur Hurlstone, the policeman who arrested Bond on this occasion, cannot remember the exact words that passed between them, but he recalls Bond wearing a pair of overalls with "State Electricity Commission" emblazoned on them, and carrying a variety of screwdrivers and pliers that made him look like a meter reader. It appears a woman had rung the police because Bond was acting suspi-

ciously, and Alan, when challenged, had been hard
pressed to explain why he was dressed as a meter
reader. Bond at the time, remember, was not a
twelve-year-old or a mixed-up adolescent. This was
Alan Bond the husband and father, Alan Bond the
proprietor of Nu-Signs who, according to the official
story, was just three years away from making his
first million. Nevertheless, this brush with the law
hardly seems to have set him back.

According to Bond's own account of his early
career, he succeeded in business because he worked
harder than his competitors and because he would
tender for the difficult and dangerous jobs that
others didn't want. In the early days he worked
seven days a week and turned his hand to anything.
Alan would paint smokestacks, scale factory walls,
even climb to the top of harbour cranes. He would
later say: "It soon dawned on me that there were
very few people who really wanted to go out and
tackle the difficult work. I found there was money
to be made in solving other people's problems."

In those days he would never ask his employees
to do things he wouldn't do himself, and he would
go far and wide when his competitors preferred to
stay at home. Bond and his painters would think
nothing of getting up at three in the morning, driving about three hundred kilometres on unmade
roads to a job, and driving back to Fremantle in the
middle of the night when they had finished it. On
one occasion, when they were painting a hotel out
at Mandurah, darkness fell before they had finished
the work. Bond disappeared for five minutes, then
came back clutching a couple of hurricane lamps.
Using these for light, they kept on painting until
midnight, and finished the job. But often there

wasn't much at the end of it. Dave King recalls that on one occasion they bought an old Bedford truck to drive a couple of thousand kilometres up to Derby, in the north of Western Australia, to do some work for the government. The roads all the way were dreadful, the Bedford kept breaking down, and to cap it all, they underquoted on the job, and ended up losing a lot of money.

Certainly Bond got about. Legend has it he painted every railway station in Western Australia, and half the country hotels to boot. It is also part of West Australian folklore that he painted the famous red Dingo sign, which stands some twenty metres tall on the side of the flour mills outside Fremantle. The huge painted sign is the first thing that immigrants to Western Australia catch sight of as they approach from the Indian Ocean on the way into Fremantle port, and had they looked hard one day in the late 1950s, they might have seen young Alan perched twenty metres up on the scaffolding. Or so the Bond legend goes. But this is another occasion on which Alan's imagination seems to have triumphed over history. According to Bond's partners at Nu-Signs, he neither painted it nor touched it up: while the company quoted to repaint the Dingo, it never got the job.

On the subject of imaginative tales, another one from those times, told to journalists several times over, concerns the way Bond prepared himself for his leap into business. He claims to have studied accountancy five nights a week for four years at Fremantle Technical College. But this seems to be something of an exaggeration. As far as one can be sure about the details more than thirty years later, it was book-keeping that Alan studied as part of a building course; and he seems to have lasted only a couple of terms—at one night a week—after which he dropped out. There is certainly no record of Alan having taken or passed any exams around this time. And the people at Fremantle Technical College are somewhat puzzled by the claim. Not long ago they decided to use Alan Bond's name in a promotion for the college on the lines of: "You too can be a success if you study at night." But they were forced to abandon the idea. When they searched through their records they could find no trace of Alan Bond ever having enrolled as a student. And when they sought confirmation from Alan Bond's private office that he had studied, they could not get it.

On a rather larger scale, the tale of Bond's early business career also owes a fair bit to the imagination. The official story of Bond's rise to business stardom, polished to perfection over the years, is that young Alan was an overnight sensation, and a millionaire at the age of twenty-one. But the reality is that it took Bond till the age of twenty-nine, or eleven years, much of the time on the verge of going bust, before he arrived at his first million. In all the years at Nu-Signs (which he virtually wound up in 1963), Bond was almost permanently strapped for cash, almost constantly pursued by his creditors, and doing anything to make money. What's more, far from having four hundred employees as Bond later told an interviewer, the company probably never had more than a dozen. Even the most charitable couldn't put it at more than thirty.

In its seven years of operation from a little shopfront in Queen Street Fremantle, Nu-Signs would sell television sets, washing machines and Chinese knick-knacks; it would renovate buildings, take on industrial painting contracts, and even branch out into fattening sheep as an alternative to its signwriting activities, and none of these things would make a fortune. Sometimes the Bond business empire would be doing all these things at once, because the general rule was that they would try anything. Bond's foreman at Nu-Signs, Lindsay McCreddin, remembers they used to sell a TV with only one channel, the Bush Simpson. Bond had got the agency for it because "he used to get around and talk to people. He would do anything to make a quid." At one stage Nu-Signs took to selling paint in bulk. Denis Sowden tells a story of Bond standing in the street, armed with a paintbrush, and a wad of butcher's paper clipped onto a blackboard, ready to deal with all comers. Whether he was shouting "roll up, roll up", he doesn't say, but in true market trader style, Bond was showing potential customers how their kitchens or sitting-rooms would look with their chosen colour scheme.

Trying to track Bond's early business career is like trying to track grapeshot. But it is certain Bond did not begin to make big money until the mid 1960s as a property developer-cum-speculator. All the things he tried on the way, from 1956 onwards, more or less failed to produce results. Indeed, in 1962, when Bond was supposedly a millionaire of three years standing, he and Nu-Signs had thousands of pounds of debts that couldn't be met and were both on the brink of being bankrupted by angry creditors; the Bond name was mud throughout Perth and Fremantle because of the way he and his company carried on their affairs.

To get business, Nu-Signs would produce unrealistically low estimates and then be hard pressed to get its money back. And this was certainly one reason why Bond's reputation was low, as he and Nu-Signs seem to have relied on some sharp practices to make ends meet. In the words of his early partner at Nu-Signs, Dave King, who seems to have left in despair at some of Bond's business practices, "there was a bit of skullduggery going on". Most of the company's business was not in fact in signwriting, but in industrial painting, which was what Bond himself organised, and here Nu-Signs was getting a lot of complaints about the standard of its work. "They were skipping paint here and there," says King, "perhaps not putting on the right number of coats. Some of our staff weren't too good either. The quality of our work wasn't there. We used to do the country hotels. We did the Esplanade Hotel down in Busselton. We started off with a forty-four-gallon drum and finished with forty-three gallons left." Says King with a laugh, "I think that he thinned it down a bit too much, and that was the old water paint, so you can imagine what happened when it rained." There had been other complaints, too, about ships which Nu-Signs had painted, and occasions on which work had to be redone. The workmen at Nu-Signs used to call the stuff in their tins "One Coat Cover Paint" because it had to hide a multitude of sins.

Nowhere was Bond's reputation worse than with the Commonwealth Government Works Department. In 1961, Nu-Signs put in the lowest tender to repaint Perth railway station—in preparation for the coming Commonwealth Games—yet still failed to land the job. "We didn't get it," says Dave King, "because our name was so bad." That they were held in such low esteem was largely the result of the job they had done on Fremantle's old quarantine station. The contract had specified that all old fittings should be reused if possible, and instead the fittings had been sold off. There followed a blazing row with the Commonwealth supervisor who was not too happy about the general quality of the Nu-Signs work either. The man who was in charge of the plumbing on the job, Tom Tate Snr, recalls that the government's man told Bond that as long as he was Commonwealth supervisor, Bond would never get another government job. To which Bond replied that as long as his name was Alan Bond he didn't want to see the man around town.

Bond and Nu-Signs also had problems with the unions. Several times during the 1950s and early 1960s they found themselves in trouble with the painters', the carpenters', or the building workers' union. Nu-Signs might have been no worse than others in the business, but Bond and his company were constantly in the Industrial Court. One month they would be accused of underpaying a worker; next they would be charged with failing to pay holiday pay or travelling allowances; next would be failing to give an apprentice proper tuition. Usually the sums of money were pretty trivial—a few pounds here and a few pounds there—but occasionally it would cost Nu-Signs a couple of hundred. On one occasion, when the case was settled in rather unconventional fashion, it cost Bond considerably more.

Ray Clohessy, long-time organiser of the Building Workers' Industrial Union in the west, and a close mate of Australia's Prime Minister Bob Hawke, explains that Nu-Signs was renovating the hospital in Derby in the far north of Western Australia. Bond was employing a large team of workers on the project and had bussed most of them up from Perth to do the job. Having taken them all that far he was naturally keen to work them hard, so he had come to an arrangement whereby the men would work weekends and he would pay them cash in hand at the ordinary weekday rate. The men were happy because they weren't declaring their extra money to the taxman, and Bond was happy because he wasn't paying overtime rates. But the harmony was shattered when someone told the union, complaining that the men weren't getting the proper union rate.

Clohessy went down to the Nu-Signs office in Fremantle to investigate, and found Alan and his mother minding the shop. On the counter, having just arrived, were three new televisions, then a reasonably scarce item in Western Australia. Eyeing the TVs, Clohessy told Bond the nature of the complaint and then pretended to offer an informal settlement. "Look, Alan," said Clohessy, "why don't we sort this out? I don't want to have to go through all the books, and nor do you. What say you hand over two of those television—one for me, and one for my mate here—and we'll call it quits?" Clohessy's mate, who was his junior from the union, was almost apoplectic at this suggestion but Clohessy managed to shut him up and Bond went off to the back room to confer with Kathleen and Frank. Then, after a couple of minutes, he came back into the shop and said: "I'll tell you what, we'll give you one."

"Well," says Clohessy today, "I knew as soon as he said that, that there was some substance in the complaint, so I told him to give me the books, and I went through them. Of course they were all perfectly in order, but none of the blokes in there had been working weekends, so it was clear they had been cooked. I mean, who sends a bunch of blokes all the way up to Derby and then has them work only five days a week?" Armed with the books and a list of all the workers on the job, Clohessy then marched out of the office, telling Bond he hadn't heard the last of it. Two weeks later he was back to bring Bond the news that the workers at the site, who had since been leaned on by Clohessy, had all complained to the BWIU about underpayment. "Look, Alan," Clohessy said to him, "I don't want you to have to pay them twice, but you're going to have to top it up to the full penalty rate." Bond agreed to pay, and according to Clohessy, it cost him £1000.

Alan Bond's own account of his signwriting career, as repeated by various journalists, is altogether more glorious than tales of watered-down paint and underpaid wages. According to him, Nu-Signs under his guidance pioneered brilliant new business methods which left the Parnells of this world standing, and revolutionised Australian signwriting. Instead of selling signs to real estate agents, for example, Bond and Nu-Signs started renting them, which brought in almost as much money for far less outlay; and instead of painting all the signs by hand he and Nu-Signs used silk screens to print them up, which made the signs much cheaper to produce. But brilliant new business methods or no, even Bond accepts that Nu-Signs was never a goldmine: he soon saw that there was more money to be made elsewhere. Bond realised, as has many a millionaire before him, that property was where real money could be made. As he put up his rented, silk-screened signs on blocks of land around Perth, and weeks later came to take them down because the land had sold for a huge profit, he came to understand that property development could bring him the riches that signwriting never would. And so Bond's real business career was born.

CHAPTER 4

The
First Million

In the 1960s Western Australia was the new frontier, a land of opportunity. Cut off from the rest of the world, and even from the rest of Australia, the state's capital Perth had the atmosphere of a large country town. But it was experiencing an extraordinary boom in population and wealth, and its physical limits were expanding ever outwards. There was a constant need for more housing and for more land to build it on, so it was a perfect time for property speculators and developers to make a killing, and an ideal environment for Alan Bond. Young Alan had all the necessary attributes of a first-rate shark: he had a talent for picking the best development sites, a flair for anticipating trends, and the vision to go for projects that others would shun. Most of all, he had limitless nerve: the fact that he never had any money was a minor consideration.

Alan Bond's first property deal came in June

1960, and involved five acres (just over two hectares) of land at Lesmurdie, out in the Perth hills. He was barely twenty-two years old and didn't have two pennies to rub together, but he agreed to pay £13,000, a small fortune at that time, to acquire it. Without putting down a deposit, the young upstart, as the boys at Nu-Signs called him, marched confidently into a local finance company, Finance Corporation of Australia (FCA), and borrowed the full amount of the purchase price. The interest rate was one per cent, or £130 a month (which was more than the average monthly wage) and the loan was repayable in one year. But Alan wasn't bothered: he just borrowed the money and set about selling off the blocks.

The land that Bond bought at Lesmurdie is some fifteen kilometres due east from Perth, on top of the Darling Range, with spectacular views to the city and the sea beyond. Today it's a classy neighbourhood, dotted with million-dollar mansions and lush green lawns. Except for the cold winter winds, it is a beautiful place to live. In the summer, when the temperature in Perth gets up above 30°C there are pleasant cooling breezes from the Indian Ocean. And in late spring it is a mass of colour, with magnificent pink roses, deep purple bougainvilleas and bright crimson bottlebrushes. But back in the 1960s, it must have needed some imagination to see what it might become. Lesmurdie was a long way from the centre of town, some of the blocks were pretty steep, and it was a dry old place as well. Indeed, looking at some still undeveloped land in the area, it is easy to see what it must have been like: a jumble of patchy scrub, bright orange sandy soil, outcrops of bare rock and grey-green gum trees.

Alan, however, gave his new property the grand new name of Lesmurdie Heights and showed how it should be done. Dick Hardman, the previous owner, had been selling the half-acre blocks at £600 to £800 each, and selling them at a trickle. Bond now shifted virtually all he had bought at about double the price, and did so within three months. He placed big advertisements in the paper, distributed handbills, and announced a "land sale" at exclusive Lesmurdie Heights. Then, come the great day, a tent went up on one of the blocks, Alan's wife Eileen positioned herself out front, and they all waited for the rush. That very first weekend, the place was swamped with customers and Eileen was almost knocked over. She remembers sitting under a beach umbrella, stuffing money into a bookie's bag as the land sold "like fish and chips". By lunchtime, so the story goes, they had taken thousands of pounds, and half the blocks had gone. All the money was repaid inside three months, and Bond had made his first killing.

Although it was hardly much of a killing, Alan had certainly made a few hundred pounds and, as part of the deal, had acquired the family house that Dick Hardman had been building on the property. What's more, he had got a taste of life as a property magnate and, compared with signwriting, it was a snack. From then on, it would be land, land, land all the way. In the meantime, however, there was just one snag—Bond had not made enough money at Lesmurdie to fund the next deal, unless he borrowed big again. And so that was exactly what he did: the second half of 1960 was a frenzy of activity, a veritable orgy of borrowing. And true to character, Bond didn't bother to wait until the first

blocks had sold before he went out and bought
more.

In August that same year, Alan and his partner
Dave King picked up another five acres in the
Lesmurdie hills, and borrowed a further £4500 from
FCA to do so. This land, which they christened
"Sunset Ridge", wasn't ready to build on and
wouldn't sell for more than twelve months, so it
would be a strain on the finances meanwhile. But
inside two weeks, Bond was at it again. Directly
next door to the original blocks at Lesmurdie was
another twenty-three acres (about nine hectares) of
scrub and orchard that hadn't yet been subdivided,
and that therefore offered the chance of a far larger
profit. The land belonged to an ageing widow
named Elsie Over, who was persuaded to sell for a
bargain price, just £9500, whereupon Bond went
back to the finance company, FCA, to borrow still
more. Once again the terms were pretty stiff—
repayment within a year and one per cent interest
per month—but they could have charged ten times
that and Bond would still have made money. When
the land was subdivided the following May there
would be nearly forty blocks, which would eventually sell, from October 1961 onwards, for an average
of £1300 each.

That, however, was more than a year away. In the
meantime, the money to clear the blocks, put roads
through, pay interest on the loans, and meet the
costs of buying and selling the land was money that
Bond didn't have. What's more, there was only one
place to find it. According to Lindsay McCreddin
and Dave King, who were, respectively, Bond's
right-hand man and partner at Nu-Signs, Bond
simply used the money from the painting business,

which was already on its uppers. As a result, he had half of Fremantle after his blood. It was a situation with remarkable parallels in later years, when Bond would take money from Bell Resources and have half of Australia's bankers on his tail. Only then the sums would be much larger.

It was poor McCreddin who had the unenviable task of going round to the creditors to plead for more time. "We had no money," he recalls, "but he bought this land. Then we couldn't pay our bills, so I went to Bunnings, the big timber merchant, who we bought our timber and paint from, and I went in to see the manager, Jack Groves. He asked me where was the cheque for their bill, did I bring it with me, and I said no, Maxine had posted the cheque. 'I've heard that story before', he said. 'Till you bring the cheque around, there's no more credit.'" McCreddin asked Alan what had happened to the money owed to Bunnings and was told it had been used to pay for the land in Lesmurdie Heights. Yet even when that land was sold, the money wasn't repaid, because Bond promptly bought some more. When McCreddin then asked Alan whether he would pay Nu-Signs' debts, Bond cheerfully told him: "No, it's cheap money."

As Bond's land deals gathered pace, the financial problems at Nu-Signs went from bad to worse because the company's coffers were constantly being emptied. According to Cam McNab, who was hired over a game of darts in 1961 to sort out Bond's finances: "Nu-Signs was in big trouble when I got there. Alan had taken quite a bit of money out of it to put into his land. Anything that it generated he took out. In actual fact Nu-Signs was bankrupt, it was insolvent. We just kept it going by not paying people. We used to bank at the English Scottish and Australian Bank in Fremantle, and we used to have to beg them for money so that we could pay the men." The accounts at Nu-Signs were also in the most shocking state. According to McNab, Alan's bookkeeping was "absolutely chaotic, incredibly bad, a bloody mess. Alan had cheque butts that were two and three years old, and they didn't have a thing written on them. He had a Suspense Account, which was pages long. Anything he didn't know about went into Suspense... It just went on and on."

When Cam came on the scene, Nu-Signs had debts of £8000 that it couldn't or wouldn't pay. The company was being sued by its creditors, and was being pursued for payment round town by its suppliers—a situation with which Alan would become familiar in his business career. Bond's policy with the creditors was to play them along, says McNab: "Most of the time he would leave it until the very last moment and pay a bit of what he owed. Then he would wait until they sent round the next summons for the rest, and then he would pay a little bit more. So we managed to spread the money round." Every time Nu-Signs paid them some money the old summons would lapse and have to be redrawn, so Bond bought himself time. But it was a nervewracking business, and Cam McNab didn't like it one bit.

Nor did Alan's father Frank, who doubtless found his son's new enterprise quite wearing. Although he was technically a partner in the business, Frank left it all to Alan and Kathleen to run. While they fought off the creditors, Frank would retire to the pub to sink a few beers, and worry over

Alan's latest escapade. "I remember him telling me," an old family friend recalls today, "how Alan used to phone him and say 'Where are you? You're supposed to be at a board meeting.' And Frank would tell me he didn't even know which one. He used to despair a bit about the things that Alan did. He was always worried that Alan was going too fast, and if it was above board." But Frank was a more cautious, gentler man. According to one of Alan's cousins, who spent many years working for Bond, "Frank was ten times a better man than Alan is. He might not have been rich, but he was a lot nicer." Or as another observer would put it, "Frank was a perfect gentleman. Unfortunately, it never rubbed off on Alan."

In these hectic years Alan was probably going too fast to keep his marriage stable, but he was hardly the househusband type in any case. And although the childhood marriage to Eileen could be interpreted as romantic, it was not exactly a conventional love story. Young Alan and Eileen started their married life living in a garage—both were aged seventeen and there was already a baby on the way. Alan had put down a £5 deposit on a £350 plot of land in the suburb of Melville the day after their wedding and then, in true Australian tradition, had built a home for the Holden, or more likely the Dodge. But a fair bit of time had passed before there was enough money to build the house, so they had stayed in the garage for the first two years, with one young son and another on the way. The first weekend of their married life, to celebrate their honeymoon, Alan had dragged Eileen off to look at development sites. And thereafter, to pass the time during pregnancies, Eileen had often clambered over scaffolding holding Alan's paintbrushes. Yet despite Eileen's apparent willingness to be a part of his business life, Alan's work came to include her less and less, and a growing family took more and more of her time.

By the time Alan and Eileen had been married five years, there were already three children on the scene, but Alan was still only twenty-two years old and he had not slowed down at all. Few young men would have had the energy to live as he did, but young Alan's appetites were apparently undimmed by the responsibilities of fatherhood. According to his business colleagues, he never grew up. If he wasn't working like mad, he was out with the lads, playing just as hard.

Even before the property deals started coming good, the extrovert entrepreneur had a succession of flashy American cars, or Yank Tanks as they were called, in which he used to cruise around town with his mates, often with a couple of attractive women in tow. People who knew Alan in those days still talk about these cars, which obviously made a deep impression on the good burghers of the west, as young Bond must also have done. One of the most memorable was an Oldsmobile which, by common consent, was the best car in Perth, as well as the most conspicuous. It would often be seen around town with someone even younger than Bond at the wheel, because he would lend it out to his friends or employees, almost whenever they wanted to use it. No doubt there were plenty of people who found such ostentatious display offensive, especially when something so valuable was treated so casually— Perth was, after all, a rather proper town at the time. But Alan didn't care what people thought of him.

And as one or two of his schoolmates observed, he was always generous with his toys.

The cars were a constant source of trouble, and not just in gaining Bond a riotous reputation, because Alan used to drive them at breakneck speed wherever he went—on one occasion with his accountant on the bonnet. McCreddin used to travel with Alan every so often down to Busselton, three hours south of Perth, and used to put it down on his timesheet as "flying time" because that's how fast Bond would drive. Before long, the would-be property king had enough speeding tickets to paper a house with and was being pursued by the police. In fact there are policemen who remember chasing Bond as almost a full-time occupation. But the boys in blue soon got his measure. Rather than bring all the offences for trial at the same time, and get only one penalty from the magistrates, they served the summonses one by one. Thus, as soon as Bond got his licence back after a month's suspension, the court would take it away from him again.

It is typical of Alan Bond that he lived in this way. In his personal life, as in business, he was always close to the edge. The mere fact that he was married never stopped him playing around, and the mere fact that he was broke never cramped his style. It was part of his charm that he behaved as if the rules were for others, not for him.

In 1962, Nu-Signs' creditors became so fed up with never getting their money that they took Alan to court and brought him to within a whisker of being made bankrupt. But Bond escaped, and his reaction was typical. One plumber to whom he owed money, Tom Tate Snr, remembers how the young entrepreneur was saved because a couple of

elderly gents from the Fremantle business community reckoned that the boy should be given a
chance—after all he was only young, and just starting out in business. The creditors came to an
arrangement with Nu-Signs and bankruptcy was
staved off. But what happened then could surely
have happened to no one else. According to the
Tates, there was a land auction the very next day,
and Alan was there. Unperturbed by the fact that he
had narrowly escaped bankruptcy, the irrepressible
Bond put his hand up for a block that cost £45,000.
Some of Bond's creditors, who had seen him in
court the day before, could scarcely contain themselves. "All these old blokes couldn't believe it,"
says the younger Tom Tate. "They had just given
him a reprieve and he lines up at this auction and
spends quite a sum of money, and they'd had it in
their grasp to bankrupt him." To which Tom Snr
adds: "Yes they'd thought he would slow down for
a while, but not Bondy."

As his old right-hand man Lindsay McCreddin so
aptly puts it, "Alan always was a dangerous man at
a sale." But there was more logic to it than met the
eye. In fact, the auction response formed the basis of
Bond's financial philosophy. According to Cam
McNab: "Very often we couldn't afford to pay the
wages, so he would go out and buy something.
People don't believe it, but that's exactly true. When
we got into strife and couldn't pay the blokes, we
would go and buy something. I remember once
having to get £20,000 in an extreme hurry, and I
mean extreme. We had to get it by the next day just
to exist—to pay wages and bills. Alan went and
bought something and I renegotiated its value so
that we could borrow against it. The local bloke had

a limit of £10,000, so he gave us two lots of £9999. That was from Custom Credit. We were very friendly with them."

By purchasing properties, Bond was always able to generate new cash. In the 1960s, land could be obtained by paying a small deposit. So, provided one could get the land immediately revalued at more than the asking price, it was not hard to borrow more money than had to be shelled out to the vendor. Land prices at the time were rising rapidly, and Bond was a persuasive man, so he could usually find a valuer who would value the land for considerably more than he was paying for it. Thus Bond bought and borrowed, generated cash, and then bought again and borrowed more when the next cash crisis hit. Often he would borrow several times against the same property, increasing his loans as land prices went up. And the finance companies handed out the money with gay abandon.

Cam McNab remembers a "lovely bit of land that Alan bought off an estate agent named Ken Dunn. It was twenty or thirty acres but it was zoned rural only, and of course you couldn't subdivide it. We borrowed money on this a couple of times. I borrowed £4000 on it and then I borrowed £10,000. I had only been up once to have a look at the land and I went up there with Don Brown from Custom Credit to show him what we wanted to borrow on. I'm not sure to this day whether I showed him the right block of land, but he okayed it. I just pointed to a bit of land and said: 'That's it, over there.' Anyway, he lent us the money to get us out of strife."

Having bought all this land to solve his cash problems, Bond had to keep it moving to avoid getting into even deeper trouble. So he and McNab started selling blocks on the never-never, or on credit terms. Instead of just handing plots over to cash buyers or to those who could borrow from a building society, they offered them to anyone who had a hundred pounds' deposit and would promise to make the payments. And, even better, they then discovered they could use the contracts of sale to borrow against. For example, they might buy a piece of land for £10,000 and subdivide it into 100 lots; they would then get contracts of sale on all the blocks for £500 each (provided they could find customers) and borrow the best part of £50,000 on the strength of it.

The finance companies were happy to play this strange and risky money game, because land prices were rising fast and because they charged exorbitant interest rates to borrowers. While money could be had from the banks at 7 or 8 per cent, the finance companies wanted 12 or 13 per cent. Their customers, meanwhile, were prepared to pay the price because they could not get the money anywhere else. In the 1960s, both banks and building societies took an extremely cautious view of property lending—they would not normally lend on land at all, and would rarely advance more than 60 per cent of the price on a house purchase. So the finance companies, who would lend 90 per cent on a land deal (and 100 per cent or more if you found the right valuer), had the field to themselves. One of the biggest among them, and certainly one of the biggest lenders to Bond, was Finance Corporation of Australia (FCA), which set up in business in Perth only in 1960. FCA specialised in land subdivisions, so Bond found them easy to deal with. But they were not the only ones. Bond went to every finance company in Perth, and they threw open their doors.

Bond and McNab could normally buy the land and turn their money round pretty fast, because subdividing in Perth in the 1960s was a fairly simple business. They didn't bother laying water pipes or sewers or electricity, it was merely a matter of putting a road through the property and then selling it off. A gravel road would do, kerbing and guttering weren't necessary, so provided they could get approval from the planners within six months, it was all plain sailing. But as soon as there were delays, there was potential disaster, because the debts were forever threatening to fall on top of them. And that's where the fun started. Bond and McNab would be in Kalamunda Shire Council or the Town Planning Board every day trying to push their projects through, and would use every trick to speed things up. "Alan wouldn't so much break the rules as bend them to the limit," says Cam McNab. "In subdivisions, town planning, he'd bend the rules to the utmost to get something done. If there was a waiting list he'd try to force his way through. Mainly because he was desperate to get a result because we needed the money. Oh, it was a hectic pace."

But once the blocks were ready to go, Bond could sell them, if anyone could. According to Lindsay McCreddin, "Bondy is the best salesman in the world. He is just brilliant, he could sell you anything." These skills, vouched for by countless others over the years, included more than just face-to-face techniques. "His marketing ideas were just brilliant," says Cam McNab, "far superior to anyone else at the time. We purchased a big slab of land in

Gooseberry Hills outside of Perth and we named it Beverly Hills. Can you imagine naming it that? Then we took out big press ads. No one had ever done that, no one had ever taken full-page advertisements for land before. Then we had big weekend sales, which no one else was doing at the time. We put bunting up all over the place and we had huge signs pointing to our land sale. I remember we sold the blocks for up to £2000 each. Right across the road they were selling for £500 a block. People could have got their land for a quarter of the price if they had investigated. But we sold all ours because of the way we did it."

With his selling ability, Alan could prosper even where fortune failed him. And the saga of the property at Guildford, with which the Tates were so impressed, provides a perfect example. Bond bought it in December 1961 for £40,000, when he was already mortgaged to the hilt, from a widow called Hilda Craven. He intended to subdivide it for housing, a plan that would have made him a fortune. But things didn't go to plan.

Rosehill, as the house was called, was a lovely old homestead set in several acres of beautiful gardens, which survive to this day. Two huge *Magnifolia grandiflora* dominate the planting, but there are also jacarandas with brilliant purple flowers, and huge mounds of orange and mauve bougainvillea, growing in bushes around the perimeter. On one side of the house, which is set on higher ground, green fields lead down to a river, with trees lining the banks. From a distance the trees could easily be willows, the spreading shade-givers in the fields could pass for oaks, and the cows swishing their tails in the long grass could be grazing in

Oxfordshire. And perhaps that's no coincidence, because the Padbury family who built Rosehill came originally from Charlbury in the middle of England, where the meadows by the Evenlode look much the same.

Having bought this beautiful spread, Bond set about trying to make some money out of it. There was some land on the far side of the river which had already been subdivided, and Bond thought he might follow suit. But before trying for all the approvals he put an advertisement in the paper offering some of the land for sale. It was at this point, according to Dave King, Bond's partner at Nu-Signs, that they discovered a small problem. A crowd of people had turned up for the great land sale, and Bond was in the middle of trying to unload a few blocks, when a local came up and tapped him on the shoulder. Pointing to a pole in the middle of the field near where they were standing, which was no more than fifty metres from Rosehill's back door, he said to Bond: "See that post there? I tie my boat up to that in winter." Bond had apparently known that the land was "low-lying" as Cam McNab puts it, but hadn't reckoned with it being under three metres of water in wintertime.

Despite this setback, Bond somewhat surprisingly went ahead with applications for a subdivision and, according to McCreddin, the planners even more surprisingly said yes. But it was only on the condition that Bond built a bridge over the river, which was going to cost far too much, so that scheme collapsed. Bond's next plan was to turn the house into a C-class nursing home, but the authorities insisted on him building nurses' quarters, and that also came to a dead end. By this time, things

were getting desperate. The property was costing
Bond almost as much in interest as all his other
ventures put together, and after two years of
schemes that got nowhere it was showing no sign of
ever paying any money back. To sell it as a homestead again would mean financial disaster; they
simply had to find a use for it. Then, just in time to
beat off the bankers, Bond came up with the brainwave of turning it into a golf course and country
club, and more to the point, he came up with a
buyer, who would buy him out at a profit.

The taker was in fact a syndicate of investors,
organised by his accountant, and including his
brother-in-law Bill Hughes. Sadly it would not turn
out to be a great investment for them. Even though
the flooding problem was fixed when the river was
dammed upstream, they never managed to get a
subdivision. They tried for the next twenty-one
years for permission to develop the land, first for
housing and then for light industry, but although
they got to the planning stage once or twice, they
struck problems with disposal of sewage, and it
never quite happened. Today, the land is still a golf
course, and Rosehill is still a country club, having
been run as such for almost the last thirty years,
without ever making much money. The house's
magnificent swimming pool, which was once
Bond's pride and joy, sadly is no more.

At a poolside party there one night, things got a
little out of hand and one woman ended up in the
water, complete with ball gown, tiara and drunken
guest. On that occasion, the party had not been
given by Bond, since the property was already sold,
but there were a number of flings that Alan did
have at Rosehill which were equally riotous. Indeed,

Leon Evans, one of Bond's business colleagues in the early 1960s, ended up getting divorced as a consequence of the goings-on there. As the story goes, Leon's wife and Alan's wife Eileen went off to Hong Kong on a shopping trip and stayed for six weeks, and while they were away there was carousing every night. Cam McNab had moved in to Rosehill with Bond for the duration, and in his words "it was unbelievable the things we did". Quite what they were, one can only speculate, but in Cam's words "the booze and the birds went on forever". And clearly, Leon Evans' wife took exception to it. Perhaps Eileen did too. But by this stage, apparently, she and Alan were already leading fairly separate lives.

It is a hallmark of entrepreneurs throughout the world that they present themselves as larger than life, so that the illusion of success is maintained. And Bond had this gambit down to a fine art: whether broke or not, he always lived lavishly, he never went second class. And perhaps it was this, as much as the business dealings, that made Bond so disliked by the Perth establishment. The old-money business community on St Georges Terrace, who knew how to behave, just couldn't believe the way he carried on. According to his partner, McNab, "Alan was despised by most people in town as an arrogant upstart. He had an obnoxious and brusque manner for a young man, and he had also trodden on heaps of toes." But worst of all in their eyes, his behaviour never brought him down—he defied their conservative ways of doing business and continued to get away with it.

In the mid 1960s, for example, when Bond bought 68 St Georges Terrace—which was to become his

Perth headquarters—he and McNab had agreed they would go to the auction to watch, but Bond could not prevent himself from buying it, even though he had no money. As the property was knocked down to Bond, the auctioneer said to the assembled company, which included the pick of Perth's business establishment: "Excuse me, ladies and gentlemen, the auction hasn't concluded yet. I believe the purchaser is a Mr Bond or a Mr McNab. I would like a bank-marked cheque for 10 per cent from you Mr Bond, and I will hold the proceedings for an hour." Alan, who had not even got round to sorting out where the deposit was coming from, leaned over to McNab and said casually: "Go over to the ESandA and get the money." Fortunately for Bond and McNab, the bank came up with the cheque. But the guardians of Perth propriety were merely the more enraged.

Throughout the 1960s the elder statesmen of West Australian business waited for Bond to go bust but, to their great disappointment, he never did. The cash crises continued, yet Bond always came through. On occasion, however, he needed help: in 1964, for example, well after the property deals were under way, Alan's father-in-law, Doozer Hughes, had to bail him out. Bond's shopping centre development in Fremantle had begun to founder because no one would rent the units they had built. Doozer, who was a councillor at the time, found himself stumping up money and a guarantee to keep the banks at bay, and then dug deep in his pocket to meet the rates bill. He told his friend Jack Sowden sourly: "I've got to go and pay the rates. I can't get any bloody money out of Alan." But this and other storms were weathered, and Alan eventually marched to his first million.

It was a classic Bond deal: a huge block of already subdivided land at Kardinya, on Perth's southern edge, was up for sale at $1.2 million. Bond wanted it but didn't even have the deposit. So he and McNab flew to Melbourne, where they went to the head office of a finance company called CAGA and borrowed the lot—deposit and all. CAGA took a share of the profit on top of its customary 12 per cent interest, Bond put the bunting up and they all made a killing. The year was 1967, and Bond was twenty-nine. He had made it at last.

A number of factors had helped him get there. In the first place, he had extraordinary drive and energy: he did not hang around debating issues, but jumped in and made things happen. Denis Sowden, a long-time family friend, says: "If he wanted to do something, he'd be doing it. You'd wake up in the morning and find Bondy's done it." But he also had an eye for a deal and, for all his academic failings, he was extremely smart at business. As Cam McNab rather pungently expresses it: "He was basically illiterate, his spelling was atrocious. He couldn't even add up or read a contract. But I tell you, he knew what a quid was. He didn't know the left from the right of the balance sheet but he had the best business brain I've ever come across."

What Bond also had was no shame; he had none of the conventional concerns about money that shackle the ordinary man. If Bond couldn't pay, too bad. If the bank gave him a hard time, no matter. As Lindsay McCreddin observes, "He would take his cheque down to the bank and if there was any trouble with it, he'd change his bank". Or as Tom Tate Snr so aptly sums it up: "He had a lot of cheek. He had to, to get where he is today."

McCreddin tells a tale of how Bond bought a new block of land up in the hills outside Perth to subdivide for housing. McCreddin was up on the property one day when Bond arrived, full of beans. "He came in and told me to get rid of the trees because they were spoiling the view. It was a beautiful view of Perth. So I arranged to get these chainsaws and two people over from the hire place. We were about to start and this man came over and asked me what we were doing. I told him we were going to knock the trees down. Well, he nearly knocked me down. The trees were on his property and he liked them the way they were. Bondy, he didn't care whose trees they were, they ruined the view from his site."

What also helped Bond was that he never worried. He seemed not only to thrive on adversity, but to enjoy the sleep of the innocent. And that, perhaps, was as important as all the other qualities put together. Bond made his first million dollars, and others after it, because he kept going whatever happened. Nothing would stop him. He had determination and extraordinary stamina.

It is worth remembering that in the 1960s, Bond's two most important business partners both quit, either because they couldn't stand the pace or because they were unhappy with the style of operation. Dave King, the partner in Nu-Signs, couldn't tolerate the customers' complaints and the creditors not being paid. So he packed his bags and left in 1963. Cam McNab for his part found that doing business alongside Bond was killing him. And thus in early 1967, he too took himself off, to Rottnest Island to run the general store.

Neither Cam McNab nor Dave King left rich.

They both missed out on Bond's eventual bonanza, in which, from 1967 to 1974 the business empire expanded enormously and the millions came rolling in. But then perhaps they didn't care—or care as much as Alan did.

CHAPTER 5

1974–
The Wrong Kind
of Person

Those who run the Royal Perth Yacht Club like to think of it as a gentlemen's club. It is steeped in as much tradition as Australia can muster, and its members insist that the word Royal be used even in casual conversation. The members guard its gates and its standards by keeping tight control over the type of people they let in, and by maintaining the sort of rules that gentlemen's clubs throughout the world rely on to keep themselves above the general scrum. Stiff-necked and stuffy, it is just the sort of place that people like Alan Bond would normally steer clear of. On the other hand, it *is* where the top people have their boats. To this day at the Royal Perth, you have to wear all white when you go sailing or face a fine. Until recently, too, if you entered the bar with a woman, a dog, or wearing a hat—or, heaven forbid, all three—you had to stand drinks for everybody present. Indeed, the same applied if your wife or your labrador put so much as a head inside the window and barked your name.

In the late 1960s, to the horror of some of its members, the unlikely figure of Alan Bond came knocking on the door of the Royal Perth Yacht Club, asking to be admitted. He had become a sailor almost by accident, in that he had been given a boat, and had decided to keep it. His father had been telling Alan he needed a hobby to help him relax. So when someone offered him a magnificent ocean racer called *Panamuna*, he could hardly say no. In his early days as a property tycoon, Bond and his company would often take cars or motor boats in payment for land, if purchasers of his blocks didn't have the necessary cash. And he had come by the *Panamuna* in precisely this fashion. It was just Bond's good luck that she happened to be the one of the largest, flashiest, and most gracious boats on the Swan River. And it was just the Royal Perth Yacht Club's ill fortune, as they saw it, that she was the queen of their fleet, carrying the coveted R1 on her sails—the number normally reserved for the club's commodore.

Bond liked the Royal Perth Yacht Club well enough, despite its eccentricities. After all, it represented the pinnacle of Perth society, onto which he longed to climb. And among its members were many people it would be useful for him to know. But the Royal Perth, unfortunately, did not take to him. Indeed there were those in the club who were outraged by his approach—here was someone not even a member of the club, buying his way into the position of number one ticket holder, and then demanding to be admitted. What's more, young Bond was someone who represented almost everything they had fought to keep out. He had a bad reputation in Perth's business circles, while personally he was brash, vulgar, arrogant, and very nouveau riche. Even according to his supporters like *Panamuna*'s previous owner Bill Lucas (who would later play a key role in Bond's America's Cup campaigns), "he had a pretty abrasive nature, and generally speaking he was regarded as a young upstart". Nor did he improve as you got to know him. One of Bond's sailing crew, Jack Baxter, remembers him at the first meeting being "small, loud and brash". His more considered view of Captain Bond, on second acquaintance, was that he was "louder and brasher by a factor of six hundred".

In the 1960s, the Royal Perth Yacht Club decided membership applications with great ritual. After receiving a detailed report on the individual candidate, a leather canister with two compartments was passed round the committee-room table, and each of the eleven members dropped a red or a black ball into the relevant pocket. The canister was then handed to a counter, who marked down the result on his sheet of paper. This in turn was eventually handed to the returning officer, who read out the names of all successful applicants. One black ball was enough to keep an applicant out, and Bond received at least one, for when his application came up for consideration, his name did not make it to the final list. Nothing more was said at the time, as was the custom, and nor was Bond's blackballer unmasked, so neither the rejection nor the reason was ever made public. But even those who argued in his favour seemed more concerned about losing *Panamuna* to a rival club, than they did about any injustice. The ebullient Mr Bond was clearly not the right sort of chap. It was rather sad that in later years, Bond would hotly deny that he had been turned down—rejection, it seems, was something he never coped with well, for all his eventual power and fame.

Oddly enough, on the Swan River in Perth, there are two Royal yacht clubs, but people who are rejected by one do not normally bother to apply for the other: the Royal Freshwater and the Royal Perth have an unwritten agreement that if an applicant is rejected by one club, he is not to be considered by the other. So if Bond did go knocking on the windows at the Royal Freshwater, he would have been given short shrift. But luckily for him and other would-be club members deemed beyond the pale, there is a third club, at Claremont, and Bond finally found a welcome there. Before long his *Panamuna* had a mooring, and was ready to cruise out onto the river and take on all comers.

Bond soon discovered that although the 44-foot *Panamuna* was the best-looking boat on the river, she wasn't quite the fastest, and it annoyed him. Whether in business or pleasure, Bond's intention has always been to win. So, when Rolly Tasker and his boat *Siska*, who were champions of the Royal Perth Yacht Club, constantly beat him, Bond did what any self-respecting entrepreneur would do in such circumstances—he went after a better boat, commissioning designer Ben Lexcen (then plain Bob Miller) to build him one. Needless to say, his brief was to build it bigger than anybody else's. As Jim Hardy, Bond's America's Cup helmsman in 1974, tells the tale, "You weren't allowed to have a boat on the Swan that was longer than 60-foot, so Ben designed the *Apollo* to be 58-foot. Alan just wanted the fastest boat he could under 60-foot, regardless of handicap. That's typical of Bondy. He didn't want to apply some racing formula. He just wanted to be fastest."

And fast she was, both in the water and in the construction. *Apollo* was built in just six weeks, and no sooner was she launched in December 1969 than she tackled the Sydney to Hobart, Australia's premier yacht race. Neck and neck down the finishing straight she fought it out with the British boat *Crusader*, owned by Sir Max Aitken, only to miss line honours by just thirteen minutes—a remarkable achievement for an untrialled boat. Now Bond had his first taste of real ocean racing and was hooked. Next would come the Admiral's Cup, and then the really big time.

The story of how Bond got into 12-metre racing is almost too good to be true. Early in 1970, just a few months after the Sydney to Hobart, Bond and Ben Lexcen were in America with *Apollo*, preparing for a tilt at America's biggest offshore race, the Newport to Bermuda. *Apollo* was being made ready at Bob Derecktor's shipyard at Mamaroneck, just north of New York City, and it so happened that *Valiant*, one of the 1970 America's Cup challengers, was being fitted out there at the time. The *Valiant* was quite radical, even for a 12-metre, not least in the way her deck was laid out, and naturally Alan Bond wanted to investigate. But when he went to inspect her, he got more than he bargained for. As he and Lexcen and three members of the *Apollo* crew peered into her cockpit at six o'clock one morning, they found a tough little number called Vic Romagna staring back at them. Romagna was an experienced America's Cup crewman and New York Yacht Club member who, thirteen years later, would be the fiercest critic of *Australia II*'s winged keel. In more ways than one it was a fateful encounter.

According to Romagna: "They were working all over the boat with cameras and the whole bit, having a really good look at everything and taking pictures." But whether they were or not—and the Australians maintain they were just curious—Romagna flew off the handle. "There were five of them and they were bigger than me but I've had a pretty tough upbringing and I said to them: 'Come on guys, get off or someone's going to get beaten up for this.' Well, they went, they knew they were wrong." But as they backed away, Bond turned to Lexcen and asked him what the hell sort of a boat was it anyway. And when Lexcen explained about 12-metres and the America's Cup, Bond's reply was effectively: "Well, we'll just bloody come back and win it off them then." At which point Ben Lexcen added the thought that they could then take it back to Perth and run a steamroller over it, so that they could rename it the Australia's Plate.

It has been said that there are two ways for the self-made businessman to gain instant respectability. One is to own the winner of the Arc de Triomphe, Europe's top horse race, and the other is to capture the America's Cup. And Bond's challenge might well have been fired by just such a search for endorsement. Certainly, those who know Bond well say he was desperate to be recognised and accepted by the establishment. According to Cam McNab: "Alan really wanted to impress people. He would have been tickled pink to have been made Sir Alan or Lord Alan. He would also have loved to have gone to a good school or to have been to Oxford or

Cambridge. He had a bit of a chip on his shoulder about his background and his education." And Jack Baxter agrees—Alan did it for the glory: "Bondy saw himself as a Cockney boy from the Swan who'd made it. He loved the spinoff of sailing because it raised him to that social level. He really wanted to be Sir Alan Bond. He was also a strong royalist. He invited Prince Philip out sailing once, and he just loved that scene."

But Bond had other motives for tilting at the America's Cup, and one of them was to take revenge on the snooty Royal Perth Yacht Club. When he telexed the New York Yacht Club in 1970 to throw down a challenge for the Cup, the members of the Royal Perth could hardly contain their amazement. But once it was clear that Bond meant business, they quickly climbed on board and grabbed the tiller. Issuing a formal challenge in the yacht club's name, to comply with the America's Cup rulebook, the Royal Perth then welcomed Bond into the fold, or at least grudgingly admitted him. "They'll have to let me in now," Bond had told a friend, and he was right. The Royal Perth would hardly let the Claremont yacht club fly the flag for Australia when they could take control.

The America's Cup till then had been the preserve of tycoons like Britain's Sir Thomas Lipton, the tea king, or Australia's Sir Frank Packer of newspaper fame; men who had built business empires, amassed large fortunes, and were happy to lose some of it out on the water. But Bond's approach was refreshingly different. He saw the America's Cup, and the massive exposure it would give him, as a chance to expand his business empire worldwide. It would put Bond's name in the

American market, give his companies access to American finance, and promote a project on which he had gambled millions of dollars of his bankers' money. The project was Yanchep Sun City, which in 1970 was his greatest dream, and by 1974, when the America's Cup was sailed, would be his greatest headache.

The village of Yanchep, if village is the right expression, lies an hour-and-a-half north of Perth, well outside the city limits. In summer it is blazingly hot, the sun beats down without mercy, and the mercury is often up around 35°C. There are flies everywhere and life can be almost unbearable. A singularly unattractive place in the late 1960s when Bond bought it, it was also a desert. In the words of one observer at the time, there was "nothing, no people, no plants, no bird life. Just sand." Yanchep had been farmed for many years, with little joy, by the Wydgee Pastoral Company, whose station manager Tiddles Cockman sowed seed on the sandhills, put down trace elements and tried to raise sheep. The sheep expired, the kangaroos prospered, and Wydgee gave up. At which point Alan Bond arrived on the scene. Seeing what no one else could see, he bought 20,000 acres (8093 hectares) at an average $70 an acre, almost ten times the farming value, and Yanchep's owners thought all their Christmases had come at once.

John Bertrand, who was a member of the 1974 America's Cup crew, remembers his first sight of Yanchep from the passenger seat of Bond's Rolls-Royce Corniche as they roared up the long coast road from Perth. There were white rolling sandhills stretching into the distance, bordered on the left by the magnificent blue of the Indian Ocean. But there was neither a person nor a blade of grass in sight. Then suddenly, as Bertrand looked again, the sandhills turned bright green, just like an oasis. "Christ," said Bertrand, looking at Bond, "have you put in irrigation?" "No," said Bond, "I've painted the sandhills to make the brochures look better." Bertrand couldn't believe it, but Bond assured him it was true. Waving his hand, he said: "just helping the grass along". Bertrand says that Bond talked nineteen to the dozen about his plans, all the way from Perth, and he remembers vividly his first impression of this pugnacious little man: "He looked like a fighter, walked like a fighter, and spoke like a fighter. He was only about five feet six inches tall but he had a neck like Muhammad Ali." He also had "the innate, terrifying charm of the true salesman", and he had used it on the Western Australian Government to sell them his dream of Yanchep.

Desert it might have been, but Bond had a vision of the future, which, true to form, he had painted so vividly that the government soon believed in it too. Although Yanchep was zoned for rural use, Bond managed to persuade the politicians to permit a massive development: a huge city-cum-tourist resort with 250,000 people. It was to be, in Bond's great plan, the Cote d'Azur of Western Australia, the Mediterranean Down Under. A hovercraft and ferry service would link Yanchep Sun City to Perth, as would a new express busway, to be constructed alongside the narrow road through Wanneroo. There would be a racetrack, a Grand Prix circuit, a new Disneyland and an Australiana Park, such that no tourist would come to Australia without paying Yanchep a visit. And for the government, there would be jobs, tax revenue and tourist dollars for the state. Bond had even taken the Western Australian Premier, John Tonkin, and his planning minister, Ron Davies, up in the Corniche to have a look at it all. Davies remembers Bond gesticulating wildly as he whipped the Roller off the road and charged through the bush to show them where the championship golf course was going to be. It was a great concept, says Davies, and the government had no trouble giving it the nod.

But promises were one thing, performance another. To realise a fraction of this dramatic vision, Bond needed $250 million, which was wildly beyond the scale of any of his previous projects. And here was where the America's Cup came in: if Bond could capture the Cup and sail the defence at Yanchep, the world would beat a path to his door and he stood to make a fortune. He could build the resort and sell at least some of the 60,000 vacant building blocks that would pay for it. So, as the 1970s unfolded, Yanchep Sun City became "Home of the Twelves", and the base for Bond's 1974 America's Cup challenge. A $2 million marina was built, along with a yachting village, complete with large open space in the shape of a 12-metre.

From the sailing point of view, Yanchep was indeed perfect. On a typical afternoon in the summer, the wind blows in off the Indian Ocean at a good thirty knots, lifting the sand and pummelling anyone who happens to be on the beach. But from other points of view it was not ideal: as the builders of Yanchep would discover, once you started to clear the scrubby grey banksias off the sandhills, the hills had a nasty habit of shifting, and the building blocks blew away. According to Jim Hardy, Bond's

America's Cup skipper in 1974, you were well advised to leave your family spread over the block if you went off to Perth for the week. That is, if you didn't want to find your land had shifted to the end of the street while you were away.

On the day that Bond's America's Cup challenge was launched, however, there was no such gale to wreck the perfect pageant. The sun blazed down on a mass of TV crews and newspaper reporters, summoned for the occasion, as a few bemused fishermen looked on. A beaming Alan Bond bustled about in monogrammed shirt and yachting jacket, pursued by anxious aides in blue and white uniform. And as the bulldozers shoved mounds of sand around in the background, over the hill appeared a full regimental pipe band, kilts and all. The pipers wailed "God Save the Queen", the Western Australian Governor rolled in, and Bond the challenger made his pitch. First he gave them the patriotic version: "The America's Cup gives Western Australia and Australia the opportunity to show people the quality of life that exists here." And then he gave them a taste of the Bond strategy: "Five hundred million people will watch the race though the media; they will see us training, they will see the clean beaches, the lack of pollution. Many of them may wish to come and live here." After the ceremony, a journalist was impertinent enough to suggest Bond might not be sailing purely for sport, to which Bond blurted out the classic reply: "Anyone who considers racing for the America's Cup isn't a business proposition is a bloody fool. There can be no other justification for spending six million dollars on the Australian challenge unless the return is going to involve something more than just an ornate silver pitcher." With 20,000 acres of scrub and sand, and 60,000 building blocks, mostly vacant, one had to agree.

A hole drilled directly through the earth from Yanchep would emerge in the United States of America, barely twenty kilometres away from Newport, Rhode Island. But the yachting capital of the USA, where the America's Cup races were sailed in 1974, and where they had been for the previous hundred years, was far more than half a world away from the dunes and dreams of Yanchep. Newport, comfortable in its role as a veritable museum of old money, strove for nothing. Some four hours from the great banks of Manhattan, where Newport's millions were either stored or made, this pretty fishing village had evolved in the nineteenth century as a playground for the robber barons. In August in particular, when business was slow in New York and the heat was hell, the air up on Rhode Island was much cooler, with fresh sea breezes to fan the face. It was to this place that the elements of New York society that mattered once used to come to be seen and have fun through the warm days and long summer nights.

They would come down from their mansions in July, preceded by a camel train of servants loaded up with the family silver, the crockery with the family coat of arms, and all the perquisites of a palatial country home. For six weeks of the year the Morgans, the Rockefellers, the Vanderbilts, and others would open up their massive marble palaces and parade their wealth. In the evenings they would hold court and give balls, while in the daytime they would sail. And every so often, when a new challenger came, they would defend their trophy, the

America's Cup. They regarded it as a private match between yacht clubs and a race for gentlemen. One wonders what they would have thought of a man like Alan Bond.

Already known in yachting circles as "The Toad" for a passing physical resemblance to that creature, Alan Bond could well have earned himself the title of "Mr Toad" in Newport that summer. He followed the races on the largest and loudest motor cruiser of them all, chartered in from far-off waters at $1000 a day. It had citrus-coloured carpet on the afterdeck, three steering systems, and parking for a sports car on the roof. But where Toad in *The Wind in the Willows* was merely boisterous, Bond was overbearing and belligerent. Opening the proceedings at an early press conference, Bond arrogantly told the world's yachting journalists: "We'll annihilate the French, and then we'll beat the Yanks." And in case the New York Yacht Club hadn't got the message he threw in a bit of gratuitous advice: "Many countries will praise you," he told the American yachties, "if you just give the cup to us."

The Americans were horrified. As the *New York Times* wryly observed: "In the aristocratic eyes of the New York Yacht Club, Bond is simply the wrong kind of person to be challenging for a trophy as sacred as the America's Cup. His money is new, made on penny and dollar stocks and later on land speculation, and his manners are terrible. Brash when he arrived here, he is now being described as being boorish and uncouth. Worst of all he appears to have come up with an extremely fast 12-meter." And it wasn't just the Americans who felt that way. Australian journalists were embarrassed by Bond's rude and unco-operative behaviour. And before long they were writing that Bond did Australia no good with his boasting, and should best shut up.

In the course of that summer, Bond annoyed virtually everyone he came across. There were some no doubt who were impressed that this thirty-six-year-old could mount a six-million dollar challenge, and bring fifty men and two boats half-way round the world to do it. There were many who liked his crewmen and their relaxed and friendly attitude to the contest. But Bond dissipated all goodwill. Around Newport he became known as "The Ugly Australian", and the American papers began to call him possibly the most unpopular challenger ever. When Bond got up to speak at a promotional dinner for the Cup, he was loudly booed by the black-tied and ball-gowned diners. Yet he seemed to delight in it all, convinced that he was right. Time and again Bond told people, and particularly the New York Yacht Club, that to regard the America's Cup as purely a sporting event was "absolute rubbish". And, as if that wasn't insult enough, he threw in for good effect: "The Americans aren't sporting about it. They have always defended it with big company money—let's see what they say about commercialism and sponsorship when we win."

Shortly before the races began, the Americans announced that their starting helmsman would be a hot thirty-one-year-old Californian named Denis Conner, whose reputation for aggressive starts was well known even then. Bond objected, and asked for Conner to be removed, issuing a press statement of almost ridiculous cheek, given his own behaviour. "We are fearful that fouling and striking tactics will be introduced to America's Cup starts. We deplore this approach which is degrading to the dignity and prestige of the America's Cup and we are most concerned that this style of racing could be condoned by the NYYC. Apart from the unsportsmanlike nature of this approach, there is a definite element of danger." Denis Conner no doubt found the complaint amusing. But the Royal Perth thought it disgraceful. Commodore Alan Edwards let it be known that Bond had belittled the dignity of a Royal club, and from that point on, he and Bond were no longer on speaking terms.

The Australian entourage had arrived in Newport with high hopes and their supporters' expectations that they would do well. And there was some reason for optimism, as it was only four years since the Australian challenger *Gretel II* had given the Americans their toughest fight in forty years. The result had not been that close on paper, since Sir Frank Packer's boat had lost four of the five races run, but the margins had been narrow in almost every race, and one had been lost in the committee room. Many in Australia were convinced that *Gretel* had been robbed. Two decisions, it was argued, should have gone the other way in the committee room, and would have done so if the New York Yacht Club did not both make the rules and then act as judge and jury. The real score, it was said, was 3-2 to *Gretel*, and there was no doubt that she would have won the last race to take the Cup.

Bond's capture of the trophy in 1974 was thus expected to be almost a formality, not least because there was now an independent jury to prevent robbery being repeated. Bond's aggressive confidence also gave credence to the assertion. The *Southern Cross*, for a start, had to be better than *Gretel II*, because she kept beating her rival in practice off

Yanchep. And, designed by Ben Lexcen, who had been responsible for the very successful *Apollo*, she was also different, so she had to be good. *Southern Cross* was the first aluminium 12-metre in the world, she was long on the waterline, and low on sail area compared with a normal 12-metre, and her keel was an odd shape. But all that merely made her more exciting in the eyes of the myth-makers, who saw in her the potential to be a truly superb performer. Sadly, however, she was not.

As the long months of preparation at Yanchep rolled on, it became apparent that *Southern Cross* was run-of-the-mill at best. Some of the crew even began to realise that her trial horse, *Gretel II*, which had flown the flag in 1970, was faster. Nevertheless, the truth was quietly ignored. No one wanted to admit that the millions spent on *Southern Cross* might have been wasted, or worse, to pass the bad news to Bond. Nor did the newspapers get an inkling. As the run-up to Newport gathered pace, American yachting journalists speculated about the Cup going back to Yanchep, and opined that the Yellow Banana, as she was fondly known, was the strongest and most serious challenger on record. Meanwhile, back home in Australia, the hyperbole went even further. Bond's boat, in the learned opinion of the Australian tabloid press, was the fastest ever seen. "*Southern Cross* closes in for the kill," announced one early headline.

The Bonds and their house guests had consequently decamped for Newport expecting to make a fight of it, if not to win. On arrival, they had installed themselves and the crew in one of the more modest mansions and had then set about enjoying themselves. According to accounts, Alan's mother

Kathleen revelled in it all, and mothered the sailors, checking their fingernails and giving them clean hankies. Eileen cooked for the guests, if not for the crew, serving up great vegetable soups and huge legs of lamb. And in the evenings, everyone partied. The crew went to bars, the captains went to functions. Eileen, with her bright green chiffon gown from Paris to set against her flame-red hair, was the toast of Newport. Fun was had by all.

But when it came to the sailing, things did not go so well. Although *Southern Cross* thrashed the French 4-0, as Bond had promised, Baron Bich's team was hopelessly prepared and in disarray. When *Southern Cross* met the real opposition it became embarrassingly obvious that she was outclassed. She sailed slower than *Courageous* and pointed lower, and she was prepared hardly a tenth as well as the American defender. Her crew had precious little team spirit, and even less real experience of 12-metre racing. They had practised for months off Yanchep, against *Gretel II*, but had never raced in anger. And when they came up against a thoroughbred 12-metre like *Courageous*, sailed by a cut-throat crew, led by the likes of Denis Conner and the sailmaker, Ted Hood, they were soon slaughtered.

The first two races were a procession: *Southern Cross* was whipped soundly. And after these two straight defeats, Bond cracked. As John Bertrand remembers it in his book, *Born to Win*: "this tough little man, the king of Yanchep Sun City—Home of the Twelves—was already running hard to save his face and his image, and he reacted as many a self-made man before him had done under circumstances that proved out of his reach. Bondy lashed out." Bond fired the navigator and the tactician, Hugh Treharne, and then rehired John Cuneo, the man he had sacked a couple of weeks earlier. But it was to no avail—the changes merely widened the margin between the two boats. In the next race, *Southern Cross* took an even bigger hiding than in the first two. "We had gone from moderate to bloody awful," says Bertrand. And sure enough, the fourth race was as bad: it was lost as well, to make it a clean sweep for *Courageous*, and a humiliation for the boat that Bond had bragged was the fastest 12 ever built.

Then the jeering and the recriminations started. *Southern Cross* was renamed the Stone Banana, and Bond started searching for excuses. Next challenge, he brightly told all those who would listen, he would perhaps steer the boat himself. After all, he boasted, it wasn't that difficult, and he certainly couldn't do worse than skipper Jim Hardy had done. But the press took a different view. Having started the campaign right behind Bond, they now began to plunge the knife in. "His win at all costs attitude", one paper noted, "seemed time and time again to take him across the line between playing it hard and playing it foul." Bond hadn't once shut his mouth since arriving in Newport, another paper observed: "He has been talking in his sleep and through his hat; he has been a critic of virtually everything, including his own crew." But even this wasn't the strongest verdict. Bond, according to one Australian yachting writer, had brought defeat upon his crew by his very behaviour. *Southern Cross* had put up her "shameful and embarrassing" performance precisely because Bond had been such a disruptive influence.

The crew were devastated by defeat, but they didn't blame him. They felt the failure had been more basic, more absolute. In the words of one of the crew members, Jack Baxter: "We really didn't know anything. We were awful but we thought we were terrific. And we got our bums kicked hard." The *Southern Cross* sailors packed their bags and went their separate ways, many without saying their goodbyes. Ben Lexcen contemplated whether to blow up his $3 million boat and sell the film rights. And Alan Bond went beaming back to Perth to face his bankers.

CHAPTER 6

The Hangover Years

When Bond came back from Newport in September 1974, the Australian economy was in the grip of a vicious credit squeeze, the cost of borrowing had soared above twenty per cent, and property companies were falling like ninepins. In July, one of the best known and most flamboyant developers, Home Units of Australia, had been rescued; in August, an even bigger property-cum-building company, Mainline, had collapsed; and come the end of September, the biggest of them all, Cambridge Credit, had gone to the wall. Bond had left Newport vowing to challenge again in 1977, but there seemed little chance that his companies would be alive in three years' time to throw down the glove. Most observers would have reckoned Bond's future to be a couple of months at most.

For Bond and for Australia, the last half of 1974 marked the start of an awful hangover. The property boom which had raged for so long had finally gone bust, and the period of pain then began. It was to be all the sharper because the party had been so good. The last two years of the 1960s and the first four of the 1970s in Australia had been one of those intermittent crazy periods, in which land and house prices go berserk and sane people begin to believe that buying property is an infallible way to make a fortune. Nowhere had the boom been wilder than in Bond's home town of Perth. There had been an atmosphere of hysteria, an impression that the last block of land in town was up for sale, and you had to buy or be left behind. All around, one heard stories of people who had made a killing, of people who had bought a block of land one week and doubled their money by selling it a week later. And then in mid-1974, when it looked like the party would never end, when even the doubters began to wonder whether they shouldn't also join in, the festivities were brought to an abrupt end. And as the cold light of dawn flooded in, everyone realised how madly they had all behaved.

Like all the other property revellers, Bond was caught by the collapse in the market and by the huge rise in the cost of borrowing. But he was, if anything, worse off than many others, because his companies had grown faster and had been fed entirely on debt. In just three years since 1971, Bond's business empire had expanded twelvefold, a reckless rate of growth, yet his borrowings had multiplied almost twice as fast as that—by more like twenty times. Now, in rough terms, the publicly-quoted Bond Corporation had $100 million of debts and a collection of assets that would fetch only $50 million in a forced sale. Meanwhile, Bond had interest payments of $10 million a year to meet, plus another $20 million a year to pay back on his loans. And there was scarcely any cash coming in to pay the bills. Bond, whose father believed him to be a mathematical genius, had managed to make such sums come right during the boom, simply by borrowing more, and waiting for property prices to rise. But now the boom was over, prices were falling, and almost all the sources of funds had gone dry.

Fresh from his humiliation at the hands of the Americans, and beset now by rumours that his empire was about to collapse, Bond came back to Perth and called a press conference. With a smile pinned to his lips, as if he genuinely believed his own message, he treated his audience to what a distinguished journalist would describe in later years as the Blizzard of Hope—which one might characterise as the barrage of optimism that blinds one to the facts. No, said Bond, beaming constantly, he had no worries about repaying the debts or meeting the interest payments on his vast mortgaged empire. No, he had not given up hope of winning the America's Cup, he would be back. And yes, he was perturbed to see Mainline and Cambridge Credit collapsing under the strain, but the fact that they had gone down merely served to prove that Bond was an infinitely stronger company. And as for the Yanchep project, that was going fine. Despite the America's Cup defeat, it was bang on budget, and selling faster than any other real estate development in Western Australia. But just in case there were doubts about his empire's future viability, he wanted to reassure people that more capital was on its way from overseas, from a source which he couldn't name. In other words, all was fine, Bond Corporation was in great shape. There was nothing to worry about.

But the reality was very different. Yanchep was not in fact selling well; indeed, it was hardly selling at all, and Bond was on the brink of disaster. Meetings between Bond and his bankers had started in earnest in July that year, and the crisis had been building ever since. Bond had made it clear from the start that he wouldn't be able to meet his interest payments when they fell due, and nor would he be able to repay the principal on time. He had asked for his loans to be rolled over. And while his bankers had not been keen to help, they were, fortunately for Bond, even less keen to pull the plug on an Australian sporting hero. So they had deferred a decision until the America's Cup was over.

Bond had spent the weeks of preparation for the Cup challenge darting backwards and forwards between Newport and Australia in an attempt to placate his creditors and to fashion a survival plan. As Jack Baxter says, only half jokingly, "He spent his weeks trying to prevent his business collapsing, and the weekends propping up his challenge." Bond was still trying, almost as the boats went down to the start, to raise an extra $250,000 to keep *Southern Cross* off the financial rocks. The challenge in Newport had been plagued by a chronic shortage of cash, there was constant difficulty paying the bills, and even in meeting the wages for the crews. Bill Lucas, who was in charge of such things, recalls at least one occasion when the money couldn't be found, but says that Bond never seemed to worry about it all. It was a thin line, says Lucas, whether Alan would carry on or not, he was under tremendous pressure, he was all but broke, yet when he breezed in from another crisis meeting in Australia, he was always the same: "just bouncy Alan Bond".

One thing that doubtless kept Bond smiling throughout these weeks was the knowledge that the banks couldn't touch his business empire while his Cup challenge lasted. However badly *Southern Cross* fared, no one would dare sink her while she was sailing for her country. And as long as he was Australia's representative in the eyes of the world, Bond was safe from any bank that wanted to send him under, especially when the banks most likely to were American. Fortunately for Bond his three largest lenders were finance companies in which a big American bank had a major share. Industrial Acceptance Corporation, to whom Bond owed some $35 million, was part-owned by Citibank, while a major shareholder in Commercial and General Acceptance, to whom Bond owed some $10 million, was the Bank of America. The third biggest lender to Bond, Patrick Intermarine, also had an American partner, Marine Midland Bank.

The American bankers' difficulty in such a situation is easy to see, and is well illustrated by a former Citibank executive's account of discussions with Bond around this time. In mid-September, it seems, with the races against *Courageous* already under way, Citibank's man in Sydney got on the phone to Bond in Newport, demanding he return immediately to Australia to discuss his $35 million outstanding debt. Bond, as the story goes, asked for ten minutes to consider and then rang back to say this: "Look, there are two ways we can handle this, and I don't care which way you want to play it.

The first is that I come back to Australia right now, as you want me to, in which case I shall have to withdraw the Australian challenge. If that happens, I can guarantee that a big American bank will get a great deal of front-page publicity for its role in the affair." One imagines he might have paused at this point. "Or, alternatively, you can hold off until I get back, and we can deal with the matter then. So which would you prefer?" There wasn't any choice, and Citibank knew it.

But just in case the Sydney-based Americans thought they might get tougher when the spotlight was off, Bond had gone to their bosses to press his case with them. In the midst of the challenge he had taken off to New York to the head offices of Citibank and Bank of America, and had marched in to see the top management there. Meanwhile, the same and other banks had been lobbied by Sir Charles Court, the Western Australian Premier, who had told them what a fine person young Bond was and how important it was for Western Australia that Bond survive. The bankers in New York would have had little trouble picking up the hidden message, if it was hidden, that their chances of doing business in Australia would be slim thereafter if they were the ones who sent Bond down. They knew that there was already little love for foreign bankers in Australia at the time.

But once the challenge was over and Bond was back home, the real fight for survival began. Bond was still basically insolvent. He needed the continued support of his bankers, American and otherwise, to stay in business, and there was still a considerable possibility that he would follow Cambridge Credit, Mainline and the others into financial oblivion. Indeed, as events began to unfold, Bond's chances of survival looked slim.

On 14 October 1974, less than a week after his first upbeat press conference in which he had reassured the world that all was well, Bond secretly flew to Canberra to ask for help. He had already been there during the America's Cup on a similar mission, but he was now in dire straits. And he was not the only one. With the banks and finance companies themselves being squeezed, the Commonwealth Government had suddenly become the place where surviving developers came looking for funds. One by one they were trooping into the nation's capital, pitching their tents outside the Treasurer's office and begging for help. The only difference was, of course, that Bond never begged—he merely explained to people why it was in their interest to do what he wanted them to do.

Bond had already called on the Prime Minister, Gough Whitlam, some months earlier, and on Federal Treasurer Frank Crean. This time he put his case to Crean once again, and then went round the corner to Tom Uren, the Minister for Urban and Regional Affairs, before finally landing up with Uren's "food tasters", as the senior public servants liked to call themselves. In each office, his line was the one that he had found so successful with the banks: Alan Bond and Bond Corporation were too big, too high-profile and too important to be allowed to crash. It would be embarrassing for Australia if he were allowed to go down. Therefore the government should buy land from Bond Corporation, and buy it immediately, to stave off any danger of collapse. Alternatively, or as well, the Treasury should relax the foreign investment guidelines so that Bond could pledge more real estate as security for his American bankers.

The politicians and the public servants listened politely, as was their custom, but shook their heads. A relaxation of the guidelines was a possibility, but money for Bond Corporation was not. They might well have added that it would be political disaster for a Labor government to be seen feeding cash to a property shark like Alan Bond. Instead, they merely pointed out that they did not believe that Australia's future depended on Bond's survival. Bond was advised to approach the Western Australian Government in Perth, which had funds and power to buy land itself. And with that, he was shown the door. But if the rebuff was bad enough, there was worse to come, for news of the secret visit promptly leaked out and fears that he was close to the brink were confirmed. Alan Bond, the press was told, had been to Canberra cap in hand. And it soon became clear that he had already been knocking on the State Government's door.

The very next day in the Western Australian parliament, Liberal Premier Sir Charles Court was on his feet to make a statement. While not normally wishing to disclose private discussions, he said, he felt it necessary under the circumstances to clarify matters. Officials from his government had met a number of times with executives from Bond Corporation to advise them about how to deal with their liquidity problems, but apart from offering guidance, they had been unable to help. There had been no deals, Court told Parliament, no government money, and no guarantees. A Liberal government, Court went on, could hardly help one such supplicant without having a queue of property developers outside its front door. Bond, however, had tried hard—Court says he lost count of the number of times that Alan either phoned him or came to see him. The Premier had been twenty-one years in Parliament and was a well-respected man, but Bond was "arrogant, aggressive and demanding". He had put forward "every conceivable scheme" by which the government could inject money into Bond Corporation, or guarantee its obligations. But Court had turned his back on any government rescue.

The day after Court's statement to Parliament, stockmarkets around the country were alive with rumours that Bond was about to collapse. Bond Corporation's share price hit the floor, with half a cent per share being the best any buyer would offer, and the Perth Stock Exchange called for information from the group about its rumoured liquidity problems. Bond came back with a strongly-worded statement, almost as if the request was an intrusion. Yes, said Bond, his company did have cash problems, like everybody else caught in the squeeze, but Bond Corporation had the confidence of its bankers and would without doubt survive. The real problem, Bond seemed to suggest, was that the pinkos in the media were placing his group, and the capitalist system, in danger by spreading fear and alarm:

> The sensational reportage accorded in recent months to our company and generally to the Australian business community has created a lack of confidence. We believe that if continued this will undermine the very basis of private enterprise in the Australian economy.

Traditionally, property companies are highly geared. Our company is more fortunate than some in having a majority of long-term arrangements backed by sound investments.

Naturally, we have experienced the effects of the credit squeeze and the downturn of the property market. We have the confidence and support of our financiers and, once through this difficult period, we see a sound, long-term future. There will be no further statements or comments issued.

Whether the bankers would have put it so positively as they contemplated their millions at risk, one cannot say, but they must have been tickled to see Bond accusing the press of magnifying his problems, because the papers had barely touched on his financial troubles. Nor were they encouraged to do so—Bond had made his statement on the condition that it was published in its entirety, and without comment of any sort.

Having received a reply, the Perth Stock Exchange had its twopenny-worth as well: Bond's statement about its finances had satisfied them absolutely—perhaps they too thought it an intrusion to ask such pointed questions—so they now weighed in on the embattled businessman's behalf. Warning the public not to listen to rumours, an odd request, since this is the currency of the stockmarket, the vice-chairman of the Perth Stock Exchange reminded people of the $1000 penalty for spreading false or misleading information, and advised everyone to wait until the accounts were published so that the facts could be established. It was an extraordinary statement because Bond was in imminent danger, and the accounts were some way off. But it was a measure of the panic that gripped the Australian financial community at the time. There was a growing fear in late 1974 that the collapse would spread from the property companies through to the financial institutions that had lent them the money. And after three or four of the biggest property developers had crashed, the spectre of collapse was looming large. Bond's statement had been right to suggest that the fall of another $100 million company would send shock waves through the system, and right in saying that there was more than Bond's future at stake. Bond, however, was lucky that this was so, for it would help ensure his survival.

The two finance companies most in danger of going under were the American-backed IAC and CAGA, who were the two biggest lenders to Bond Corporation. Both now risked being crushed by the property market collapse, because they had lent so heavily on land during the market's spectacular rise. In the words of one CAGA director, the boom had seen "halcyon days, when to touch property was to make money". Property lending had meant high interest rates, four per cent above what the banks would charge; fat fees for procuring the loans, often ten per cent of the principal amount, and big profits from taking a share of the action. And neither CAGA nor IAC could resist the lure: they had lent recklessly, and were paying the price. They now had millions of dollars lent to almost every basket case in the country. Both had Home Units of Australia as a major customer, which had nosedived in July 1974, and both had Mainline, which had crashed in August. In addition, IAC was lead banker to Cambridge Credit, the biggest casualty of all.

Both, of course, also had Bond. So when the problems at Bond Corporation came to a head in November 1974, IAC's and CAGA's first concern was to ensure their own survival. It was Bond's good fortune that if the finance companies ditched him they would hasten their own demise. In November, Bond Corporation was due to make a major interest payment on its $10 million debt to CAGA, but did not have the money. Far from insisting on payment or declaring default, CAGA decided the best policy was to sit tight and say nothing, so they gave Bond three months' stay of execution and rolled the loan over until February. The immediate danger had been averted.

But an even more pressing problem had been IAC, which itself needed rescuing if Bond were to survive. IAC was in an even bigger mess than CAGA because it had raised $100 million in record time when the credit squeeze began in October 1973, and had then found the money burning a hole in its corporate pocket. To get rid of it, IAC had gone on a six-month spree, lending money to all and sundry in the property market, including Bond, and had lost heavily. It already had $80 million of bad or doubtful debts, and Bond was now threatening to add $35 million more to the pile. But luckily for IAC and for Bond, the big American-owned Citibank was prepared to rescue its prodigal son, to safeguard its own name. According to John Thom, now Citibank's top executive in Australia, "We had never in 120 years walked away from any company for which we were responsible—even 20 per cent responsible and had we started then, our depositors throughout the world would have been rushing to get their money out." So, after two phone calls to the USA, and within forty-eight hours of Thom's arrival at IAC, there was US $140 million of new ammunition in the vaults at IAC to defend it from the onslaught.

With his chief bankers solvent once more, Bond's task was to convince them that he should keep using their money, even though he couldn't pay the interest. And here his talents as a salesman served him well. In one crucial meeting, Bond carried the day. "Even on his optimistic valuation criteria the company had assets of $90 million and liabilities of $100 million," says one of his bankers today, "and we all knew that the real position was even worse, because he had almost certainly overvalued his assets and understated his liabilities, but what could we do?"

The bankers could do nothing but listen, their hands tied, as Bond set about persuading them that in this situation there was no better man for them to trust than Alan Bond himself. Who, after all, would be better placed to find buyers than he? And who would be better at selling the assets for a top price if a buyer could be found? There was no choice, he argued, but for them all to sit tight and wait for the market to settle down. They would sell bits of the Bond empire whenever the price was right, and before long everyone would get their money back. The bankers shuffled their papers and mumbled their approval, knowing that Bond was a better liquidator of his assets than they were, and knowing too that they already had other companies like Mainline and Cambridge Credit to break up and sell off. "After all," says one of the bankers, "what could we do with Yanchep Sun City, what could we do with a couple of grossly-overvalued insurance companies that were practically insolvent? We didn't want to be landed with them, so we decided to let him sell them. We had nowhere to go."

Indeed, they had not. In later years, Alan would tell his cousin Eric how in one meeting the bankers tried to get tough. Bond got up from his chair, threw a huge bunch of keys on the table, and said: "Okay, you take care of it all." Then he turned his back on them and walked towards the door. The bankers stopped him before he touched the handle.

CHAPTER 7

The
Survival Game

Bond had managed to get his key bankers on side, but his problems were by no means over. In fact, the fight had just begun. February 1975 was looming as a month when several big payments had to be made. And it was clear to all that Bond would not be able to make them. Just then, in the city bars where bankers and brokers meet, bets began to be taken on when, not whether, Bond would go bust. The favourite date was 5 February, which was the deadline for a payment of $2.2 million on a parcel of shares that Bond had bought in a big iron ore producer called Robe River. Bond had agreed to buy the shares on extended terms some eighteen months earlier, and now did not have the money. Nor did he have a hope in hell of raising it. It seemed to be just a matter of counting down to zero. But as Alan Bond would prove fifteen years later, he was never an easy man to write off.

Once again, he was lucky that it was not just the future of *his* empire that was at stake. For, on the other end of Bond's $2.2 million, waiting for payment, were some of the best-known companies in Australia, who would set upon each other in a most unseemly fashion if the money did not materialise. The companies concerned were creditors of a mining house called Mineral Securities, which had crashed in spectacular fashion in 1971, who were now arguing bitterly about who had most right to be paid. Some had apparently jumped the queue in an attempt to get preferential treatment; others were alleging sharp practice. It was all getting out of hand. The only way to avoid a fierce battle in the courts, with the top names in Sydney and Melbourne suing each other for years, was for everyone to get their money. And that was where Mr Bond came in. For he had agreed to pay exactly that amount for Robe River which would send everyone home happy.

A number of people were therefore hoping that Bond could find his $2.2 million. And none was hoping harder than the liquidator of Mineral Securities, Jim Jamison of Coopers & Lybrand, the man to whom Bond actually owed the money. Jim Jamison was desperate to avoid a messy court battle with the creditors, and desperate to be shot of the liquidation, which had already dragged on for more than three years. But he was also fighting for his reputation. It was Jamison who had sold Bond the Robe River shares on tick and Jamison who had been pilloried in the courts for doing so. His critics had said even then that Bond had no money, and wouldn't be able to pay. And now it looked as though they might be proved right. Jamison was therefore determined to stitch up a deal.

There were, however, few bankers in Australia keen to lend to Bond at this point. And there was also a particular problem in finding this $2.2 million, for Bond had contracted to pay ninety-three cents for each Robe River share—and as 5 February drew nigh they were selling at only half that price in the market. Any banker lending funds would thus have security for just half his money, and it seemed impossible that the cash would be found. But Jim Jamison and an enterprising man called Bill de Boos, from the Bank of New South Wales, came up with a plan which, for sheer brass nerve, was quite outstanding.

Bill de Boos had a sentimental interest in finding Bond the funds because he had helped get the Robe River project off the ground in the first place. And his bank had an interest too, because some of the Wales's biggest customers were Minsec creditors, waiting for payment. What's more, the Bank of New South Wales had actually lent several million dollars to Bond Corporation, which it hoped to get back. De Boos's proposal was that his bank should lend $2.2 million to Bond, so that he could pay his creditors. But there was a catch which gave the plan its twist. The Wales would only take a risk on half the money, which it would secure against all the Robe River shares. The other half would have to be guaranteed by the creditors themselves. So if the deal fell apart, they would ultimately have to stand the loss. The creditors were virtually being asked to write themselves a cheque and pretend they had been paid.

The attraction of the scheme, if it had any, was that everyone *might* eventually get paid in full. The drawback was that they could be merely prolonging the agony, since Bond might never be able to pay. There was also the small matter of the liquidator's fee: Jamison would, quite legitimately, be paid his half-million dollars as the money made its way round the circle, so that the creditors would get very little guaranteed cash out of the deal.

It was on this extremely complicated money shuffle that Bond's survival now depended. De Boos had taken the proposal to his board at the Bank of New South Wales to find that they "weren't exactly jumping for joy". But he had got their agreement, provided that enough Minsec creditors could be persuaded to share the risk. So in the weeks up to the vital February deadline he had set about finding others to man the lifeboat. He remembers it now as being an extremely stressful time. No one wanted to climb in with him; many felt Bond had sailed recklessly into the storm and deserved to go down.

On 5 February in Sydney, the financial press gathered in anticipation of the midnight showdown. Speculation about whether Bond could find the money had been rife for weeks, and most had concluded he would not. Towards 8 p.m., the journalists installed themselves in Jim Jamison's offices in O'Connell Street, having been tipped off that it would go to the wire. Back in the newsrooms, no doubt, the financial obituaries had already been prepared. And the waiting began.

Bond, meanwhile, was also waiting, around the corner at his own offices at No. 1 Castlereagh Street. And so too was Bill de Boos, sitting in his office at 60 Martin Place with Peter Lucas from Bond Corporation, hoping that the phone would ring. He had told the switchboard to leave a line open to his office after they had shut down for the evening, and had put calls out all round Australia. He had even tracked down one of his targets to the lounge at Perth airport. But the phones stayed silent. No one wanted to help in the rescue. And as the midnight hour drew nigh, it became painfully clear that de Boos had failed to get the money together. Picking up the phone, de Boos rang Jamison and asked for more time—enough to sew it up. Jim Jamison conceded just one more week, and then went downstairs to tell the assembled journalists that there were a few more details to sort out, he had granted an extension of seven days, but that it was all looking hopeful. Whether such optimism was entirely justified is not clear. But Bond had been reprieved again: it was not quite five minutes to midnight, but at 10.55 p.m., it was close enough for comfort.

As to what happened in the next hectic week, no one seems now to be entirely clear. But the ANZ Bank (who had clients in property and feared what would happen if Bond collapsed), helped with the odd half-million dollars, and Bill de Boos did finally drag enough people kicking and screaming into the lifeboat with him. Even then, there were those who wanted to change their minds and jump out. De Boos remembers one meeting in particular at Coopers & Lybrand's offices where Jamison went round the table asking each creditor in turn what their particular problem was. But the syndicate held together: when people dropped out because they lost their nerve or because their boards wouldn't back them, others were bullied to stay in or to take their place. The Bank of New South Wales picked up more of the risk as the week went on. And as they ground towards that second midnight deadline of 12 February, fingers were crossed that this time they did have a deal.

That second night was, if anything, more chaotic than the first, for Jim Jamison had rashly promised his wife Mary that he would look after their two very young children while she went to the opera. And, not surprisingly, he had been unable to get home. At 8 p.m., the two youngsters were therefore delivered to the Coopers' offices by the chauffeur, who had kindly bought them a bag of jelly beans each. Thrilled at the prospect of going to Daddy's work, and expecting to be looked after attentively by their father, the scene they found was hardly what they might have expected. There, as they burst into the Coopers' boardroom, were two dozen creditors, accountants and lawyers, wrestling with the details of a $2 million rescue deal that none of them wanted to be involved with. The air was thick with cigar smoke, there were sleeves rolled up, braces round the ankles, green eyeshades, and a sea of paper. And in the middle of it all was their "Father Bear". For the three-year-old James and his slightly older sister Emma, the excitement was all too much. James fell flat on his face, the jelly beans went flying and twenty-four creditors, lawyers and accountants got down on their knees to scrabble for the scattered sweets. Perhaps, though, it was a welcome relief from tension, because as the evening wore on, tempers began to fray. There was one document that all had to agree to, and individual words were becoming a problem.

Down in the press room, a small army of reporters from the financial press had moved into Jim Jamison's office where they had been given the key to the drinks cupboard to keep them quiet. But as the grog now ran low and print deadlines drew nearer, they too began to get edgy. Out at the American Club, having dinner with friends, Bill de Boos was also becoming nervous. He had told his right-hand man, who was back in the Coopers' boardroom, to phone as soon as the deal was done, as he confidently expected it would be, but 8.30 had passed, then 9.30 and then 10 o'clock, and still no word had come. He was concerned that something had gone wrong at the last minute, that the whole rescue package had fallen through. Then, around 10.30 p.m., the barman approached his table looking flustered. The man at the other end of the telephone had refused to say who he was, but his one-word message "Eureka" was enough to tell de Boos that the rescue had been completed. Bond had been saved. This time, he had been some ninety minutes away from disaster.

Bond's executives had played only a minor role in the escape, in that they had not actually put up the money. But they had nevertheless impressed the bankers. One of them, George Carmany from Ord BT, who actually held out against the rescue, rated Peter Mitchell, Bond's figures man, and Tony Oates, Bond's legal expert, as "better than anyone in any Australian merchant bank that I had come across". Jim Jamison also had nothing but praise for Alan Bond: he had conducted himself perfectly, and not broken his word. The entrepreneur, indeed, had been irrepressible throughout. He had been on the phone to Bill de Boos at all hours of the day and night, to tell him of his latest brainwave about how the rescue should be handled. And he had never worried once: he had been supremely confident that he would come through, and had not even considered the possibility that he would fail. His personality was electric, said de Boos, his powers of persuasion extraordinary.

But while the Robe River crisis was now weathered, the Bond empire was still not safe. There was still no cash to pay the interest bills and the company's debts still far exceeded its assets. Ever-optimistic, Alan Bond had told the world that large amounts of money were on the way to help bail him out. But the cavalry constantly failed to arrive. In November, Bond had promised $4.7 million from a new preference share issue, but that had come to nought—since no one in their right minds wanted a share in Bond Corporation's problems. In December, he had said $16 million worth of land sales were imminent—but those had not materialised either. And then, in May 1975, he had boasted of an even more remarkable solution. Just three months after Bond Corporation had failed on its own account to raise $2.2 million for the Robe River shares, Alan proudly announced that he had negotiated a $100 million letter of credit from an American bank, which would enable him to refinance his empire from top to bottom. Unfortunately, the letter failed to arrive—lost, no doubt, in the post.

By such devices, Alan Bond both bought time and helped keep the banks at bay, much as he would fifteen years later. He gave them proposals to study, documents to look at, business plans to consider. And it all helped keep his financiers in the game. And then, in June 1975, Bond did lay his hands on some cash at last, and so further improved his chances of ultimate survival. And this time, his rescuer was Sir Charles Court's Western Australian Government. For not only did Bond manage to sell the government some land, when there were virtually no other buyers in the market, but he managed to sell the piece of property that he most wanted to be rid of: the Santa Maria estate, just north of Perth.

Santa Maria was something of a *cause célèbre* in Perth in the early 1970s. A massive slab of land, some five thousand acres (2023 hectares) in all, it was on the northern outskirts of Perth, about twenty kilometres from the city centre. Typical Perth real estate, with masses of banksia scrub on dry sandy soil, it was not much good for growing anything. But it was near enough to the middle of Perth to make it a possibility for building. Bond had bought it at the height of the boom in 1969 for $3.6 million, around ten times its rural value, in the hope that the zoning could be changed for development.

Having found a valuer who said it was worth $1 million more than the purchase price, Bond had borrowed the money he needed for the deal and sold the land into a new company, West Australian Land Holdings, which had been set up five days earlier for the purpose. On the way, he had received a $100,000 "finder's fee", as his personal commission for negotiating the purchase. Then he had launched the company's shares on the Stock Exchange as a brilliant investment opportunity. The prospectus that had sold the project to the public was a classic—a triumph of hope over reason. The land was clearly only a good investment if houses could be built on it, since it had been purchased at ten times the agricultural value. But the State Government had declared publicly that the land would not be developed. Bond's prospectus, however, just kicked that problem aside and leapt blue-skywards. It pointed out, as it had to, that:

> The property is zoned 'rural' and is hence not available for urban development, and the Metropolitan Region Planning Authority has through press statements declared that it is not its present policy to rezone the land.

But then continued quite unperturbed:

> In the circumstances, the directors cannot predict when rezoning will be effected. When rezoning is effected the company intends to develop the holdings as a composite industrial and residential complex.

Throughout the prospectus, a sparkling picture emerged of the inevitable future of this "excellent land with good potential" on which one "could reasonably expect a steady capital accretion". And the opposition of the planners was played down.

To give Bond his due, however, he seems to have made the impossible happen more than once in his career. And the planning concept eventually produced for Santa Maria some eighteen months later was both attractive and remarkable for its time. It envisaged a new town, with pedestrian walkways separated from the traffic, heaps of open space and residential developments planned round lakes and lagoons. There was to be a golf course, shopping centres, schools, hospitals, and everything needed for its proposed 75,000 residents. There was also a sweetener for the politicians. At a time when house and land prices were roaring out of control, Bond was promising that building blocks at Santa Maria would be released to the public, fully serviced, at half the price being asked in the Perth metropolitan region.

But there were a number of problems, not the least of which was one of image. Bond was Perth's most notorious land developer and would make a killing if the deal went ahead. And the Labor Government did not want to be seen to bend the rules to help him. Perhaps all would have been fine if things could have been done quietly, but that was not possible, because Perth's professional planners were adamant that the project should be stopped. Unfortunately for Bond, Perth's Metropolitan Planning Authority had decided too that the city should be developed in corridors stretching out from the centre, and Santa Maria was slap bang between two of them. What's more the land stood right on top of Perth's last remaining source of pure drinking water. And if Bond's development were allowed to proceed, the water could be contaminated.

There the story might well have ended, but Alan Bond never took "No" for an answer. He intended that the promise of his prospectus should come true, so he commissioned his own planners to attack the corridor plan from a professional standpoint. And he then started lobbying the politicians, with great energy, and some success. But as the debate began to warm up, and Labor's Planning Minister, Herb Graham, started to express mild public sympathy for Bond's position, a major political row broke out, with rumours of bribery and corruption.

Graham had hired his own consultant to examine the corridor concept for the government, and somewhat unwisely had picked Perth's former chief planner, Paul Ritter—who had condemned the corridor plan as "inconsistent, unimaginative and unrealistic". Perhaps not surprisingly, the whispering had begun with Ritter's appointment, amid suggestions that Ritter had been picked because it was known what he would say. But the Planning Minister had then dignified the rumours with a response. In the midst of an ABC television interview, Graham suddenly burst out without apparent provocation: "They have been saying some shocking things about me, that I have some sort of an implication somewhere, that I have interests somewhere. These are a pack of lies, of course. I don't like to use that word but it's perfectly true—a pack of lies." It was not long before Liberal Party politicians and the newspapers had a field day with what Graham called these "filthy rumours". And nor was it long before Herb Graham went to his leader to return his portfolio.

The Santa Maria row rumbled on for some time after Herb Graham's resignation and Bond finally lost the battle to get the land developed. By mid-1975 there was no chance of Santa Maria being built on in the near future, or indeed at all. It was eating its head off in interest, and there were no buyers in the private sector who wanted a part of it, particularly at $780 an acre. But in times of hardship, politicians can have their uses. In June 1975, when Bond's fortunes were at almost their lowest ebb, the new Western Australian Government took four thousand of Santa Maria's five thousand acres off Bond's hands for just over $3 million. It was not, as the new Liberal Premier, Sir Charles Court, pointed out, as much as Bond wanted. But it was slightly more, per acre, than Bond had paid, and the advantage was in any case in the purchase rather than the price.

There was a legitimate question as to why Court's government had bought the land. The funds they used had been granted by the Commonwealth, primarily to build up banks of land for housing—so that land could be released onto the market during the boom to keep down prices—but Santa Maria was not housing land at all. And while Perth needed parks, which the Santa Maria land was supposed to become, it hardly needed its largest park at the price of $780 an acre, or at this distance from the centre of Perth. There are no figures to say how many people now visit the Santa Maria land each year, but as one Perth planner disparagingly puts it today: "It's not as though it's anything special, it's just a load of banksia scrub." The stated reason for the acquisition—to safeguard Perth's water supply—also seemed a little odd, since the planning powers existed to prevent the development anyway.

Bond, however, wasn't complaining. Although Peter Beckwith, one of his executives, had earlier opposed such land purchases by the government as a socialistic interference with free enterprise and an attack on the capitalist system, one had to move with the times. And no doubt it was ideologically sound enough if the funds were being used to prop up a property developer rather than to reduce his profits. Whatever, it was cash for the bankers and a slice off the interest bill. Furthermore, Bond hadn't only sold Santa Maria: the Western Australian Government also bought 15,000 acres (6070 hectares) on the southern edge of Yanchep for nearly $2 million. It was more than Bond had paid for all the land at Yanchep, all 20,000 acres (8093 hectares) of it, some six years earlier. Yet the land was still zoned rural, and it has not since been built upon.

CHAPTER 8

1977–
Down and Out in
Perth and Newport

For four years, from 1975 to 1978, Bond's empire continued in business only by the grace of God and the goodwill of his bankers. Each annual report to the shareholders carried a message which in accounting terms was the equivalent of: "We hope to see you next year, but don't bet on it." In each of those four years, the accounts of Bond's many companies were prepared on the basis that the businesses were still "a going concern"—which, in the code of accountants, is tantamount to saying that they were no such thing. The shareholders of Bond Corporation Holdings were treated, almost for the first time, to a glimpse of the truth. And it was bleak. The 1975 accounts set the tone:

> The company has been faced with the curtailment of nearly all its programmes, certain of

the company's loans have passed maturity date, and in other instances, interest remains due but unpaid. Other loans will mature over the next twelve months which the directors believe will be treated in a similar manner. The continued support of the group's lenders is needed so as its obligations can be met or satisfied as and when they fall due.

While the Bond empire still seemed to be afloat—to the extent that the accounts said its assets were worth more than was owed against them—a closer look revealed this to be an Alice in Wonderland view. In terms of hard cash—that is, what Bond immediately owed compared with what he could lay his hands on, his empire was $21 million short. What's more, although the books appeared to balance, his assets were still in there at boomtime values rather than their current market price. The reality was that if the bankers forced Bond to sell things quickly there would be nothing left at the end except millions of dollars of unpaid debts.

Had the bankers known when they started that it would be a four-year fight to get their money back, they might have cut their losses and pulled the plug on Bond then and there. But if they had, Alan would have come out a rich man, and they would have had to settle for crumbs. For Bond had structured his empire in such a way that his private company, Dallhold, stood first in the queue for any share-out of Bond Corporation's assets. Bond certainly at this stage considered cashing in his chips himself, but it wasn't in his nature to give up so easily, and he doubtless believed that the rollercoaster of success would take him up again as quickly as it had brought him down.

So, just as he had previously staked everything to build his business empire, Alan Bond now threw in all he had to defend it. On at least three occasions during the long fight back, he pledged his personal fortune to the banks to persuade them to pay the wages. Meanwhile, all work stopped on his huge new house in Perth, and his ocean racer *Apollo* was taken into hock by the builders. He even took his children out of private school. But the personal privations did not last for long. After all, you can't be a successful entrepreneur unless you behave like one. By 1976, though the empire was still losing money hand over fist, Bond was spending again, and looking, to the unpractised eye, as rich as he had ever been. In the driveway of the home in Dalkeith, Alan's black Rolls could be seen parked next to Eileen's white one. Alongside them stood a whole array of cars for the children, plus a speedboat on a trailer. And down on the Swan River, the tourists could once again be seen cruising past Bond's building site, seeing for themselves how things were progressing with the palace.

The new house had been started some eighteen months before when the property boom was still in full swing. A huge, white affair on six levels, at the water's edge in Perth's smartest suburb, it didn't have the Palladian pretensions of some of Perth's more recent mansions, but it was big enough to count among Western Australia's major construction projects. And it was certainly one up on the garage where its owner had started married life, or the house in Perivale where he had grown up. By the time it was finished, it would have eight bedrooms, five bathrooms, a billiard room, a ball-room, a swimming pool, a tennis court and garaging for eight cars. The taps were of course gold plated, the floors the finest Italian marble. Total cost, for the building alone, was well over $1 million, which would be more like $5 million today.

Geoff Summerhayes, Bond's architect, had landed the job of designing this extravagance after working on several business projects for Alan. By this stage quite a good friend of the Bond family, it had not always been so. His first impression of young Alan, whooping it up around town in a purple V8 convertible during the early 1960s, was that he was a bit of a yahoo, and the stories he had heard subsequently about his business style had hardly changed his mind. When Bond had become a successful property developer, Summerhayes had approached him for work. Summerhayes, at this time, was already an architect of some repute, and was ten years older than Alan, who was still in his mid-twenties, but he remembers feeling "incredibly intimidated" throughout their first meeting. Bond had a power and a confidence about him, and a directness in his language that allowed him completely to dominate their encounter. At the end of the meeting, says Summerhayes, the young Bond took him into a tiny room to show him a spinning globe with a map of the world printed on it. Bond spun the globe with his fingers and declaimed, as if he were Napoleon: "This is the old world." Then he stopped the globe, flicked off the top to reveal a drinks cabinet, and said: "This is the new world, have a drink." Summerhayes was quite bemused by it all.

One of Bond's characteristics, Summerhayes discovered in the course of working for him, was that he almost always quibbled about payment and tried to beat people down on their bills. There had been a dispute over fees for a big apartment project that Summerhayes had run, and now there was another over Bond's new house. Costs overran because there were so many changes, and Bond then refused to pay Summerhayes his full percentage. Dreading the thought of a battle with Alan, Summerhayes didn't make a great issue of it and, as a consequence, never got his money. In settlement of one lot of fees, Bond offered him free air tickets to Newport to watch the 1977 America's Cup, but these never materialised. In settlement of the other, Summerhayes took half-a-dozen blocks of land. Some blocks at Yanchep were offered, but Summerhayes turned them down. "I've got three of the bloody things already," he supposedly told Alan, "and I never even wanted one."

Yanchep Sun City, poor old Yanchep, was by now looking less and less like Bond's colour brochures, and more and more like a desert. By the mid to late 1970s, it was losing money at a terrible rate, sales had virtually dried up, and such residents as were there were complaining bitterly of broken promises. They had been told by selling agents in the eastern states and in England that they would find schools, yet there were none. They had been told there would be doctors, but there weren't any. They had been led to expect jobs but a large number of people remained unemployed. And there wasn't even a bus service to link them to Perth, let alone the monorail, ferry or expressway which they had been led to expect. But none of this, said Bond, was his fault. Everyone was going through hard times, and everyone had to put up with it. He would do everything he could to help, but they would do better to fight than to whinge. And as for their being unemployed, he suspected, as self-made men have a habit of doing, that most of them did not want to work.

Bond might well have come clean that Yanchep was a disaster for him as well. The promised 250,000 residents had by this stage barely tipped 3000. There were debts of $16 million or more on the project, for which Bond was responsible, and unpaid interest was piling up by the week. For all that his bankers were patient, the millstone of Yanchep still threatened to drag him down. He needed desperately, come 1976, either to find a buyer or to win the America's Cup. And typically he was confident he could do both.

Given the state of Bond Corporation and its various companies, it was remarkable that Bond could find the money for another challenge, although there was help this time from the Western Australian Government and cash from Bond's private coffers. But Bond not only put together a syndicate to mount a campaign, he raised enough for a new boat to replace the sluggish *Southern Cross*. And once again, to some people's surprise, he got Ben Lexcen to design it. Lexcen had left Newport in 1974 in the depths of despair, blaming himself for the Australians' 4-0 hammering, and had gone to Europe to start a new life. Bond had tracked him down and rung him there, asking him to design a new 12-metre. Lexcen, in his life story, describes what happened next:

We had an argument on the phone, and I was really angry, so I slammed the receiver down.

It takes more than that to put Bondy off; he's determined. He called me back ten times. He kept ringing me, and I kept hanging up. We had this long-distance phone fight, he just wouldn't give up.

Eventually the phone calls had stopped, leaving Lexcen feeling rather foolish: he did, after all, want to design another America's Cup yacht. But then, without any warning, the ever-persistent Mr Bond had pitched up in person, and bounced out from behind a cereal rack.

I was in the supermarket in Cowes, spending my last money on a packet of cornflakes, when Bondy walked in all bright and breezy. He said: 'You've got no money.' I said, 'Yes, I have.' He said, 'You're broke, and you're coming home with me.'

So Lexcen returned, and designed *Australia*, a similar boat in many ways to America's *Courageous* which had thrashed *Southern Cross* in 1974. Most of the old team were recalled to sail her, including a few who had vowed never to challenge with Bond again, and off they went to Yanchep once more to prepare—but not before Bond had made the big announcement on the opening day of the Royal Perth regatta. Jack Baxter remembers it well. They were sailing in *Southern Cross*, because *Australia* was still being built, and Bond insisted on taking the helm. The excitement of lording it over his old sparring partners at the Royal Perth clearly put Bond on a high. He slashed through the fleet, which contained just about every boat in the club, scattering them as he went. Most of them were half the size of his huge 12-metre. "It was like dodgems with a samurai sword," says Baxter, "absolutely terrifying."

By the time they got to Newport, Bond was a lot cooler than he had been in 1974. And he was considerably less abrasive. "He wasn't the boy thumbing his nose at the big boys, any more," says Baxter, "he was there to do a job". And the challenge was altogether better run, not least because one of Bond's top executives, the calm and competent Warren Jones, was now its full-time manager. Jones not only kept Bond off the boil, he instilled a little more professionalism into the crew. They were told the day that Jones took over that they answered now to him—any deals they had done with Bond were cancelled; he was the boss. Flash parties and uniforms from here on were out: the money would be spent on getting the boat and the people right.

Bond's challenge this time nevertheless had some similarities to that of 1974. Once again, for example, there was a row about the origin of the boat. To ensure that Bond could defend the Cup at Yanchep, in the unlikely event that he won it, he had formed his own yacht club at Sun City to make the challenge—the Royal Perth, after all, would never consent to trekking up there if they had charge of the affair. But, beneath the name Sun City Yacht Club, which Bond had painted on the back of the boat, was *Australia*'s port of registry, Fremantle. And, to Bond's anger, some journalists insisted on describing her as the Fremantle boat—which, of course, did not publicise his Yanchep project. Bond promptly announced that he would not talk to reporters who referred to his challenger in this way, since Fremantle was "a union run port full of red-ragging socialists". And this produced a minor explosion in Alan's home town. As the Mayor of Fremantle pointed out, their money had been good enough for Bond while he was after his first quid, and some of Fremantle's taxpayers had even supported his challenge. "I don't care if he puts Sun City or Tokyo on the back of his boat," said the good Mayor, Bill McKenzie, "but it seems to me that in fame and fortune, Mr Bond needs to improve his manners."

With the Americans, however, Bond kept himself out of trouble, largely because his rival in 1977, Ted Turner, was far louder than Bond could ever be. Ted Turner was a self-made entrepreneur, like Bond, who hated the establishment and its petty rules, and thumbed his nose at pomposity whenever he could. He had bought a baseball team, the Atlanta Braves, in 1976, for $10 million, and promoted it on television by dressing as a jockey and racing an ostrich around the perimeter before a game. Known variously as the Mouth from the South or Captain Outrageous, he was the last of the great amateurs—determined to have fun at all costs, yet talented enough to win on the way. The press and public loved him. The New York Yacht Club regarded him with horror.

When Turner wasn't quoting Cicero, he was telling reporters with an entirely straight face that he was Magellan reincarnate. He was, in the words of Doug Riggs, who wrote the excellent book *Keelhauled* on the history of foul play in the

America's Cup: "loud, crude, vulgar and outrageous, a public drunk, a public womaniser and sometimes a public nuisance. He was also straightforward, totally unaffected, unpredictable, enthusiastic and engagingly frank about his foibles." In Newport, in 1977, you couldn't move without seeing young female chests bearing the slogan: "I'm turned on by Turner." And on the social scene he was also in great demand, even if he misbehaved himself. Manhandled by a society hostess one night at the posh Bailey's Beach Club, Turner said loudly to her: "What you need, lady, is a good fuck." He had already been banished from the Reading Room, a high-class Newport watering hole, for bellowing. It was hardly surprising that the New York Yacht Club found him hard to take. One American yachting writer joked that the Cup Committee would prefer to wear blue jeans and motorcycle boots on the course than select Terrible Ted to be their defender. But Turner had seen off all their better-bred candidates with the greatest of ease. And now he was planning to see off Bond.

Before the 1977 race, Turner proclaimed to UPI's Terry Anzur, with a touch more style than Bond had done in 1974, that *Courageous* was unbeatable. "We're fast, we're perfect. She's the most perfect 12-metre that ever sailed, and I can't think of anything I could do to be any better. My biggest problem now is to keep from getting a big head. You don't think I have one, do you?" And he then added, apparently taking no heed of his own warning, "There will never be a time in my life as good as this. I'm so hot I just tell my guys to stand by me with their umbrellas turned upside down to catch the stuff that falls off."

Sadly for Bond and *Australia*, it was true. Turner and *Courageous* were far too good for them. The races were comparatively close, with two-and-a-half minutes the widest margin, but the result—4-0 to the Americans—was a whitewash again. Lexcen blamed the choice of sails and swore that *Australia* was not at fault. The next series in 1980 would prove him almost certainly right. But meanwhile, there was the victory to be celebrated and Turner was determined to enjoy it in style.

By the time the boats got back to port, Turner was astride the bow deck to give the salute. He had already had a few beers. He then, according to Doug Riggs, partook of the champagne or rum or aquavit, or most likely all three, and turned a fire hose on the NYYC committee boat to show them who was boss.

> His legs were getting a bit wobbly by then. He had to be escorted to the press conference at the National Guard Armory on Thames Street by two Newport policemen. Someone placed two bottles of aquavit in front of him at the table on the stage. Someone else, perhaps a NYYC official mindful of the TV cameras, placed them under the table. Turner reached for one of them, discovered it missing, then slowly disappeared from his seat, only to emerge moments later with the bottles in hand and a silly grin on his face.

Thus he sat until his time came to speak by which time his brotherly love had reached global proportions. "I never loved sailing against good friends any more than the Aussies," said Ted. "I love 'em.

They are the best of the best, the best of the best."
Moments later, he was carried from the stage by his
crew, shoulder high, heroically drunk, empty bottle
still in hand.

CHAPTER 9

Bouncing Back

Bond came back from Newport in 1977 in far better shape than he had in 1974. His challenge for the Cup had been sunk again, but on the business front, things were at last looking up. He had sold out of Robe River in mid-1976, at a profit of more than $4 million, proving, he said, that it had always been a good buy. And now he got rid of his greatest remaining problem, Yanchep Sun City.

The lucky buyers were the Japanese Tokyu Corporation, who had unwisely bought a half share in Yanchep back in 1973, and had then found themselves locked in to the project. Bond's initial approach to Tokyu was either a brilliant bluff or an extraordinary exercise in wishful thinking, for his suggestion was that he should buy them out, for several million dollars, and then inject a mass of new funds. Quite how he would have kept his promise had the Japanese said yes, is not clear, since he had no money at all, but fortunately for Bond, they offered to buy him out instead, paying Bond Corporation $7.1 million in cash, and taking over all of Yanchep's loans to boot. Bond then easily surmounted the only obstacle to the deal, namely Australia's new rules on foreign investment which banned foreign companies from owning real estate.

As he had done when he was in trouble in 1974, Bond called on the Prime Minister, now Malcolm Fraser. The suggestion was that the government might like to buy his very desirable Sun City development, putting Yanchep into a government-funded foundation, with all future "profits" earmarked for charity. Not surprisingly, Malcolm Fraser said no; there were better ways to spend taxpayers' money than to take on Yanchep's losses. Bond then fell back on his second line of defence, which might well have been his favoured position from the outset. If the government would not help Bond Corporation out of trouble, then surely they would allow it to help itself. Surely, they would at least permit Bond to sell his shares to the Japanese, given that no one else was willing to take on the project. And, with the minimum of humming and ha'ing, the government this time gave Bond the approval. In March 1978, the sale of Sun City went ahead and Bond bade goodbye to his dream, saying how sorry he was to see it go. Inwardly, no doubt, he was delighted to have got it off his back.

Bond was now almost solvent once more: in three years he had sold almost $70 million of assets and cut his borrowings by four-fifths. He was now ready to start all over again. Even better, he had a deal that would put him back on top. The opportunity stemmed from troubles in the United Kingdom,

where the big oil producer Burmah Oil had got itself
into financial difficulties and was selling off most of
its assets. Burmah had grouped together a number
of companies in South Australia which were explor-
ing for oil and gas in the Cooper Basin, most notable
of which was Santos, the operator of the Cooper
Basin fields.

The Cooper Basin lies deep in the Australian interior, almost at the heart of the continent, and it is
one of the hottest, driest and most inhospitable
places on earth. But in such places, particularly in
Australia, wealth is often found. By 1978, when
Bond made his play, Santos had already struck natural gas there, with the hint of better things to come.
No one had yet found oil, but the gas was already
being pumped down pipelines to Sydney and
Adelaide, and earning some return for the huge
amounts that had been invested. There was not,
however, enough cash flowing out to pay the interest
on the $36 million that Burmah wanted for the Santos
shares. Nor were there any buyers in evidence—or
none apart from Alan Bond. He alone thought they
were cheap, and could see opportunities.

Buying Santos was a reckless move for Bond
because the investment threatened to produce
nowhere near enough cash to pay the bankers. If he
was to get his hands on the cash flow from the
Santos gas contracts, as opposed to the paltry dividends that were paid to shareholders, he would
need to get control of the company, or capture the
Santos board, and there was no guarantee he could
do either—he was only buying 37.5 per cent of the
shares. Meanwhile, he had agreed to buy without
even arranging the finance. And to be blunt, he had
no money.

Bond himself hadn't a clue at this stage where he would find the money. No bank would put up 100 per cent of the funds for such a deal, when there was insufficient income to pay the interest bill, and few bankers were keen to lend to Bond anyway. Alan Bond, meanwhile, had no money of his own to speak of. He had even borrowed the $1 million deposit. Now he was hoping that something would turn up before the payments fell due. Fortunately for him, it did.

On 24 September, four weeks after Bond agreed to buy the shares, and six weeks before the first major instalment of $10 million needed to be found, Santos struck oil in small quantities. The share price started to climb, and Bond was able to pick up some money. It is possible on the stock market to sell shares that you do not already own or, in the jargon, to sell short. And that is what Bond did with Santos. He raised the money for the first instalment by selling some of the shares that he hadn't yet paid for — the shares he was about to buy.

There were many difficulties in doing such a deal, but the main one, however, related to timing. Australian Gas Light, the company which was buying the shares, wouldn't pay for them until they had been delivered. But there was a Catch 22, in that Bond couldn't get his hands on the share certificates until he had paid Burmah for them first, and he didn't have the money to give to Burmah until AGL paid him. There was one possible solution—if all the parties got together on the same day, and completed the two transactions simultaneously, all would be well. They could all keep one hand on the cash or on the share certificates as the paper passed round the room. And so it was arranged. Bond's brokers, the purchaser's brokers, the Burmah representative, Alan Bond and one of his top executives, agreed to meet in Sydney at the appointed time. The day came, the man from Burmah waited, the brokers waited, the time ticked on. Three o'clock came, the banks pulled down their shutters, it would be hard now to complete the deal. Finally, an hour-and-a-half late, the Bond party arrived, apparently the worse for wear. The brokers were so unimpressed that one vowed never to do business with Bond again.

On later instalments, there were also problems in raising the money, but what made them surmountable was that the price of Santos shares continued to rise. Hard on the heels of the September oil strike came revolution in Iran and a surge in energy prices. Then came a rush for resource stocks. Just as Bond and McNab had raised money on land in the 1960s, Bond was now able to persuade a finance company to lend 100 per cent of the purchase price for the Santos shares, taking only the shares as security. Before long, he was sitting on a sizable paper profit. But he soon ran into trouble with the South Australian Government who didn't relish the prospect of a company like Bond controlling their gas supplies.

The South Australian Government realised that Alan Bond would need to get control of Santos for his investment to make sense: only then would his empire get its hands on the cash flow it wanted. They suspected that controlling Santos would not be the end of it. They feared, with some foresight, that Bond would then use Santos to raise far larger loans which would prop up Bond Corporation's share and property deals. There was then a danger, they reasoned, that a repeat of the 1974 crash would force a savage increase in energy prices in order for Bond or the South Australian Government to clean up the mess.

The South Australian Government had said little when Bond moved in on the company, but before long they were threatening dire action. Then, within months, they were proposing new legislation to force Bond to reduce his Santos shareholding by more than half. And at this point, an almighty row ensued, for not only did they plan to seize some of Bond's shares, but they intended to pay far less than market value for them. The Australian *Financial Review* branded it "asset confiscation of the worst sort ever seen in this country". Bond called it nationalisation without adequate compensation. Editorials said it brought Australia into disrepute in the eyes of the world. Almost everyone, except the South Australians, thought it parochialism run riot.

But seven of the ten directors of Santos supported their government, and tales from the boardroom gave some backing to their case. Some of these directors, who had not been appointed by Bond, were clearly not enamoured of the way Bond had behaved since the takeover. There had been protests about the $100,000-a-month fee that Bond Corporation wanted to charge the company for the services of Alan Bond and two of his top executives, Peter Mitchell and Tony Oates. At least two Santos directors thought this was "money for nothing", and the payment had been stopped after three months. There had been further dispute when Alan Bond had suggested that Santos might buy two companies in which he personally owned a major stake. And there had been more difficulties when

Bond had suggested that Santos's money be deposited with Spedley Securities, a merchant bank run by Alan's friend Brian Yuill. It was alleged, to put it bluntly, that Bond was already trying to generate money from the company for his own purposes—including to pay for the takeover he had just made.

But that was only the start of the complaints. As the South Australian Energy Minister, Hugh Hudson, revealed in Parliament, there were other matters which made Bond and his company, in his view, unfit and improper persons to be running the state's energy supplier:

> Any assessment of the accounts indicates clearly that the Bond empire has had significant financial difficulties over a number of years and now, as a company, stands in a very weak financial position. The Bond Corporation does not have the financial wherewithal, the managerial competence or the knowledge of hydrocarbons to be in control of an energy company, particularly one that is vital to the future of South Australia. I am confident that the local directors will not deny any of the details of the fears I have expressed. Mr Bond, in dealings with the Government, gave some indication of the pressures Mr Bond and his associates have put on the other Santos directors. If Mr Bond feels in a position of strength he will attempt to govern by fear. Once he knows the cards are stacked against him he will plead and give assurances without limit. Mr Bond

has personally threatened to sue the Government and to sue me personally. He also threatened the Premier with a campaign of vilification throughout Australia against the Government. Mr Bond's actions on the Santos board have no doubt been of a similar nature. I believe it has only been the patience, determination and subtlety of the chairman and other local directors that has postponed action by Mr Bond to dump enough local directors of Santos to ensure his complete control of the board.

Despite the rows outside Parliament and in the national press, the South Australian Government had its way, and a law was passed, forcing Bond to cut his Santos shareholding to 15 per cent of the company. Bond called on Canberra to come to his rescue, but they could not or would not. He then took action through the courts, to prevent the South Australians forcing the sale of his shares, but the courts wouldn't help either. Finally, he threatened to take his case to the Privy Council in the UK. But it was all in vain. Bond was forced to sell the shares as the new law required him to do. By this time, however, he was able to sell on the stock market at a far better price; for in the year since he had bought the Santos shares, they had nearly trebled in value. So, although he had technically lost, he appeared to have a profit of some $60 million to comfort his companies. Not only was he solvent again, he was richer than he had ever been. And that applied both to the public company, Bond Corporation, and to Alan Bond himself.

One of the joint venturers in the original purchase of Santos had been Dallhold, Alan Bond's master private company, through which Alan and his family had picked up an $8 million personal profit on the deal. In addition, Dallhold had taken a $700,000 fee from Bond Corporation for helping to guarantee finance on the purchase of the shares. There was no question that Dallhold was entitled to some money, since it had put up a proportion of the funding. But it appeared to outsiders that Bond had been more than generous to himself when the hat was passed round.

CHAPTER 10

━━━━━

A Nice
Little Earner

There is a long history in Alan Bond's business career of assets being juggled between different companies in his empire. There is also a long history of the money ending up in Bond's hands at the end of it. He has dealt constantly between his public and his private companies, selling assets backwards and forwards, charging fees, receiving commissions, providing services in exchange. Big institutional investors have refused to buy Bond Corporation's shares as a consequence: you could never know where the profits would end up, they said, but you always suspected that a large portion would find its way into Alan's pocket.

In a way, Bond's love affair with other people's money dated back to his first property deals in the early 1960s when he had used money due to creditors of Nu-Signs to pay for land he was buying in the hills. But his passion had first become a problem when his empire went public. With outside share-holders, Alan Bond suddenly had a large pot of other people's money which he could dip into at will. Since he controlled the public company, Bond Corporation, he could use its shareholders' money for his own private gain; provided, as a general principle, that he kept shareholders informed of what he was doing.

Thus, in 1969, when his first public company WA Land was launched to the public, Alan Bond's private company had charged a $100,000 finder's fee to the new shareholders for negotiating the purchase of the Santa Maria property. Thus, again, in 1971, his private company had been able to make a $250,000 profit by selling to the public company, WA Land, an office block which it had bought in Perth some eleven months earlier. Again, in 1974, Alan was able to sell his shares in what was then his main private company, Bond Corporation, to WA Land for $17 million—six months before the crash almost toppled his business empire. And with the Santos deal, he had once more made a handsome profit for his new chief private company Dallhold.

There was, without doubt, a clear conflict of interest in all of these deals in that Alan Bond controlled the companies on both sides of the trans-action, but was taking decisions that involved paying other people's money to himself. It was impossible to be sure that he had not misused his position for personal gain. On occasion, indeed, as with the purchase of Perth's Palace Hotel, it seemed clear that he had.

The Palace Hotel, on St Georges Terrace in the heart of Perth, was for many years one of the city's most famous landmarks: a fine Victorian building with scrolled balconies, it had long been protected from demolition by a National Heritage listing. A number of developers had looked at the site and talked about buying it, but had been unable to make the sums add up because of the requirement to retain the hotel intact. Then in June 1978, after several months of negotiations, Alan Bond announced that Bond Corporation had acquired the site for $5.5 million. It would eventually be an excellent investment for his shareholders, and also become the site of Bond's new headquarters. And nor would it do Alan and his mates any harm in the meantime.

According to the Australian taxman (in evidence to court almost ten years later) Alan Bond and the three other principal directors of Bond Corporation helped themselves to a personal profit of $899,000 each on the Palace Hotel deal, at the expense of Bond Corporation shareholders. This windfall cost them an initial outlay of precisely one dollar each.

The manner in which it was done was fairly complex, but the principle was simple. Bond and his three key directors, Peter Beckwith, Peter Mitchell and Tony Oates, cut themselves in on the public company's transaction, and turned it into a nice little earner for themselves.

When Alan Bond announced that Bond Corporation had bought the Palace site he was not telling the full story. Only 45 per cent of it was actually being parked in the Bond Group, and the rest was being dumped in a couple of $2 companies picked off the shelf for the purpose. One of these companies, Rowdore, which was given 10 per cent of the site, had as its four shareholders and directors Messrs Alan Bond, Peter Beckwith, Peter Mitchell and Tony Oates—the four men who ran the Bond Corporation empire. They had each paid one dollar for one share in Rowdore the day before the site was acquired. Two years later, they would sell their shares to Arkindale, the other shelf company in the Palace Hotel deal, for a total of $3.6 million, thus poking into the piggy bank a nice little profit of almost $900,000 per person. One might feel that this was an entirely improper thing for directors of a public company to have done, but the four Bond directors would later argue that it was perfectly above board.

According to the taxman, Bond Corporation not only guaranteed Rowdore's debt, it paid all the bills. In this way Bond's men got a free ride: their company, Rowdore, did not even have a bank account until two years after the Palace Hotel was purchased. There was, therefore, no question in the taxman's mind that the transactions "lacked commercial reality". Nor did the taxman have much doubt about what the scheme was all about. An internal Taxation Office document produced to the court stated:

> It is difficult to escape the conclusion that the whole series of transactions were part of a profit-making arrangement on the part of the four directors.

Bond and his three co-directors were removing $3.6 million from the shareholders of Bond Corporation and giving it to themselves. They maintained that the shareholders both knew about, and approved of, their actions. But in practice that argument was hardly sustainable. Only a financial genius could have worked out the size of the profit that Bond directors picked up, or the way in which they had made it. And one would have needed considerable financial acumen even to be suspicious. Shareholders were shown a few pieces of the jigsaw, but were given no hint of what the complete picture looked like. They were not, for example, pointed to the most significant fact: that the four directors were making $3.6 million at the shareholders' expense.

In 1989 I interviewed Tony Oates, one of the four Bond executives who benefited from the Palace Hotel deal, expecting to find him embarrassed by what he and his fellow directors had done. But he showed not the least shame. His line to the taxman had been that lots of companies were doing the same, and that he had merely been "keen to build up his asset position for the future". He was no more repentant when I spoke to him on ABC TV's *Four Corners*:

Q: In 1978 Bond Corporation bought the Palace Hotel?

A: Yes.

Q: Did you make a profit of $900,000 personally on that transaction?

A: No I did not.

Q: $899,000?

A: No I did not.

Q: The taxman says you did.

A: Paul, can you tell me what relevance this has to the financial health of Bond Corporation Holdings?

Q: Why should I not believe that in making that money you were not lining your own pockets at the expense of shareholders?

A: I suppose that you're entitled to take that view. I suppose again that if you want to deal with the issue on a superficial basis that is an assumption you could make. But please tell me why and what has this to do with the affairs of Bond Corporation today?

Q: The Companies Act lays down duties of directors to act in the interest of all shareholders. By making $900,000 profit for yourself in the course of a public company transaction do you think you were acting in the interests of all shareholders?

A: Paul, the conduct of the directors of this company is, I would suggest to you, of the highest standard. We take pride in the way we run the company. We disclose to our shareholders what we do, as we did in this case.

Q: Can you point to the page in the accounts where you tell them that you bought a share for one dollar and sold it for $900,000?

A: No, because there was a general disclosure about it.

Q: But, just a moment, not a specific disclosure, was there? Can you just confirm that, there was not a specific disclosure?

A: There was, in the sense of one dollar for a share, no there was not. There was a

general disclosure that there was a
dealing with a number of directors of the
company.

Q: Not that you had made a profit at their
expense?

A: No, there was not.

Not only did the Bond directors not disclose the
substantial profit they had made, or the way in
which they had made it, but Alan Bond had misled
his shareholders about the role of Arkindale, the
second shelf company in the Palace deal. Arkindale
was important to the Bond directors' defence
because it gave the Palace transactions some
appearance of propriety: on paper they had sold out
to a company that had nothing at all to do with
Bond Group. Yet there was the strange coincidence
that on the very same day that the Bond directors
had sold out to Arkindale, Arkindale itself had been
bought out by Bond Corporation.

At the annual general meeting of Bond
Corporation in November 1980, Alan Bond told
shareholders that Arkindale was an "unrelated"
company. He also reassured shareholders that the
total amount Bond Corporation had paid for the site
was far less than it was worth. But, to put it deli-
cately, Mr Bond was being "economical with the
truth". In practice, Arkindale was not only
connected to Bond Corporation, it was controlled by
it. Arkindale was just a front. The four Bond directors had thus paid $3.6 million of Bond sharehold-
ers' money into their own private bank accounts.

The two controlling directors and shareholders of
Arkindale, which according to Bond was an

independent company, had for many years been closely involved with Alan Bond and the Bond Group of companies. One of them, Ron White, had been Bond's close business partner since the late 1960s, and was at the time of the Palace Hotel purchase a senior Bond Corporation executive. He later took over the running of Dallhold, Bond's private business empire. The other, David Tremain, was also a high-flying Bond executive who was, at the time, Dallhold's company secretary. He had been with Bond since the early 1970s.

One might well ask why, if it was to be only a patsy for Bond Corporation, Arkindale existed at all. The Bond camp argued that it was there to keep the transaction off Bond Corporation's balance sheet, so that the company looked healthier to shareholders and bankers—itself a deception of a sort. But the taxman believed it had a different purpose, that it existed:

> ...to hide the transaction from the public shareholders of Bond Corporation. It is believed that Arkindale Pty Ltd and Rowdore Pty Ltd were brought into the agreement to enable the four shareholders to achieve a personal benefit. This view is taken because after all the various transactions referred to in this report had been finalised the position was more or less unaltered. On the other hand the effect brought about by the moves had resulted in Bond, Beckwith, Oates and Mitchell personally benefiting to the extent of $899,999 each.

One could argue on that basis that the four relevant directors of Bond Corporation were unfit to run a public company. They had failed to act in the interests of their shareholders and had misled them. Indeed, Bond's own legal counsel would make precisely this point in a subsequent court case when Bond tried unsuccessfully to gag publication of an article in the Perth *Daily News* by investigative reporter Martin Saxon, who had bared the bones of the deal. If Saxon's allegations were true, Bond's counsel would argue, the four directors had made the profits by "stealth, non-disclosure and in breach of diligence" and were therefore not fit to remain as directors. Nevertheless, publication of the allegations was allowed, the judge considering there might well be "a reasonable basis on which the facts and the imputations (could) be justified".

At no time did the directors show the slightest contrition about what they had done. Their attitude when confronted with details of the Palace Hotel deals was that they had behaved impeccably and, not only that, they deserved the money. Peter Beckwith, indeed, seemed to believe that *he* had been cheated. In an affidavit filed in 1988, he said that he was "not only disappointed, but angry" when Alan Bond asked him to sell his share of the Palace Hotel site. He had said to his boss:

> I am not interested in selling and I don't think Tony and Mitch will be either. If you pay us $10 million then I might sell.

Beckwith could not in 1988 recall Bond's response—

perhaps hoots of laughter, or extreme anger, considering that Beckwith had acquired his share in the site for $1, according to the taxman. But he did remember that he was even more upset when the price that he and Bond settled on, of $1 million for each director, was knocked down by $100,000 after Alan insisted on a valuation of their 10 per cent of the Palace site.

> I recall at the time that I felt cheated at losing $100,000 but Alan Bond was adamant that he was not going to place himself in a position where he could be criticised for allowing Bond Corporation Holdings to pay more for the Rowdore shares than could be independently supported by the opinion of a person who was not a party to the transaction, particularly where the vendors were all executive directors of Bond Corporation Holdings.

Beckwith could not produce the valuation to the court, but he nevertheless painted a touching picture of Alan Bond doing the right thing by his shareholders, while he, poor Beckwith, was cheated out of the proceeds of his brilliant investment which he did not, in any case, wish to sell.

Beckwith's affidavit formed part of an explanation as to why none of the four directors should pay tax on their nice little earner. He and Oates argued before the court that they made a capital profit on the sale of a long-term investment, and so should be free from income tax. But their case did not succeed. Details of the settlement were never made public, but Oates's appeal against his assessment for tax on the money he had earned was "dismissed by consent".

It is one of the great unsolved mysteries that the dealings surrounding the Palace Hotel site were investigated by Western Australia's Corporate Affairs Commission without action being taken. It seemed plain, on the published facts of the matter, that the four men acted both improperly and in breach of their duties as directors of a public company. Yet one should perhaps not be surprised, for it was neither the first nor the last time that Alan Bond had got away with what appeared to be improper behaviour.

From the point of view of public servants who police such matters, it may well have appeared that Bond was too big to touch. It would not be until 1986 that the Palace Hotel dealings were investigated, and Bond by this time would tower over the state and its Premier. He would be locked into multi-million dollar deals with the government, he would be the west's biggest businessman and a national hero. He would hardly be an easy target. And nor would the prizes for pursuing him be particularly large. There would be little incentive, therefore, to risk career suicide by mounting a case against such a man and failing to drive it home.

Left: Alan and Geraldine in the early 1940s, at the house of a neighbour who minded them.

Right: The ten-pound Poms. Kathleen, Geraldine and Alan arriving at Fremantle, 5 February 1950. Alan is wearing a thick sweater and tweed suit in 35°C summer heat.

Perivale School, 2nd class, late 1940s. Alan is in the back row, second from right, complete with handkerchief in breast pocket.

Class VIa, East Fremantle Primary School, 1950. Alan is third from the left in front row, frowning, arms unfolded. Squinting at the sun or wishing he were home?

Washing the decks on *Apollo*, his new ocean racer, prior to the Sydney-Hobart race, December 1969. *News Ltd*.

Ocean Beach Hotel, Cottesloe, 1960. Dave King, Bond's business partner at Nu-Signs, is on the right with his wife; Nu-Signs' accountant Ron White and his wife are on the left; Alan and Eileen are in the middle. Ron White was only briefly at Nu-Signs, but rejoined Bond in the late 1960s.

No airs and graces. The Bonds at home, 1974. Clockwise from left, Craig, Susanne, John, Eileen, Jody, Alan. *News Ltd*.

On *Southern Cross* with Prince Philip off Yanchep, March 1974, six months before the first America's Cup challenge. *News Ltd*.

Left: Bond with *Southern Cross*, August 1974. "Anyone who thinks racing for the America's Cup isn't a business proposition is a bloody fool." *News Ltd.*

Right: Why shoes? It's only a Rolls Royce … *News Ltd.*

Striking it rich with Santos in 1978. Perhaps Bond's best-ever deal, all on borrowed money. *News Ltd.*

The proud head of the *Australia II* syndicate holds aloft the spoils of victory at Newport on 27 September 1983. Skipper John Bertrand stands far left; designer Ben Lexcen is on the far right. *UPI.*

America's Cup winners, Alan Bond and skipper John Bertrand, triumphant on *Australia II,* September 1983. *News Ltd.*

The world's best salesman makes his pitch. The new Bond headquarters was Perth's biggest building. Built over the Palace Hotel, its site also proved a goldmine for Alan Bond and three top executives. *News Ltd.*

Alan Bond and Ronald Reagan at the White House after *Australia II's* America's Cup success. *UPI.*

A hero's welcome in Perth, October 1983. For the America's Cup victory parade, 200,000 people lined the streets. *News Ltd.*

Mates. Prime Minister Bob Hawke holds the hero's hand aloft, November 1983. *News Ltd*.

Bob Hawke, Brian Burke (centre) and vice-patrons of the famous John Curtin Foundation, which linked the Labor Party to Western Australian big business. John Roberts of Multiplex is next to Brian Burke; Rod Evans Perth City councillor, is far right in back row; John Horgan, chairman of WADC, is at left of Alan Bond. Laurie Connell is on Bond's immediate left. *Bell Publishing Group*.

You can't go bust if you own a brewery – or so they said until Bond came along. In the 1980s Bond bought Swan and Castlemaine Tooheys and then Heileman to become the world's fifth largest brewer. *News Ltd.*

Bond's blimp. Airship Industries was one of several bad buys that drained money out of Bond Corporation in the late 1980s. *News Ltd.*

CHAPTER 11

——

Having Fun

By all accounts, Alan Bond was no more restrained in his personal life than he was in business. The parties at Bond's offices in the 1970s were famous around Perth. And if he no longer drove round Fremantle with girls in the back of his open-topped purple V8, he was only marginally more discreet. There were mistresses from time to time for whom he would buy a car, a flat, or sometimes both. In his personal life, as in his business dealings, it was in his nature that he did what he wanted, and left worrying about the rules to others.

Alan Bond in the late 1970s was a millionaire many times over, even if his empire was continually strapped for cash. But he certainly had no airs or graces. Though he might have taken elocution lessons and had his teeth capped, he was still plain old Alan Bond underneath. Some thought him common. Others liked his lack of pretensions: the fact that he remained an ordinary bloke. He had no great gastronomic or cultural leanings: he liked Chinese food and was mad about Clint Eastwood movies. He didn't often drink, didn't smoke, and never gambled. Nor did he have much of a sense of humour. He was a hopeless raconteur and hated comedy films.

As for fun, he went water skiing, he sailed, and for a time, played tennis. But the tennis was not entirely for pleasure. Even at the age of seventeen, Alan had made it his business to get to know the right people. He used to tell his fellow apprentices at Parnell's, with no great originality, it's not what you know, it's who you know that matters. And now, in the words of more than one friend, he collected people who counted. Tennis was part of this pattern. He took up the game, according to his coach Arthur Marshall, because he discovered that in America anybody who was anybody knew how to play—and not only that, did business on the court. Bond took a week's crash course of lessons, so as not to make a fool of himself, and then, says Marshall, expected to become a champion. "He came at it like a bull at a gate. He wanted everything to happen very quickly. He was incredibly impetuous. He gritted his teeth because he was so determined to succeed." Bond was no Lew Hoad, but he did have guts. He came to his 6 a.m. tennis lesson one day, having been up all night at a party. Marshall tried to put him through the ringer, make him squeal for mercy. Bond rushed all over the court, turned blue, green and then purple, but never flinched.

Quite what drove Bond on was a mystery. He devoted his enormous energy to making money, yet he had enough to last a lifetime. He told interviewers that his health was the most important thing, yet his lifestyle seemed destined to destroy it. He claimed to believe in religion, but there were few outward signs of him practising any. If there was a god he worshipped, it seemed to be the God of Power, or perhaps the God of Success. There was no question that he loved the thrill of the chase, the excitement of the deal. No question that he needed the adrenalin it released. But what he seemed to want more than anything was to prove himself, to impress, to be loved for what he had done. These seem odd ambitions, since he had spent so much of his time thumbing his nose at his schoolmates or the Establishment. But some of those who know Bond best say that he was always desperate to be accepted by that same Establishment he feigned to scorn. Martin Rowley, who was a high-flying executive at Bond Corporation in the early 1980s, says that Bond wanted to be patted on the back for his achievements. He wanted, above all perhaps, to be Sir Alan. Others, like Cam McNab and Jack Baxter, reached the same conclusion.

In 1978, Bond did achieve recognition, though for his sailing rather than business exploits, and from the Antipodean establishment, rather than the Queen. He was made Australian of the Year. Twelve months later, he received what some would regard as greater acclaim. After a day's sailing on Sydney Harbour, he came off his yacht to find himself face to face with the TV cameras, and was told in that oft-repeated phrase: "Alan Bond, This is Your Life". Back in the television studios, where proceedings continued, he could hardly contain himself.

Bond, the viewers were told, was the man who had challenged twice for the America's Cup, the penniless Pommy immigrant who had made a fortune, the signwriter who had built a multi-million-dollar business empire. But to look at him was to find this hard to believe: he was like a twelve-year-old boy who had won a game show or who had been singled out for praise in front of the school. Far from looking like a millionaire, it appeared that he had just bought his wardrobe at Woolworth's. He was dressed in flared trousers that were too short for him, and trussed up in a blazer that was too long. Perhaps it was the outfit, but it was impossible not to notice that he was the most extraordinary shape—he was mostly round, and his legs appeared extremely short. But it was Alan Bond's manner which stood out more than anything. He had a sheepish grin fixed on his face and, as he listened to the anecdotes, and the account of his rags-to-riches success, he hopped from foot to foot and waved his hands, as if he was standing barefoot on hot bricks.

It was impossible, looking at Bond then, to dislike him; impossible, too, to believe most of the stories of his business career. He seemed a simple, enthusiastic lad, who was tickled pink to be the centre of attention. He looked a bit of a spiv perhaps, with his long sideburns and untidy hair, but aged forty-one, he looked more than anything like a boy who had never grown up.

His family were there to share the joy. His mother, Kathleen, looking proudest of all; his son Craig like an even more awkward version of his father; Susanne in a tight crimson satin trouser suit. And Eileen, in high heels and black trousers, looking remarkably thin, with her red hair piled up on top of her head. There was no sign of Alan Bond's sister, Geraldine, nor of his old schoolmates. There were no creditors from Nu-Signs, police constables from Fremantle, or blackballers from the Royal Perth Yacht Club to spoil the fun. The stories were funny and affectionate, the sunny side of the truth.

It was hardly the forum in which to do it, of course, but no one asked Eileen and the children what price they might have paid for Alan's success. Had anyone put the question, and secured an honest reply, they would have been told that Eileen regretted being forced to bring up her family almost single-handed. They might also have discovered, as some already knew, that Eileen and Alan lived almost separate lives, that they stayed together because Eileen was a Catholic, and that to live with Alan you needed "flexibility, lots of it". Or they might have found out that Eileen would not give others much of a chance of succeeding with a marriage like hers. But whatever the precise wording of the message, the meaning would have been much the same. The price of success had been high. Bond's private life was not the happiest. It was just as well that there were money and fame to compensate.

It was as well, too, that Eileen was a strong person, because a lesser woman would not have survived so well. She was straightforward and loud, but at the same time breezy, cheerful, and fun. She was also, like Alan, a law unto herself. Not so much a breath of fresh air as a whirlwind, Eileen Bond had been known to jump fully-clothed into a swimming pool to liven up a dull party, and could frighten builders' labourers with her coarse language. Universally known as Big Red, thanks to her hair and her size, she had acquired the nickname in Newport, USA, where the Rhode Island

Red is a breed of chicken, because she had squawked around on a purple moped with her red hair streaming in the wind. Though not then as outrageous as she has since become, you could still hear her coming. She liked to take a drink, and had a striking taste in clothes. She would think nothing of mixing emerald green silk and masses of diamonds with her vivid red hair and leopard skin trousers. She was uncomplicated and friendly and the Americans loved her. So, too, did many who worked for Bond in the early days. But she was not everyone's cup of tea.

As a partial guide to the sort of person that she was, or perhaps to the sort of person that she was not, a planner who worked for Bond in the 1970s tells a story about going to Yanchep with her and Alan to look round the site. Having driven up there in Bond's Rolls-Royce at breakneck speed, and having careered across the sand dunes in the same style, they eventually settled down in a beach hut to eat lunch. Eileen had bought three or four takeaway chickens, which they ate with their fingers off paper plates. After they had finished, they wiped their hands on masses of paper to get rid of the grease. There was a huge pile of rubbish left over: paper, plates, bones and all, but it was a simple matter for Eileen to clear. She scooped up the mess in one big armful and flung the whole lot out the door, scattering it to the twenty-knot winds.

Apart from the fact that they both did much as they pleased, and were both somewhat larger than life, Eileen and Alan appeared to have little in common. In most ways, their lives barely touched. While Eileen loved parties, friends, and drinking till dawn, Alan got his kicks out of doing deals. He had

no time for her hectic lifestyle, was not a social creature, and given the chance, would talk business
morning, noon and night. Business was his life. He
drew his friends, such as they were, from the teams
that he did things with—whether it was sailing or
running Bond Corporation. He was, says American
banker George Carmany, who knows the family
well, a man's man in all senses of the term. And his
lifestyle confirmed it. Bond Corporation was domi-
nated by men, its top managers were men, and
those it did business with were the same. Alan
jetted round the world doing deals with men and,
insofar as he came across women, he did so
normally in pursuit of pleasure. He lived the
hundred-mile-an-hour life of the international
entrepreneur, and he enjoyed it. Back home, in the
meantime, Eileen tried to ignore his infidelities,
brought up the children and became bored.

To fill the gaps in her life, it seemed, she spent
money. She told an interviewer in 1980 about a
recent trip to hospital when a friend had brought
her a bottle of her favourite Veuve Clicquot champagne. The cork shot out and hit the ceiling, and,
said Eileen: "It was marvellous. I sent the little
golden cap on the cork to a jeweller in Sydney to
have it set in 18-carat gold and now I wear it on a
chain round my neck. That's the sort of thing I do to
relieve boredom." On the same stay in hospital she
had observed that all the other women had their
menfolk around them. So she had rung Alan in
London to berate him for not being by her side.
Tongue in cheek, and perhaps as a subtle message to
her husband, she told the journalist that she had
said to Alan: "All the other women have studs."
"What kind of studs?" Alan had enquired, perhaps

fearing the worst. "Diamond studs!" Big Red had replied. "Well," said Alan, "don't worry darling, as soon as you get out, you go and get diamond studs." And so she did, the biggest pair of diamond studs she could find in Perth. "Serve him right for leaving me bored in the hospital."

For all his absences, Alan was an interested father. He took great pride in the achievements of his children, and gave them encouragement and support. He also, on some accounts, did better than that. Geoff Summerhayes, who was close to the family over these years, says Alan would always try to sit the family at table for breakfast. "For all the things he might or might not have been, he brought his family up that way. Breakfast was the meal of the day when he wanted everyone together. He realised that he wouldn't be home most evenings." His children, it seems, loved him, but wished he were there more often.

The wives of Bond executives had to cope with pressures similar to those experienced by Eileen. Bond and Bond Corporation demanded that the job be priority number one, so its top executives were constantly away, sometimes for six or seven months a year, and were constantly under pressure. On occasions, the wives would complain. And Alan would give them short shrift. Martin Rowley, who was an executive assistant to the Bond Corporation board in the early 1980s, says: "I've seen him say to the women at dinner parties that he, Alan, had bought them everything they owned. For a number of reasons I don't think the wives liked him. I don't think the wives thought of Alan as being the greatest guy ever." But Bond's executives were more than loyal. "Warren Jones would have crawled half-a-mile over broken glass for Alan if he had been asked to," says one former Bond insider.

If Alan did not always treat his top men well, they either loved him enough or feared him sufficiently to accept it. Even in private most would not shout back. But sometimes Bond would bawl them out in public. According to Martin Rowley, "Alan always had to be seen to be making the decisions and having the upper hand at meetings. We guys were meant to be with him as a team. If you were at a meeting with legal advisers and tax advisers, and Alan said we'll do it this way, and you said you couldn't do it that way, he'd abuse you in front of everyone. You could never tell Alan that he was wrong in front of other people."

Bond's anger rarely lasted long: he had a temper but he was not given to sulking. He also did not often sack people: like all good leaders, he was loyal to his chosen men—unless he felt they were being disloyal to him, and then the ties would be cut without ceremony. After four or five years with Bond Corporation, Martin Rowley decided he would go solo and see what he could build for himself. On a flight to Melbourne one morning he told Bond Corporation's Managing Director Peter Beckwith of his plans, making it clear that he would not actually leave for three or four months. "Peter said, 'That's good, Marty. We encourage entrepreneurship.' That was on a Friday. I got back to Perth on Sunday and Alan rang to tell me not to come to work Monday. Eventually I caught up with him and we spent from eight in the morning to eight at night talking. It started off very aggressive and we ended up as friends. Alan was just angry about me leaving."

When others became angry with him, Alan could

almost always talk them back on side. In his book *Born to Win*, the 1983 America's Cup skipper John Bertrand recounts how Bond could move people down the pecking order in the team, yet get them to react as if they had been given a better job. It even happened to him: "In the end I resigned as tactician and went to see Alan Bond. In one hour, Bondy converted me from a disgruntled second-in-command to a supremely happy mainsheet hand. Alan Bond had made me feel good about it."

Bond's greatest talent, whether with bankers, sailors or businessmen, was his power to persuade. Michael Grace, who came up against the man in the early 1980s, when Bond was barging in on Grace Brothers in an attempt to take them over, says: "If he wanted something it was very hard not to say, 'Yes, I agree with you, Alan.' He just had that charm, that charisma, that complete belief in where he was going." But he would also never take no for an answer: "No matter how many times we said, 'That doesn't suit us, Alan,' he just brushed it aside and kept going ahead. And then when we said: 'Look, we can't do that legally,' he said: 'Oh, we'll find a way round it.' It did not enter his negotiating position that it couldn't be done."

For all his charm and charisma, Alan Bond gathered few friends. In the words of John Bertrand, he was "formidable, shrewd, innovative, multi-talented and a fantastic salesman". But he was also isolated: "not so much a loner as a lonely man." Just as he had been outside the crowd in his schooldays, so he was now in the 1970s. It wasn't easy to see him unless you had business to discuss. And the bigger the empire grew, the more that became a problem.

Geoff Summerhayes says Alan would sit down by him at parties and ask how he was, but would never wait for the answer. "He would slap you on the leg and say: 'Before you start, I'll just tell you what's happening.' And then he would talk non-stop for half-an-hour about his latest deals." Summerhayes remembers one party at Perth's Parmelia Hilton, just after Bond had found emeralds up north somewhere. "He had this handful of stones in his handkerchief. He came up to me and said: 'Don't tell anyone. I don't want people to know what I've found, but these are fantastic.' And he showed them to me. I noticed as the night slipped by that he was showing them to everyone."

John Bertrand tells a bizarre, in some way rather sad, story in a similar vein. One night Alan and his America's Cup crew were at dinner and Bond was becoming more and more bored. Suddenly he started to recite to the assembled company a list of everything he owned. "I own this, I own that, I will soon own…" It was like a little boy bragging about his father's riches or boasting that he had better toys than anyone else: a rather pathetic insight into what drove Bond on. It seemed he was obsessed by the desire to possess and control.

Yet perhaps Bond had good reason at this stage to be counting his assets—if only to see what he would have left if the bankers were again tempted to pull the plug on him. For in 1983, as he prepared another tilt at the America's Cup, he was once more in financial trouble. It was the same old story: he had used his new-found riches to buy more assets, and had then borrowed yet more money and hit trouble again. After the Santos success, he had indulged in a bewildering array of share deals and corporate raids, which had made more paper millions for Bond and his companies. He had bought gold, he had bought copper, he had bought coal. His companies, too, had bought into retailing, with less than spectacular success. And then, in 1981, he had made the largest personal takeover bid in Australian corporate history, paying $164 million in cash for Western Australia's Swan brewery. It was the state's most blue-blooded company, and its purchase marked Bond's entry into the corporate big time. But, typically, it also nearly marked his downfall.

From the crash of 1974 Bond had learnt a lesson that he believed would keep him from ever facing ruin again. To get through the slumps in the property market, he needed a business that would earn cash in the bad times as well as the good. And one product fitted the bill better than anything else— beer. Whatever the weather, whatever the economic climate, Australians liked to drink. In Swan Brewing Bond picked perhaps the best brewery in Australia. It had modern plant, it had 95 per cent of the state beer market, and little in the way of borrowings. It was perfect.

But Swan Brewing was also huge. In fact, it was Western Australia's biggest home-grown company, twice as big as Bond in terms of its stock market value. To take it over, Bond had to borrow more than he had ever borrowed before—not far off $160 million. And just as he did so, interest rates rose. Once again, Bond found himself in a cash crisis. Once again, on Fridays, there wasn't enough money to pay the wages. Bond's new bankers, the Hong Kong Shanghai Bank, moved into the company and cracked heads. Spending was cut, all Bond's remaining shares in Santos were sold, along with other

CHAPTER 12

1983–
Sailing To Glory

With three unsuccessful challenges for the America's Cup behind him, Bond decided that in 1983 he would give it one last go. His record thus far was hardly inspiring, having notched up just one win in thirteen races, but he was determined to try again, and being the person he was, he believed that he could win. Quite what encouraged him to think so one can only surmise. But he was adamant that 1980 had been just a holding operation; 1983 would be his year.

It had taken no time at all to get the '83 challenge under way. Moments after *Australia* had sailed to her fourth defeat of the 1980 series, at the hands of Denis Conner's *Freedom*, Bond had roared up in a speedboat with Warren Jones at his side and bounced into the midst of his defeated crew. His first words were a cheery: "Don't worry boys. That was great. We gave it our best shot." And in almost the next sentence he was telling them the good news—they would come back in 1983 with a major challenge. "We'll have the budget and the boat," Bond told them. "And we are going to win the America's Cup. Right?" The crew cheered, but few would have given a prayer for Bond's chances. Only months after his 1980 success, Conner already had his plans for the Cup's defence drawn up. He would build two brand new 12-metres and trial them for more than a year beforehand, first off Newport, then through the winter in California, and finally back in Newport again. It seemed to be somewhat unnecessary, given that in his old 12-metre, *Freedom*, Conner had just sailed fifty-two races against the best that the world had to offer, and had only lost five times.

But one man in the Bond camp, apart from Bond himself, was not yet prepared to concede defeat, and that was the yacht designer, Ben Lexcen. A huge, bearlike man, with thick pebble glasses, and almost no formal education, Ben had a fund of wonderful stories, an encyclopaedic knowledge of classical music, and a great flair for coming up with brilliant ideas. But his lateral thinking sometimes took him very wide of the mark. His first 12-metre for Bond in 1974, *Southern Cross*, had been a dog, while his next effort, *Australia*, had been ordinary at best. Now, however, Ben was back at the drawing board in search of something special. Or, more precisely, he was building model boats at a test tank in Holland, where he had gone with $400,000 of the Bond syndicate's money, and a brief from Alan to do whatever he wanted.

Ben Lexcen, who died in 1989, was in many ways similar to the man who backed him; he was certainly one of Bond's few true friends. But in his case the myth-makers had concocted an even more remarkable story than they had cooked up for the Fremantle signwriter. For a start, Ben had been christened Bob Miller, and had only changed his name to Lexcen in the 1970s for reasons that were never entirely clear. He had been born out in the New South Wales bush in a town called Boggabri, where his parents had stopped off in their wanderings. For the first few years of his life he had been humped from town to town, and from log camp to log camp, while his father and mother looked for work, and then, at the age of six he had been dumped in Newcastle, a couple of hours north of Sydney, to be brought up by his grandparents. Grandad, who was soon looking after Ben single-handed, was "a silent old codger" who left the boy pretty much to his own devices, except for insisting that Ben get some formal education. It was not until the age of eleven that Ben first went to school. He stuck it for just two years, made it to top of the class, and learnt to write. But he never mastered what children call running writing, and nor did he learn to spell.

From an early age, Ben busied himself with boats, and before long they became his passion. In his teens he was a national dinghy-sailing champion. Soon after, he was racing eighteen-foot skiffs to success and building his own, brilliantly fast conveyance. Bigger yachts followed, and his reputation as a designer began to grow. Rags turned into riches, his Ferraris started to fill the driveway, and the list of successful boats grew longer. But the passion to excel, and the despair when he did not, remained unchanged. He still wanted desperately to design a winning 12-metre. And he now unleashed all his manic energy onto that task.

When Lexcen set off for the test tank in Holland, to the Netherlands Ship Model Basin at Wageningen, he tried to clear his mind of what he already knew; he wanted to experiment. But for a strategy to guide him, he opted to work on the design of *Australia*, the boat that had challenged in 1977 and 1980, while at the same time searching for something more radical. Time was no great problem, nor was money, for Bond had given him a free hand and an open cheque book. The facilities and technical back-up were also unrivalled. They would build twenty-foot models of Ben's designs, and tow them up and down the seven-hundred-metre testing tank by the mast, feeding the data into a computer to assess the results. Then Ben would modify the design, or go back to the drawing board, and try again.

Ben had already tried putting wings onto the keel of a smaller yacht, with no great success—the boat had gone faster downwind, but slower in every other direction. Now he tried putting them on a 12-metre, and the results were spectacular. It took six or seven different versions, and a month or two of fiddling to get everything right, but by the end Lexcen had a boat that he thought was "really wild". The new winged keel was not especially attractive—it looked like an ordinary keel which had been fixed to the boat upside down, and its wings looked like a pair of duck's feet—but the test tank said it was a winner. On the computer's calculations, the boat would go to windward five per cent faster than a conventional 12-metre.

Lexcen, quite naturally, was beside himself with joy, because he appeared to have made a major breakthrough in 12-metre design. He summoned Alan Bond, Warren Jones and skipper, John Bertrand, to Holland for a secret viewing and, as Bertrand recounts in *Born to Win*, turned his enthusiasm on them full blast. Lexcen told them: "We're not just going to win the America's Cup, we're going to win it by miles. We're going to win some of these races by twenty minutes."

The claim was extravagant: it could just be another of Benny's brainstorms, but the computer results seemed hard to fault. And once the boat was built it became clear that Lexcen's optimism was more than partially justified. For on *Australia II*'s maiden voyage off Fremantle, it transpired that she had another, more exciting, characteristic than sheer speed: the boat's skipper, John Bertrand, now found as he took the helm that she could turn in quite remarkable fashion. In fact, she could turn faster than any other big boat he had ever sailed. This manoeuvrability alone could win them the series, because an advantage gained at the start in a 12-metre duel, when the boats twist and turn and jockey for position, was often enough to secure victory. But there was yet another edge that *Australia II*'s secret weapon would give them, and both Bond and Bertrand knew it: she would frighten the Americans. Perhaps she would even unsettle the super-confident Denis Conner.

To exploit this psychological advantage, but as much to prevent anyone making a copy of their pocket Exocet, the Bond camp kept the winged keel under wraps at all times. Lloyds of London, who had to approve construction of the boat, were even shown plans for *Australia II* with a conventional keel. And when, in 1983, the Superboat, as by now she was called, was shipped to Newport for the start of the series, she was unloaded with a green canvas modesty skirt to conceal her private parts. From then on, she was surrounded by armed guards and protected by an electric pen whenever she was in harbour. Plans were made by rivals to photograph the keel from the air as the boat heeled over in the wind; and a diver was even caught near her mooring. But the secret of the magic keel remained intact.

It was high summer in Newport, towards the end of June, when the elimination races began. *Australia II* surged out of the harbour into Rhode Island Sound each day, with her Black Swan spinnaker bulging in the wind. And every evening as she came back, the message was the same, the list of the vanquished longer. She ran rings round her challengers, beating them not just on boat speed, but also through the sailing skills of her crew. After ten years of practice, the men who handled *Australia II* were now a match for anybody. By the end of the second round of races, the Bond boat had notched up twenty-one victories against only three defeats. And even the Americans were worried.

Denis Conner had spent hours watching *Australia II* perform, and the stopwatch showed him what Bertrand already knew. She tacked in five seconds, half the time a conventional 12-metre would take. And to judge by the race results, she sailed well too. Conner's design team had told him to expect that *Australia II* would go faster than his boat *Liberty*, because she was lighter than a conventional 12-metre, and would make less leeway. But Conner knew that the Australian yacht would also excel because his boat had problems: not to put too fine a point on it, *Liberty* was a tub when she was going downwind. And now, as the real battle drew near, it was obvious that after 132 years the unthinkable could happen: America could actually lose. Conner's navigator, Halsey Herreshoff, even said it out loud: if *Australia II* was allowed to continue in the competition without penalty, she would not only be chosen as the challenger, but she would almost certainly win the America's Cup. The logic was clear: *Australia II* had to be stopped. The New York Yacht Club now devoted its energies to having her excluded from the challenge or handicapped out of the race.

It should be said that the America's Cup had a history of argument and foul play, and the New York Yacht Club had often managed to arrange the rules in its favour. For example, in the very first race for the Cup in 1871, the British challenger had crossed the Atlantic to find a fleet of fifteen American schooners from the New York Yacht Club lined up on the starting line against her. The British had duly raced, under protest, and lost, but had complained quite rightly that fifteen to one was grossly unfair. The next time, the British challenger had turned up to find only one opponent down at the start, as the new rule stipulated. But the Americans had then played a different trick, changing the defending yacht from race to race: in light weather, the Americans had put up a boat built to perform in light winds; in heavy weather, they had fielded a more sturdy boat to beat the British. The Americans had won again, the British had complained, and once more the rules had been changed. But the arguments had continued down the years. And now the battle lines were drawn for the biggest argument of all. From here on, the bickering and scheming over the winged keel would amply demonstrate the truth of Denis Conner's observation: "There has never been any sportsmanship in the America's Cup. Anyone who thinks there has is just kidding himself."

The fact that *Australia II*'s keel had been measured twice and passed by a committee of experts did not concern the New York Yacht Club. It was clear to them that the boat had been rated incorrectly, and the secrecy surrounding the Australian boat simply strengthened their convictions. Even at the official measurement on her arrival in Rhode Island, *Australia II* had been protected by guards at the boatshed, and the measurers had been sworn to silence. Why else would that have been done, except to hide her obvious illegality? the NYYC asked. But there were technical arguments to back up the Americans' case, and a section of the rule book which supported it. There was, it is true, no doubt among the measurers that the official formula rated *Australia II* as a valid 12-metre. But one of three men running the ruler over her in Rhode Island, an American named Mark Vinbury, had suspected that the formula might not have measured her fairly—a subtle difference. And he had wondered in particular, whether the wings might be "a peculiarity" which should be separately considered. As Vinbury and others pointed out, the wings on *Australia II*'s keel gave the boat extra, unrated, draught when she heeled over, because the wings stuck down below the keel's lowest point. It was arguable that this extra draught should be rated. The Americans said it should; Bond, naturally, did not agree.

On 3 August, after rumblings behind the

American lines, the first shot was fired. Bond stepped ashore after a hard day's sailing, to hear that the NYYC had officially complained to the International Yacht Racing Union (IYRU) that *Australia II*, as she stood, was not a legal 12-metre. If the IYRU agreed with them, there could only be two results. Either the Australian boat would have to accept a penalty, or Bond and his crew would be pitched out of the game. Bond was almost white with rage at hearing the news. This was no longer sport, it was war. But he was confident of victory, and he relished the battle: he had been spoiling for this particular fight for a long time.

A Texan banker once described doing business with him as "like wrestling with a pig in shit, and the pig loves it", and so it was now, for Bond was in his element. During an early lull in the hostilities, three of the top officers of the New York Yacht Club called on Alan at his Newport mansion to arrange a truce—or so they said. By way of a reply, Bond gave them such a shaking that one of the party, the NYYC's Commodore, Bob McCullogh, had almost to be carried out. McCullogh said they were just trying to be civil but Bond shouted, threatened to smear the club, to pull it through the mud, and to drag its name through the gutter. It was all too much. Another of the American deputation, Bus Mosbacher, recalls asking Bond: "What can we do to calm things down, to end all this controversy and get back to sailing?" And Alan just said, according to Mosbacher: "End the controversy? No one would know we were here if it weren't for the controversy."

The war over the winged keel made sailing that summer almost an irrelevance. It was one of the great confrontations of our time, at least in the eyes of the press. Here on the one hand was the plucky challenger, who would never give up, and now looked like snatching the prize. And there on the other was the stuffy defender, who had cheated its way through history and now couldn't lose with dignity. As the battle raged on, the Americans sank deeper and deeper into the pit of unpopularity while Alan Bond and Warren Jones soared higher and higher into the clouds of innocence. The letters poured in, supporting Bond, as the brickbats hailed on the heads of the hapless NYYC. The papers had a field day.

The Americans tried every trick in the book that summer to ensure that the Australians did not make it to the starting line. Not only did they allege that the winged keel had been designed by Dutch scientists rather than by Ben Lexcen—which would have caused *Australia II* to be disqualified, since the rules stated that she must be designed solely by Australian nationals—but they tried to trap or to bully the Dutch into admitting it. Both attempts backfired in spectacular fashion: the scientists at the Wageningen test tank confirmed that Lexcen had designed the wings and then complained about the New York Yacht Club's antics. At the height of the whole unseemly farce, telexes were published by the Bond camp revealing that the Americans had even approached the Dutch with the stated intention of buying the keel themselves. Whether they genuinely wanted to, or whether it was just a ploy, hardly mattered—it did not look good alongside their protests that the keel was unfair.

The Americans' original attempt to have the keel declared illegal by the IYRU fared no better. Alan Bond's British double, the loud and colourful

Peter de Savary, announced before the matter even reached the relevant committee that he had asked the IYRU about winged keels fourteen months earlier and had been told they were perfectly legal. The Americans had therefore lost on both fronts. But still they would not accept defeat.

With only three days to go to the opening race, the NYYC committee voted to cancel the 1983 America's Cup series unless Bond signed a document swearing that he had complied with all the rules of the challenge. Bond took one look at the document which demanded quite ridiculous assurances and told the NYYC what unprintable things they could do with it. He told them, too: "Whether you race or not, I will be at the line, and so will CBS, NBC and the rest. So take your choice."

In reply, the New York Yacht Club approached the chairman of the challengers' liaison committee, and demanded that another challenger be put up in *Australia II*'s place. The committee's chairman told them to get on with the races, and at last the Americans were forced to face the decision whether to fight or run. On the eve of the first race, the full America's Cup committee of the NYYC met on Bus Mosbacher's boat, *Summertime*, to decide whether to cancel the series, as they had threatened to do. It was an angry meeting: most of the fifteen members present believed the winged keel to be unfair; most believed they would be sending Denis Conner out to lose the Cup for them for the first time in 132 years; but most also realised that to run away now would make the New York Yacht Club a laughing stock. The NYYC had no choice. As Bus Mosbacher now says: "The issue was decided on the front pages. We had headlines like 'The New York Yacht

Club waives the rules to rule the waves'. I guess we had to keep a stiff upper lip and go out there."

The 1983 series was thus decided on the water, rather than in the court room. And it turned out to be a corker; in the opinion of Ed Du Moulin, manager of the *Liberty* syndicate, the best and most enjoyable series ever. If anyone could pull off an American victory, it was Denis Conner: competition was life's blood, said Conner in his autobiography *No Excuse to Lose*, and he was the vampire. He slept only four hours at night, never took a day off, and was never sick. And in the twenty hours he was awake every day, he devoted himself to being the best sailor in the world. Conner told his crew to put winning the America's Cup above everything— family, money, sex, religion, social obligations, the lot. But he would need all his skills this time, because, against *Australia II* even Neptune would be a long shot. Or so it looked as battle began, but before too long, things were turning out quite differently.

The first race went to Conner in *Liberty* when *Australia II*'s steering failed. The second race went to the Americans as well: this time when a pin holding up the mainsail broke on the Australian boat. And already it was looking like the same familiar tale of over confidence and incompetence combined. After nine years, and fifteen races against the Americans, they had still only picked up one victory. And their so-called Superboat had scored none out of two. As for Denis Conner, he looked anything but psyched out: after the second race, the old vampire of competition cruised into Newport Harbour, at the head of the huge spectator fleet, with his arms in the air to acknowledge the cheers. The New York Yacht Club elite might have liked him little better than

Bond, but the great gladiator of sailing looked set to save their bacon nevertheless.

Race Three put a smile back on Australian faces when *Australia II* at last got her act together and beat *Liberty* to the finish. Better than that, she won by the biggest margin of any Cup challenger ever, as proof of what she could do when things went right. But almost at once, disaster struck again: Conner in *Liberty* ran away with Race Four, and now only one more win was needed for the New York Yacht Club to clinch the Cup. There were three races for the Americans to do it, to pick up just one victory, while *Australia II*, to come out on top, had to win them all. Given a strike rate thus far of two victories in sixteen tries, it looked an impossible task.

But Alan Bond enjoyed impossible odds, according to those who knew him well, and he now rallied his troops. One wonders whether he believed what he told the newspapers that day and, if he did, where he found his faith. But his message was defiant: don't write us off, he said, we will win, and win gloriously, just like our boys did at Gallipoli. Some smart journalist pointed out that Gallipoli far from being glorious, had been a defeat, but Bond was not deterred. He came punching back with the reply that the boys had fought hard then and they would fight hard now: we won't give up, said Bond. And sure enough they did not. *Australia II* won the next two races to level the series at three-all, giving the Americans in Race Six the biggest hiding they had ever had. It was now a tie with only one race to go—a Hollywood scriptwriter's dream, except that no one would have dared contrive such an improbable story.

Even now, most people in the United States

hardly knew that the America's Cup was taking place, and far fewer were getting excited about it. The big US television networks weren't interested at all, and nor, by and large, were the bulk of their viewers. The Americans were used to winning at sports, and certainly didn't think of such contests as any test of their national virility. But back in Australia, this final showdown was watched as if the country's future depended on it—there was no question of the Australian networks ignoring it, or of people not bothering to turn on. Six million stayed up all night to watch it run. Others with the money or the luck made the pilgrimage in person. The Australian Treasurer, Paul Keating, graced Bond's high-speed launch *Black Swan* with his presence, having hustled off from a meeting of the International Monetary Fund in Washington to watch it live at Newport. Meanwhile, on another boat, Australia's former Prime Minister Malcolm Fraser was also waving the flag. *Australia II* was no longer the project of a loud-mouthed, little-loved Perth millionaire. She was suddenly the nation incarnate: all Australia sailed with her.

Of course, it was not true to say that the whole of America ignored the Cup, for in Newport the final race was a magnificent occasion. Overhead there was the buzz of fifty helicopters and fixed-wing aircraft, and the drone of the Goodyear blimp. On the water were a US Navy destroyer, a host of coast-guard vessels, and a fleet of pleasure craft to compare with that assembled for D-Day. This, after all, was the climax, the deciding race, with the chance that history would be made. The spectators would not be disappointed.

The start was tight, with no clear advantage, then

straightaway the two yachts parted company, choosing to race on different sides of the course. When they came together again, after thirty minutes, *Australia II* was just in the lead. Immediately, they parted again, and Conner struck lucky—or perhaps had gambled well—because he found a windshift that gave him an advantage. As they rounded the first mark *Liberty* was twenty-nine seconds in front and looking good. By the second mark the gap had widened to forty-five seconds; by the fourth mark Conner and *Liberty* were close on a minute ahead, and it seemed all over. Surely now, he had the race sewn up unless he made a terrible mistake or *Liberty*'s gear broke. Surely now the Cup was won, it would go back to America again. On the Australians' tender, *Black Swan*, Ben Lexcen could watch no more. Convinced it was all over, he went below deck and looked through a porthole at the faces of the men from the New York Yacht Club on their launch *Fox Hunter*. They looked tense, but confident. And then, suddenly, they must have frozen with horror. For Denis Conner apppeared to have just committed the cardinal sin of yachting.

In sailing, the first rule of match racing is that when ahead, if you can't cover your opponent with a coffin lid, then you must at least sit on him, and keep one foot on his neck. That way, once you're in the lead you stay there. But almost one minute behind Conner, the Australians had taken a different course, and Conner had chosen not to follow. There was now the risk that the Australians could pick up a better wind than he, and slip past *Liberty* on the run, and that was exactly what happened. Out on her own, the Australian boat suddenly began to fly. She first drew level, then overtook the

American defender, and as the two boats rounded the last mark, it was *Australia II* not *Liberty* who was ahead. There was now just the one leg to go to the finish and the Australians were forty seconds in front. As they came down this last straight the Americans threw in everything they had, tacking almost fifty times to try and pressure John Bertrand and his crew into a mistake. But as the red hull of *Liberty* swung each time into the tack the white nose of *Australia II* up ahead moved with her, like a shadow. The grinders, the men on the winches, were being pushed beyond the limits, and so were the nerves of the crew. On board *Australia II* they hardly dared look at their opponents; no one said a word except to call the wind. Then the gun roared as the first yacht crossed the line. They had held on, they had done it, they had come back from the dead: Australia had won the Cup.

Almost at once it was pandemonium. Sirens blared, hooters honked, *Black Swan* turned up the Aussie battle cry—Men at Work's "Down Under"— and the champagne showered over all and sundry. In the near riot that greeted the Bonds as they returned to harbour, Eileen had a $50,000 diamond and gold Cartier watch torn from her wrist, but it could hardly dampen her spirits. Denis Conner came back to shore with tears in his eyes to tell Jim Hardy, Bond's skipper from 1980, that he couldn't have sailed any better. On the opposition boats, the champagne stayed in the fridge, and the rum punch came out instead: they would get drunk quicker that way. That night for the Australians it was fireworks, Swan Lager and a party the likes of which poor Newport had never seen.

The scene back at the New York Yacht Club's

headquarters on Manhattan's West 44th Street, by contrast, was a study in gloom. There was no television in the vast pillared building—club etiquette did not permit such a thing—and nor was there a radio in the men's bar, but someone in the kitchen had found a transistor radio to keep them in touch, and one of the members rang his wife for a running commentary on the race, which she gave as she watched it on cable TV. Now that it was all over, the building resembled nothing so much as a morgue. At least in Newport they could go out and have a party, and drown their sorrows in style, but here it was awful. In the huge dark rooms and silent corridors, one or two members embraced, even burst into tears. There was a vain attempt to mark the passing of the Cup with a toast, but even that fell flat. Having unscrewed the famous trophy from the table to which it was fixed, they discovered that the champagne ran through the bolthole in the bottom. Then, as darkness fell, the Brinks Mat security men came to fetch the Cup to ferry it up to Newport. The hierarchy of the Club had wanted to present the trophy to the Royal Perth Yacht Club in New York, in the privacy of their galleon-windowed headquarters. But Bond would have none of it. He wanted the world to see his victory crowned. He had waited ten years or more for this triumph, and he planned to make the most of it.

Back in Australia, the rejoicing had already begun. It was like the end of World War II. Those who had gone to bed in despair, with *Australia II* apparently beaten, woke to find a nation gone mad. Green and gold flags and bunting sprouted everywhere. Cars hooted their horns as they cruised round the streets, the bottle shops sold out of

Australian champagne, and perfect strangers threw their arms round each other to celebrate. Prime Minister Bob Hawke, who had watched the race in his hotel room and then high-tailed it down to the Royal Perth Yacht Club, himself led the celebrations. Before dawn came up over the Swan, the people's PM had excelled himself—shaking champagne bottles to make them spray a golden foam, leading choruses of "Waltzing Matilda" and eloquently declaring a de facto national holiday. "Any employer," said Bob, "who sacks a worker for not coming in today is a bum."

To Bond, Hawke sent a telegram of congratulation: "We said we could do it. Our word was as good as our Bond." The trophy should be renamed the Australia's Cup, he suggested. After all, victory had united the nation. The *Sydney Morning Herald*, in an editorial, went even further in banging the drum of national pride: "The crew of *Australia II* has shown all Australians that we can do anything if we try. We have proved that in technology, courage and tenacity, we can compete with the best in the world." If Australia had put a man on the moon, the excitement could hardly have matched it. No one dared say it was only a yacht race. Nor did anyone point out that the "we" who had won the Cup was a little-loved millionaire from Western Australia. For in winning the America's Cup, a new national hero was born.

CHAPTER 13

WA Incorporated

After his America's Cup success, Bond returned to Perth to a hero's welcome. As the victory motorcade proceeded along St Georges Terrace, with Alan and Eileen leading the way in an open-top Rolls Royce, two hundred thousand people packed the pavements or shinned up trees and lamp posts to get a better look. The crowds cheered, the tickertape rained down, and all paid homage to the state's new favourite son. The newly-elected Premier, Brian Burke, took the microphone to say in emotional tones that Australians walked beside Bond with pride. He might well have added, in the vein of mediaeval kings: "ask for whatever you wish—even up to half my kingdom", for that was the scale of the debt that he clearly felt. Not only was Bond bringing home glory and the Cup, he was carrying with him the promise of a bonanza for Western Australia. After all, the America's Cup defence in

1987 would be held in the port of Fremantle, and the tourists would come flocking in their thousands to watch. There would be prosperity for all in Western Australia. Not least, of course, for Alan Bond.

Bond by now must have been well aware that there was good business in being a national hero. But he could hardly have realised what dividends he would be able to reap from Brian Burke's new Western Australian Government. In 1983, as the victor listened to Burke's panegyric, Alan Bond was already a big man in the state. Five years later, he would be a colossus. By this time it would be said, only half jokingly, that Bond owned everything—the breweries, the newspapers, the television stations, the tallest office buildings, Kalgoorlie's Golden Mile, even the government. Perth would in five short years become Bond's town. The America's Cup victory would play a large part in this, but so would the Labor Government. For Premier Burke had decreed that the State and big business should work together to make Western Australia rich. And big business meant Bond.

Looking at the incredible mess that Burke, Bond, and another big businessman Laurie Connell have bequeathed Western Australia, it is hard to believe that WA Incorporated once had a philosophy that both press and public believed in. Brian Burke had campaigned to election victory in 1983, with enthusiastic support from the media, on the promise of a new entrepreneurial style of government that would boost the state's economic growth and lower taxes. In this Burke dream world, a team of dynamic young ministers, led by the plausible and presentable Burke, would harness the expertise of the business community to make the public sector more efficient; at the same time, his government would provide millions of dollars for the go-getting private sector to invest. Where Sir Charles Court's Liberal administration in the 1970s had promoted oil and mineral development to make the state rich, Burke would in the 1980s bring new wealth to Western Australia by developing the sunrise industries of tourism, finance and high technology. Taxpayers would benefit because their taxes could be lowered, and Western Australian business would prosper because it would be given first pick of the best projects.

Described this way, Burke's plan for an alliance between business and government seemed perfectly reasonable. And, had the Japanese or the French public service been hired to pick the winners, the promised prosperity might well have been delivered. But in WA, whose population is less than two million people, the practice was a disaster. Questioning the loyalty of anyone who stood in his way, Burke removed or bypassed many of the state's senior public servants, filled his administration with political supporters, and then allowed a bunch of self-interested businessmen to guide the government's actions. The final cost of WA Incorporated may never be counted, but it will run to hundreds of millions of dollars of taxpayers' money—wasted on a variety of share and property deals and government-led rescue operations which had one key thing in common: that public money should never have been committed.

Western Australia is physically vast, but it is well to remember how small it is in other ways. Its networks operate on a scale where a handful of people share power—to create private sector jobs or to dispense state contracts—and all either know each other well or know of each other. It is hard, in such circumstances, to prevent the process of government being corrupted, however honest the politicians, however correct the public servants. But Brian Burke made the task harder still because his administration dismantled some of the checks and balances that normally keep the system on the straight and narrow. By removing senior public servants (thus putting those who criticised him in fear of their jobs); by allowing state-owned sites to be sold or contracts to be given without a public tender process; and by permitting the Western Australian Development Corporation to operate outside parliamentary scrutiny, Burke removed three of the key safeguards on which good government relies.

But the Burke administration's most important contribution to the failure of the system was even simpler than that, and it stemmed from dealings with Perth's business elite. To the cynic, the concept was clear—big businessmen would help pay for Labor's election challenges and assist the party into office; an elected Labor Government would then send contracts and opportunities in the big businessmen's direction. While the official line was never so bluntly stated, the message was clear nevertheless: government and big business would link hands to develop WA, and both would benefit from the partnership. The letters sent out to potential business donors weren't quite so crass as to promise favours for supporting Burke, but they guaranteed a hearing for any problems, plus the possibility of an audience with the Premier for those who put their hands in their pockets.

Burke's corporate fan club, eventually launched in 1984, read like a Business Who's Who of Western Australia. Known officially as the John Curtin Foundation, in ironic memory of that most correct of Labor prime ministers, it contained the majority of Perth's rich and powerful. The state's two largest property developers, Alan Bond and his mate Laurie Connell, were both there; so was their friend John Roberts of Multiplex, Western Australia's biggest builder, who had built Bond's house and handled all his developments, and who was granted state contracts; so, too, was the man whose company did the electrical contracting work in Multiplex's buildings, Mick Michael of Milec. Then from the official side of town there was Perth's Lord Mayor, who was also Chairman of the City Planning Committee, and who happened to be the same Mick Michael. There was also the Vice-Chairman of the Planning Committee, Rod Evans, who doubled as a property investor. And finally there was the chairman of the West Australian Development Corporation, John Horgan, the man who would have extensive power to hand out large Government contracts. There is a photograph of the dozen-or-so founders, lined up like a football team, on the day the John Curtin Foundation was launched. Sitting right in the middle is the Labor Prime Minister of Australia, Bob Hawke. Next to him is the Labor Premier of Western Australia, Brian Burke, smiling possibly at the thought of the benefits that this new club would bring. And ranged around them are the corporate movers and shakers of Western Australia, of whom half had surely never voted Labor in their lives but could now suddenly see the point of doing so. There, too, is Alan Bond.

It need hardly be said that Alan Bond was not a natural supporter of the Labor Party. He had warned his shareholders in 1972 of the creeping cancer of communism; he had followed up in 1977 with his tirade against Fremantle's red-ragging socialists; and on every occasion until Burke came on the scene, he had shown a preference for the ruling Liberal Party. When Bond had served briefly as a Perth City councillor in the early 1970s he had called on a prominent Liberal politician Ray O'Connor to smooth the way for him. And in 1974 he had not only donated $20,000 to the Liberals' election fund, he had made the services of Bond Corporation available to ferry Liberal voters to the polls and to spruce up the party's advertising. One of the slogans to which he had given the green light was "Power-Hungry Whitlam Must Be Stopped", guaranteed to have incensed any true Labor supporter. But by supporting Burke, it was not so much that Bond was abandoning his political principles as reinforcing the fact that he had none. Bond was interested in power rather than in politics. He supported whichever party was in government, if it could help him make money. And, after 1983, support Labor was what Bond certainly did. Exactly how much he or his companies gave may never be known, but one donation of $250,000 to the ALP for the federal election campaign in 1987 has been admitted. It was pledged, as we now know, at or after a private lunch attended by the Premier Brian Burke, the Prime Minister Bob Hawke, and a handful of Perth's biggest businessmen—Laurie Connell, who matched Bond's $250,000, Dallas Dempster, the casino builder, who also gave $250,000, and John Roberts of Multiplex, who put $200,000 into the pot.

No doubt, Bond's companies helped out on Brian Burke's state election campaigns as well. The fact that his was a Labor administration was no problem—as long as it was good for business.

The first major deal between Bond and Burke's new Labor Government was sealed in Perth, on the morning after the America's Cup was won. Bond's executive assistant Martin Rowley was in the Bond Corporation offices at 7.30 a.m. drinking champagne in celebration of the victory. He would spend the evening at a Labor function sitting between Prime Minister Bob Hawke and State Premier Brian Burke. And in the hours that filled the gap, he persuaded the Western Australian Cabinet to spend $42 million on a company that Bond wanted to unload. The company, Northern Mining, had a 5 per cent share in a diamond mine in the north of Western Australia, which Bond had been forced into buying by circumstances beyond his control. To get him out of trouble, he now wanted far more money than it was worth, and the Western Australian Government obliged. There were problems with the cash flow; there were problems with why the State should be buying into diamonds in the first place, but Martin Rowley dazzled the politicians with a few fast tacks of his own. He took out a small leather pouch and scattered the jewels across the table in front of him, inviting his audience to inspect the highest quality diamonds outside South Africa. The politicians, it seems, were enthralled. When asked today whether the $42 million was excessive, Rowley answers: "They only paid cost but there were questions about whether cost was the right figure." He laughs as he remembers it. "It was probably a good deal for Bond Corp," he adds, and laughs again.

The story of the government's purchase of Argyle Diamonds from Bond is no different in principle from a dozen other deals that followed it: the same group of mates was involved; the same benefits flowed to rich and powerful businessmen; and the same misguided political rhetoric justified the careless use of the public's money. All that marked this one out was that it was the first, the one that put WA Incorporated on the map. It was utterly appropriate that Alan Bond should be a founding partner; perfect too that the other businessman involved should be Laurie Connell of Rothwells. The two of them were in at the birth of WA Incorporated, as they would be at the death.

By the early 1980s, Laurie Connell and Alan Bond were already the best of mates, and had been for many years. They had first done business together in the mid-1970s when Connell was a money market operator at Martin Corporation, and from there the relationship had blossomed. It was Connell who had put Bond back on top after the 1974 property crash, by lending Bond a million dollars for a downpayment on the Santos deal. And it was Connell, too, who had helped get the money for the Swan Brewery acquisition. Now it was Connell who gave Bond a hand with getting rid of his stake in Argyle. Laurie's role in the deal was to act as the government's financial adviser. It was he who now put the price tag of $42 million on the Argyle parcel of shares, and he above all who persuaded the government to buy. For his services to the taxpayer, of course, Mr Connell would be handsomely rewarded but not, strangely enough, by the Government. As Premier Burke pointed out to his Cabinet at some length, Laurie was generously providing his advice to the Government free of charge. He might have gone on to say that this was because the altruistic Mr Connell was being paid a massive fee—between $3 million and $5 million—by Alan Bond's Bond Corporation. But Burke omitted to tell them this crucial piece of information. So here was the adviser supposedly acting for the Government, in practice working for Bond. As the Royal Commission into the WA Government's dealings with WA business would be told eight years later, there was evidence that Laurie Connell's role in the deal was "to justify the purchase price to the Government rather than to conduct an independent valuation". Had Burke informed Cabinet of the true position, the deal would almost certainly have been stopped in its tracks; that, at least, is the view of WA's then Attorney General, Joe Berinson.

It did not of course escape notice in Perth at the time that Bond's great friend Laurie was the government's valuer in the deal. Nor did it pass without comment that many millions of taxpayers' money had apparently been wasted, since one could have bought a similar stake in the Argyle venture on the stock market for more like $28 million, through another quoted company which had an interest. And it was just a short step from there to suggest that the two were intimately connected. But there was little that the Liberal Opposition or the other critics could do except kick and shout. The fat fees were confidential, they were told, and the price was fair: the shares were worth what a willing buyer would pay in the market, and since the government had paid $42 million, that was clearly what the shares were worth, QED. All that the protests managed to elicit was an explanation from Burke as to why Laurie Connell's firm had been chosen in the first place. But in the light of Connell's spectacular crash some years later, even that was quite a significant answer:

> ...the high standard of advice was evident in the clarity and precision of information on a wide range of matters, including aspects relating to the capital savings, infrastructure commitments, production and marketing of diamonds involved with the Argyle project. The firm also recognised early the entrepreneurial initiative and direction of the new government, and like any other highly-motivated private company made submissions to the government in relation to business opportunities that would benefit the state.

The answer was also significant for what it refused to say. Twice now, the Premier had been asked who had made the decision to engage Laurie's services. And twice he had dodged the question. Only when questioned a third time was the request phrased tightly enough to block any escape. When it was asked of the Premier who, *specifically*, had recommended Laurie Connell as the government's adviser, Brian Burke had no choice but to own up:

> The retention of the firm of LR Connell and Partners was decided by the government on the recommendation of the Premier.

In other words, Burke had done it himself, but was obviously embarrassed to admit it.

Laurie Connell is the sort of character often euphemistically described as "colourful". He was not, when first introduced to Burke, Australia's richest businessman, as some would later make him out to be, and nor was he the most respectable. In 1983, the best that could be said about him was that he was a fast money merchant, a big noise in this small-town society. He was also something of a legend. As the son of a bus driver, Laurie was a working-class boy made good, someone who had worked his way up from nothing. A short, stout man, he had at one stage been a fairground boxer, taking on all comers. Now, in Perth banking circles, he did much the same, only this time as king of the bare-knuckle businessmen. Connell had his own merchant bank, Rothwells, and a string of private companies investing in glamorous hi-tech projects with apparently limitless potential, which one eventually discovered would never be realised. He also had his own idea of style. He hired trains to take his pals racing, gambled big, and stood drinks for everyone on the racecourse when his horses won.

But that was the extent of whatever glamour the man possessed. There were aspects of Connell's past that he preferred not to talk about. In 1975, for example, he had been warned off Western Australia's racetracks for two years by the WA Turf Club. Connell had been caught trying to pull off a classic sting, betting in Kalgoorlie on a horse race being run in Melbourne, when it was alleged he already knew the result. The victims were only bookmakers, it was true, and police investigations had not produced enough evidence to support the charges of criminal conspiracy, which they were eager to bring. But it was rather more than a clever coup: a couple of policemen had helped put on the bets, and a live radio broadcast of the race had been delayed, fooling the bookies. The investigating steward, Max Blight, had reported to the Turf Club inquiry:

> There is absolutely no doubt in my mind from this inquiry and from information supplied that there has been a conspiracy and a fraudulent trick committed at Kalgoorlie racecourse, and I know the detectives enquiring into the matter are of the same opinion.

In view of this history, there should perhaps have been some doubt about Connell's suitability to be the government's financial adviser, especially when the other party involved in the Argyle deal, his friend Alan Bond, had such a great deal to gain. And Brian Burke who should have been aware of Connell's Kalgoorlie track record.

But suitable or not, there was no question that Burke and Connell were close. At the very least he had the Premier's ear—he could literally pick up the phone and get Burke on the line. More graphically, in the description of one of Connell's close advisers, Laurie operated like Burke's outer office. Those in Perth who couldn't go to Brian Burke direct to get things done would go to Laurie instead, and he would fix it for them. And Connell never ceased reminding people of this fact. He would make statements to his close colleagues at Rothwells to the

effect that: "The Premier's my mate, senior ministers are my mates. I can get on the phone to Graham
Richardson or Paul Keating, I go fishing with Bob
Hawke. I've got leads to Corporate Affairs, I've got
leads to the NCSC, I've got leads to the police. I've
got money, and I can get things done. So I want it
done, and I want it done now." Connell clearly
frightened his colleagues. He might also have frightened the politicians. The longer Burke's reign went
on, and the richer Connell got, it seems, the more
offensive and overbearing he became. According to
one close adviser, he behaved as if he was untouch-
able, all powerful, and had the Premier's protection.
And so to a degree he was: he certainly had people
in high places who could bring him the results he
was after.

But Bond was no shrinking violet either, and nor
was he without influence. While some of the biggest
deals organised by WA Inc involved the firm of
Bond and Connell in partnership, there were others
where Bond played the cards himself. A former
Bond executive's sterilised version of events is that
Brian Burke was a friendly, approachable person,
whom Bond would ring up to say: "We're going to
do this and we'd like your support." But the reality
was that support often involved government action,
and Bond had the ability to get his way. One top
public servant says that it looked to him as if Bond
told the government what to do. Bond, as many
Western Australian politicians would testify, was
always a pretty dominating person, forceful, aggressive, and prone to bully if he didn't get what he
wanted. "He flew off the handle at people, and could
be really intimidating." And Burke found him hard
to resist or fend off. "Burke hated confrontation.

He wanted to be everyone's mate." In 1984, the same public servant had a taste of Bond's methods when he advised against a property deal that Bond was proposing to the government. "The next thing I knew was that Alan Bond was on the phone and I was copping his wrath. He was going mad, abusing hell out of me, going up the wall and shouting at me, saying we'll never get anything off the ground in Perth if you take this sort of attitude."

It is not clear whether Bond used the same tactics successfully with Burke. But he did manage on several occasions to persuade the Premier that the interests of Alan Bond and Western Australia were the same, that what was good for Bond was good for the state. In 1983, for example, Bond Corporation, through a subsidiary, had plans to build an office and hotel complex in Bunbury, one-hundred-and-sixty kilometres south of Perth. The development had been inherited from a company called Austmark which Bond had taken over; it looked as if it would never get off the ground, because there was difficulty getting hold of the finance. But, ever obliging, the Burke Government came to the rescue, and made the sums look suddenly healthier. Not only did they guarantee, before the building was up, to lease all eleven floors of the office block for government use for the next twenty-five years, they agreed to pay absolute top rates for the privilege. The rent they agreed to pay, at around $150 per square metre, was more than twice that commanded by any other office space in Bunbury. It was also on a par with the cost of prime properties on Perth's top street, St Georges Terrace. The space worked out as even more expensive than the Premier's office.

The attraction of the deal to the Labor Party was fairly clear—Bunbury was a marginal seat in Western Australia, and one that often held the key to electoral success, so spending money in the town could win valuable votes. But it was a staggering decision for a government to make: Bunbury is a little seaside town, a long way off the beaten track, with a population of just 26,000. The government did not have nearly enough people to fill the offices even if they were cheap, and the high rental merely made it doubly absurd. To meet its commitment, the government decided to move large numbers of people down from Perth. But even so, two of the eleven floors of the building were still vacant in 1990. Mr Bond, meanwhile, was laughing. So, indeed, was a fellow member of the John Curtin Foundation, John Roberts: his Multiplex company built the Bunbury tower, despite tendering higher than at least two of his three competitors.

The Bunbury office block incident was by no means the only occasion on which Bond persuaded Burke's men to come to his rescue. Indeed, there was a similar helping hand held out to another Austmark development, which would eventually become the headquarters of Bond Corporation. Now an attractive building, soaring fifty-two storeys above Perth's streets, in 1983-84 this proposed tower block was also looking like a non-starter unless a partner could be found. Bond had managed to persuade the previous Liberal Government that they should guarantee to take a quarter of the space, or thirteen floors, but even that had not produced anyone willing to share the financing. So now, with the Burke Government in place, and other options apparently exhausted, the state-owned R&I Bank stepped into the breach and agreed to a fifty-fifty deal. Only later was it revealed that the proposition had been put up by Jack Walsh, the government's chief business fund-raiser.

Bond also seems to have achieved special consideration for Observation City, a hotel complex which he built on the beach at Scarborough outside Perth. The plans for Observation City, and one or two other big projects in the area, were already causing huge local rows in 1983 when the State election campaign was in full swing. Brian Burke was therefore well-received when he promised a huge open-air meeting on Scarborough Beach that his Labor Government would prevent any high-rise development from going ahead. There was no doubt that, given the will, he had the power to make the promise come true. Thus it was both a surprise and a disappointment when the Labor Government's new planning rules, framed only months later, allowed the local council to approve Bond's high-rise hotel—with Burke in the meantime praising Bond for bringing jobs to the area. Quite possibly, the project was a good one. But this relaxation of the rules was not extended to anyone besides the America's Cup winner. Another high-rise development in Scarborough, with planning permission already granted, was stopped by Burke's Planning Minister; Observation City remains the only high-rise on the coast.

When Bond was questioned on Perth's Radio 6PR about why Burke had overruled the local council on Observation City (which his Planning Minister had done, but only on detail), he gave an answer that sums up how he saw himself in relation to government. It was absolutely right and proper for Burke to do what he did, said Bond: "The local authorities become dictators, the shire councils become dictators. You've got to have a firm hand to get things done." Yet when he was reminded of Burke's suggestion that the Premier did favours for Bond and others in the interests of Western Australia, the altruistic entrepreneur was most indignant: "I don't care what he says about other people, but I do care when he says he is doing favours for me. The reverse is the situation. I'm causing employment opportunities in this state. If they don't go in this state, we can put our investment capital elsewhere. We're not compelled to put it in this state. I think he's misconceived in his comments quite frankly. I mean we're doing things for him, not him for us." Apart from bringing jobs to the state, or so Bond said, his companies were of course contributing considerable funds to Brian Burke's election campaigns, though that was probably not what Bond had in mind. But it later transpired that Bond Corporation might be doing rather more in relation to some local politicians. There were allegations raised in late 1990 that Peter Beckwith had arranged for a $30,000 bribe to be paid to a Stirling City councillor to help the Observation City proposals get through. This allegation arose, somewhat bizarrely, from a conversation with a prominent Liberal politician which had been secretly taped by the Premier's brother, Terry Burke. Police had apparently investigated the allegations in the late 1980s and had decided to take no action.

Bunbury and Observation City, however, were small beer compared to the saga of two development sites in the heart of Perth's business district, where tens of millions of dollars, and many arms of state and city government were involved. In the 1990s the two sites, which once supported the Perth Technical College and the David Jones department store, will become one magnificent linked development, worth hundreds of millions of dollars, and their history will doubtless be forgotten. But students of rotten government should be made to remember them. Not only did Connell and Bond receive a free ride at the taxpayer's expense, they benefited from major planning concessions given by the Perth City Council which, in blunter language, broke its own rules. The saga was a paradigm of WA Incorporated at work, not least because it involved a major role for Western Australia's State Superannuation Board.

The State Superannuation Board looms large in the annals of WA Incorporated for one simple reason—it had vast amounts of the public's money which could be raided for development schemes, and it had a soft touch for a chairman. Brian Burke had fixed his eye on the Superannuation Board almost from the beginning. He had come to power in 1983, with his dream of dynamic government, convinced that there was at least a billion dollars of public funds lying idle—"lazy money" which the government could put to work with the entrepreneurs' help. And nowhere was more money lounging around than in the State Superannuation Board, which controlled the investment of public servants' pension contributions. The SSB seemed to do no more with its cash than tuck it away into fixed-interest securities and slowcoach stock market investments. Clearly, it needed to be set free.

There was a problem in how to liberate the SSB's millions, since the Board's trustee status allowed the funds to be invested only in the most conservative manner, but that difficulty was soon solved. In 1984 the SSB's then chairman was swept aside, after an investigation into the SSB's management practices, and Len Brush, one of Burke's closest advisers was installed in his place. Mr Brush promptly instigated a new investment strategy, which circumvented the rules on trustee status, allowing the Board to invest in property and high-risk entrepreneurial stocks. And with that, the game was on: Brush gave himself the freedom to strike whatever deals he liked, with whom he liked, whenever he liked, provided the Premier agreed. A succession of disastrous investments followed—disastrous not just in terms of the loss of millions of dollars of public money, but also for Mr Brush himself. In 1987 his meteoric rise ended as abruptly as it had begun. Len Brush, close adviser and friend of Brian Burke, was forced to resign, having become the subject of a major political scandal.

While negotiating with a rich and powerful property developer, Robert Martin, to back a number of Martin's projects with the State Superannuation Board's money, Brush accepted three separate cheques for himself from Martin, to a total value of $150,000. According to Brush, the money was a perfectly proper personal loan, at commercial rates of interest, secured by a mortgage. But, even if it was, Brush seemed never to have considered the appropriateness of accepting it.

Stupidity, impropriety or illegality aside—and Brush was acquitted on charges of official corruption—Len Brush did not obviously possess the qualifications one would expect of a man who was in charge of hundreds of millions of dollars of the public's money. He was, indeed, a loyal friend and adviser to Brian Burke, and his wife Brenda had for many years been Burke's constituency secretary, but his worldly achievements would not have taken up much space in *Who's Who*. He had been variously a public servant in Victoria for thirteen years, a small-time accountant and tax adviser, and latterly the proprietor of a modest stationery business. Now he was negotiating head-to-head with the likes of Connell and Bond, and giving them access to the public's millions. He seems to have had no investment committee to guide him, no colleagues to hold him in check, no requirement even to clear major deals through the Western Australian Cabinet. It was quite typical of Burke's government that it should have been so, and quite typical of Perth that, for so long, no one else seemed to care. But when the details of the Perth Technical College and David Jones site transactions eventually came to light, at least some people began to see why they should have paid more attention.

The details of each deal were, as always, quite complex. But the principles were simple, as was revealed in Parliament: taxpayers' money was doled out to millionaire property developers; private profits were made at public expense; the government dealt on uncommercial terms with the Big Boys in town. The Perth Technical College site was sold by the Western Australian Development Corporation in October 1985 to a partnership comprised of the State Superannuation Board and a company called Midtown Properties. Midtown was in turn owned jointly by Bond and Connell. The sale cut across a tender process already under way in which thirty-five other bidders had expressed an interest.

That, however, was not the most remarkable feature. As the former Liberal leader Bill Hassell would point out in the Western Australian Parliament two-and-a-half years later, the significant point was that Len Brush and the SSB had put up all the money:

> *Bill Hassell*: Mr Bond and Mr Connell did not have to put up one red cent. They provided no money.
>
> *Barry McKinnon*: Nothing?
>
> *Bill Hassell*: Nothing. The purchase from the WADC was fully funded by the State Superannuation Board. Bond Corporation and Connell, although part-owners of the site from 20 December 1985, were not required to pay for their share and, presumably, paid no interest, this being capitalised by the SSB against later recovery on completion of an agreed development plan for the site. Note, Mr Speaker, that this arrangement gave Bond Corporation and Connell a free ride on any capital appreciation of a key St Georges Terrace property at the time of a strongly rising market.

Capital appreciation on the Perth Tech site was handsome indeed: a year after it had been sold to the SSB/Bond/Connell consortium for $33 million, the site was valued, perhaps rather optimistically, at more than three times that, or $100 million plus. Having paid no interest on the loans, Bond and Connell had been helped, risk-free, to a huge profit. Bond Corporation, in addition, still had the prospect of earning large fees as developer of the project once the whole thing got under way. Yet, according to Bill Hassell's account in parliament, in this remarkably one-sided deal, the SSB had not even obtained security for the money it had lent.

In some ways the story of the David Jones site was still more remarkable. Bond and Connell had bought this site, just across the road from the Perth Technical College, from one of their entrepreneurial mates, Yosse Goldberg, in 1981 (whose own empire, like so many others in the Bond/Connell orbit, has since turned to dust). They then persuaded Len Brush and the State Superannuation Board in March 1985—or perhaps he persuaded them—to buy a quarter share of the project, and to fund the development. Once again, Bond Corporation was slated as project manager and developer, for which it would receive large fees. And once again, the SSB put up all the development costs, and capitalised the interest. Bill Hassell again takes up the story:

> About the same time that the SSB purchased its 50 per cent interest under the chairmanship of Mr Brush with the approval of Mr Burke, it also purchased a 25 per cent interest in the Central Park property—of which the other partners were Bond with a 50 per cent interest and Connell with a 25 per cent interest. Mr Speaker, you will be amazed to know that in that deal also, neither Mr Bond nor Mr Connell were required to put up a red cent. They put up nothing. In that deal it was even more dramatic. In that deal there was a ten-year agreement under which Mr Bond and

Mr Connell would not have to put up any money—a ten-year agreement, one which is so scandalous that the current Deputy Premier has remarked on it recently and has acknowledged that they are frantically trying to negotiate with Bond Corporation to get out of it.

I say that massive preferential benefits have been given to Alan Bond and Laurie Connell over these deals. I say that the evidence is there that that is so because the transactions are, on the face of them, not commercial in their character. I say that those deals are so scandalous that the Deputy Premier of the State—the present Deputy Premier, not the Opposition— has criticised them.

Peter Dowding: He has not criticised them. He made his comments in respect of one of them.

Bill Hassell: He has said they would not have been approved by Cabinet if they had gone to Cabinet. That is important.

The Deputy Premier had in fact revealed, after the departure of his boss Brian Burke to diplomatic pastures in Ireland, that the deal had been personally agreed to by Burke himself, and that the Cabinet knew nothing about it. (His new boss, Peter Dowding, confirmed this.) He then added words to the effect that it was an appalling deal for the SSB, which would give them great cash flow problems, and which ought to be unwound. He might have put it more pungently than that: the SSB was putting up all the money, but was getting only half the profit.

What the Deputy Premier did not say was that the chairman of the State Superannuation Board, Mr Brush, had been silly enough to accept a loan of $30,000 from Laurie Connell's bank at roughly the same time as the David Jones and Perth Technical College deals were being negotiated. This had emerged publicly two months earlier, just before Brush's trial.

But the SSB and Brush were not the only players in the David Jones saga: there was a fortuitous decision by the Burke Government to site Perth's $23 million bus station nearby and to link it to the new development, which greatly enhanced the site's capital value. And there were planning decisions in Perth City Council which helped increase the project's worth even more. Delving into the mire of complex planning decisions is a dangerous business, but in the colourful language of one councillor, when the David Jones project went through the planning process, the council "sold out to the developers. The city was taken to the cleaners."

There was in Perth at the time an established plot ratio of 5:1, which essentially allowed the developed space to be five times as large as the site area. But, on the basis of providing open space, Bond, Connell and the SSB, or Central Park Developments as they were now known, were given a better ratio of 6:1. That was worth maybe an extra $100 million to the developers, but it was fairly standard. The concessions on car parking, however, were not.

Perth City Council's policy was that no public parking at all should be created in this central area of the city because of the traffic congestion it would cause. The most that the building could therefore have expected, was three hundred spaces for the

tenants using the building. But the developers in
this case got almost four times that amount. As one
councillor pointed out, this was "totally against
Perth's existing and proposed Vehicle Parking
policy". It was also in defiance of the advice from
the Chief Planner and the City Engineer. The council's professional planners warned that there would
be long queues up Perth's main street as cars waited
to get into the car park, and predicted disruption of
bus services; they could therefore not support it.
A former chief planner of the city, Paul Ritter,
complained that the massive car park was
"disgraceful, and contrary to every good planning
principle". Even the Transport Minister wrote a
letter to the Perth City Council to express his
concern. In spite of everything, the developers had
their way. And beyond that: when it came to assessing with the 6:1 plot ratio how large the offices
could be, the car park was not even counted as
developed space. So with concession loaded upon
concession, the council wasn't so much taken to the
cleaners as shown the way: after that, it managed to
get there by itself.

The question of how all this could have come
about is not easy to answer. But perhaps the explanation lies in the fact that Perth was that sort of
place. It was a town where networks of influence
operated to grant favours, a town where a handful
of powerful men with perceived common interests
held sway. And the climate of the times was permis-
sive: there were fortunes to be made; there was
plunder to be had; there was a state to be developed; there was enough for all, as long as red tape
didn't tie everyone down.

But it seems too that the carpetbaggers had

gained a foothold in Perth's City Council. A study conducted in 1986 by Dr Ian Alexander, who is now a member of the Western Australian Parliament, pointed out that the Town Planning Committee was stacked with councillors who had financial interests in property development. Of fourteen such councillors on the full council in the early 1980s (before the David Jones decisions were taken) no fewer than eleven had worked their way onto the Planning Committee, and to good effect, it seems. During those same years, projects in which a councillor had a financial interest were turned down less often, and granted concessions more often, than other projects. In fact, they were granted concessions ten times more often. Furthermore, those concessions were typically against the strong advice of the City Planner. The Town Planning Committee, one could say, looked after its own.

None, however, did better than Alan Bond. Given that he had considerable persuasive powers, that he was an excellent salesman, knew the right people, and was the biggest name in town, there were good reasons not to stand in his way. But whether he was dealing with Burke or with the Perth City Council he seemed after 1983 to be forever getting what he wanted. With the R&I Tower, for example (which became the Bond headquarters), Bond Corporation even now holds the Perth all-comers record of a 7:1 plot ratio. Causing a great row at the time, this planning concession was worth an extra fifteen floors to Bond and ultimately some $80 million on the value of the development. Half this bonus was gained by promising Perth City Council that the famous Palace Hotel facade, out of which the new tower rose, would be preserved and that the building would remain a hotel. Yet when Bond decided later that the ground floor would become a banking hall instead, none of the bonus was retrieved and the extra floors remained. One might of course ask: Why?

Perhaps the answers to why Bond was able to wring such concessions, and why he was able to get Western Australia to give him what he wanted lie in the fact that no one dared stand up to him. His money, his power, and his will were too strong; the state's Premier, Brian Burke, and the city's council were too weak. *L'état, c'est moi*, Mr Bond told them. And they lay down before him. But in his arrogance would lie the seeds of his downfall. The government and Mr Bond would eventually fall out. So would Mr Bond and the people of Australia. So, even, would Mr Bond and the banks.

CHAPTER 14

Borrowing Big

Alan Bond's triumph in the America's Cup had made him a household name almost throughout the world. And in America, in particular, he had won tremendous admiration. Now, both his fame, and the style with which he had achieved it, gave him an entrée to almost every company and every bank in the West. He had once said: "get me inside any boardroom and I'll get the decision I want", and now he proved the truth of his boast. He was able to borrow money and strike deals on a scale that he could never have contemplated before his Cup victory. His refusal to accept defeat seemed to convince the bankers that he would win for them, too, if they backed him with their millions. They must have thought that whatever the obstacles, Alan Bond would be able to pull it off, for he never gave up.

The conqueror of Newport was thus encouraged

to milk his victory for every last billion. And the result was a remarkable expansion of the Bond business empire. On the day that *Australia II* sailed into the history books, Bond Corporation had fewer than 2000 employees, its net assets were only $230 million, and it could not even make it into the ranks of Australia's 100 largest companies. Five years later, Bond's empire was twenty times the size, having almost doubled its reach every year. It was Australia's largest media company and one of the world's largest brewers. It had property in New York, London and Hong Kong, gold in Kalgoorlie and South America, telephones in Chile and satellites in space. There were oil wells, airships, newspapers and TV stations. In short, it spanned the world. But it also had debts to match, for it had grown fat on OPM—other people's money.

There is an old Scandinavian story about a cat that became hugely fat because it ate everyone it came across—two gentlemen called Skohottenot and Skolinkenlot, seven maids-a-dancing, and a number of others all disappeared down the hatch— and the growth of Bond Corporation in those five years was much the same. But at the end, Bond looked like the huge fat cat standing on its head. Swaying to and fro above the company was the vast body of debt, balancing precariously on the small amount of real money that Bond Corporation called its own. Bond's empire had grown huge by swallowing others; but every time that happened, it was the banks who had footed the bill. Five years after the America's Cup, Bond and his companies had gobbled up ten, twelve or perhaps even fourteen thousand million dollars of the bankers' money. And as those bankers sat waiting for the Bond body corporate to disgorge the eight, ten or twelve thousand million dollars that remained, they must all have been asking themselves why on earth they had fed him so much.

By 1988, the banks had lent Bond and Bond Corporation the equivalent of $700 for every man woman and child in Australia. It was a staggering amount, and one might well ask how Bond got hold of it. Bond's persuasive powers were part of the answer, but he was not the only entrepreneur in the 1980s to walk out of the bank a richer man than when he had gone in. Corporate borrowing in Australia during the last decade became a popular national pastime. And Bond just led the pack because he was prepared to take bigger risks and knew how to sell his dreams. He went to the banks with big stories and coloured pictures that made the bankers' eyes gleam, and they threw open the vaults. He went in as Bond the super salesman, and came out as Bond the super borrower. But he was an old hand at the game. Only the noughts had multiplied. He had done the same thing with the finance companies in Perth in the 1960s. And the banks were really no more sophisticated. They were just men, motivated by money. Bond was needy, they were greedy. It was the perfect match.

The ordinary person often finds it hard to believe that, in certain circumstances, bankers actually like to lend money—and the more they can lend the happier they are. This may seem a preposterous idea to anyone who has tried to borrow a few dollars from the local bank manager, but all good con men, property developers and entrepreneurs know it to be true (which is why they become rich and we do not). The first principle of borrowing money is that it gets easier the more you want to borrow, especially when the economy is booming. If you only ask for a couple of thousand, the bank manager will kick you onto the street unless you mortgage your house and prove your income, because all he can see is the risk. But if five hundred million is the sum you have in mind, the bank manager will pull you into his office and get down on his knees, because then he starts to think about returns. When the sums get large enough, avarice takes over: the man and the bank are blinded by the dazzle of the profits. They might even press you to borrow a thousand million, since that will make them more, and if it's takeovers that you have in mind, then that's no problem, because they are going to get their cut.

To the banks, the great attraction of lending to entrepreneurs like Bond was that they were prepared to pay. In the words of one American banker who lent Bond very large amounts of money in the 1980s: "He liked to move in a hurry, so the fees were always pretty reasonable." Or as one Bond insider put it: "I have never known a company that paid so much for its money." The fees that Bond Corporation was prepared to pay its bankers soon became enormous. Ten million dollars on one deal was entirely possible. Fifteen million dollars was not unheard of. And on top of that, the banks could charge a three per cent margin over prime interbank rate, which meant that they took a straight three per cent profit on the total value of the loan. Multiply that three per cent by one billion dollars, and you have thirty million dollars' profit every year at the stroke of a pen. It should now be obvious why Bond was the bankers' favourite, and why they were glad when he asked for more.

But it wasn't just the banks who were after the fees that such huge loans would bring. It was the bankers themselves. To the whizz-kid bankers in their pin-stripe suits, closing or not closing the five-hundred-million-dollar deal could mean the difference between buying or not buying the new Porsche, or between getting or not getting the million-dollar waterfront mansion. Salaries were (and still are) typically tied to performance—the more business you brought in, the more money you made. So who could be surprised if the boys were keen to innovate? Especially when the merchant banks who advised on takeovers, arranged leveraged buyouts, or put together the fancy financing packages frequently did not put up the five hundred million dollars themselves. When it came to corporate lending, the banks were often divided into two separate sections, or two separate companies. It was the investment or merchant banks who pulled in the big clients, created the opportunities and wrote the business. And then it was the parent bank who typically produced the money. Risk and reward were thus often separated in the system, creating in the process irresponsible lending.

But other, larger, factors at work in the 1980s made borrowing a breeze. In essence, the banks were desperate for business: lending to the Third World, and even to the oil producers like Mexico, Venezuela and Nigeria, had become off-limits. Brazil wouldn't or couldn't repay the billions it had borrowed; nor could the Poles, the Yugoslavs, the South Koreans and another dozen besides. So there was a flood of money that needed to find a home. The same amount of cash kept flowing into the system, but half the borrowers had disappeared. At the same time, many corporate borrowers had found new ways of meeting their needs: they had discovered they could borrow more cheaply than they could from the banks by selling bonds to the public direct, which only governments, public authorities and the likes of Exxon had hitherto been able to do. Soon the banks found some of their better customers were no longer knocking on the door.

Trends like these, which made bankers less and less fussy about whom they lent to, were magnified in Australia. Until 1984, Australia was one of the world's financial backwaters, cut off from the rest of the world and its nasty habits. There were strict limits on how much any bank could lend in relation to its capital, and how it could lend it. It was not possible to import or export money to or from Australia without the greatest difficulty, and foreign banks were banned from operation (at least as bona-fide banks). But after 1984 everything changed. The market was deregulated—via the unlikely intervention of a Labor Treasurer, Paul Keating—the rule book was thrown out the window and the new rule was no rules. Suddenly the banks could lend what they wanted, how they wanted, to whomever they wanted, and a bevy of foreign bankers was let into Australia to do business. Suddenly the scene was transformed. Not only did the home-grown banks now have to fight for depositors, they had to fight for people to lend to. It became a borrowers', and particularly a big borrowers', market.

In the five years from 1984 corporate credit in Australia grew by twenty-five per cent every year. The entrepreneurs almost certainly picked up the lion's share, simply because they asked for the money and were prepared to pay the price. In the words of one merchant banker: "after deregulation the banks kicked in the doors to lend to people, especially if they got a sexy rate". And so it was that the fast-money merchants flourished: Equiticorp, Chase, Ariadne, Hooker, Qintex, IEL, Holmes à Court, and others rose like shooting stars. But Bond, of course, outshone them all. By 1989 it was almost a rarity to find a banker who did not lend to him or his companies. The Bond Group's former Treasurer, Robin de Vries, would be asked in a London courtroom how many bankers knew the corporation through dealing with him, to which he would answer that he couldn't be sure, but that he estimated it to be about fifty.

There was no good reason, however, for Bond to borrow himself to death, because some of the deals he made in the 1980s were brilliant in both concept and execution. His talent for property, seen on a small scale in the 1960s, made millions for Bond Corporation in the 1980s; he bought well in oil, in nickel, in coal and gold. But his problem was that he never knew when to stop—in much the same way as in the 1960s, he was a glutton for growth. He kept promising to digest his acquisitions, to slow down, to reduce his debts, but the actions never matched his words. Deal was piled upon deal, acquisition on acquisition, debt upon debt. The future of the company was constantly punted on the next big play. And when the inevitable mistakes were made, the great pyramid of borrowed money collapsed. It would appear that Bond began to believe his own legend. When people had criticised him in the past, he had so often proved them wrong. Now, it seems, he began to believe that he must always be right.

It would prove a fatal error.

The start of the Bond empire's extraordinary expansion and the key to its subsequent growth can be found in a deal struck in 1985, when Bond Corporation acquired the huge brewing company Castlemaine Tooheys. The critics couldn't believe that Bond could raise the money; others thought he was crazy even to try. When he did seize control, the voices then said that he had paid too much. But the purchase, in fact, was quite a coup, for the business was a good one. Bond told people that he was looking twenty to fifty years ahead, and that the breweries would provide a solid base from which he could attack the world.

Castlemaine Tooheys, when Bond came on the scene, was a sleepy old family firm which was unchallenged as the beer market leader in Queensland and New South Wales. It also had almost no borrowings, despite some $600 million worth of assets; its shares were cheap, and there were two or three big shareholders who might be persuaded to sell out. It was thus a tempting takeover target, and even the Castlemaine directors realised it. Yet when Bond started buying the shares, rather than worrying, they were convinced that Bond Corporation was far too small to swallow them, and sure that no bank could conceivably put up the money. Beyond that, Alan Bond had been trying to sell Swan Brewery to them only months before, and he was thought to be in his usual cashless state. It was hardly necessary, therefore, for Bond's Peter Mitchell to tell reporters in June 1985, as the Castlemaine share price roared upwards, that Bond was not the buyer.

Bond and his team had in fact been planning the

attack for a year or more, having decided in May 1984 that Castlemaine was just what they needed. Not only would the breweries' huge cash flow fund the takeover, it would also finance Bond's forays into property, gold, and shares where there were big dealing profits to be made. And, having settled on the prey, Alan Bond had then set about stalking it. He had lunched several times in the London board-room of Castlemaine's biggest shareholder, Allied Lyons, and made friends with Sir Derrick Holden-Brown—who agreed that they should work together in some way, at some stage. His executives, led by Peter Mitchell, meanwhile had concentrated on getting the funds into place.

The deal they were trying to bring off was the largest takeover in Australian corporate history, and would cost Bond Corporation $1200 million, or four times what the Bond empire was worth. But if that was thought to be an obstacle, Bond easily surmounted it. Once he and his executives had persuaded the Hong Kong Shanghai Bank that it should put up the $1000 million needed for the war-chest, the struggle was almost over. Having convinced the bankers that the sums made sense, Bond Corporation picked up 20 per cent of Castlemaine's shares on the stock market and another 25 per cent from Allied Lyons, whom Bond had been cultivating. Then, by dint of an offer which was three times what the share price had been at the beginning of the battle, the rest of the shareholders came quietly. Corporate Australia could only gasp with admiration at the nerve of it all.

Bond Corporation had just bought itself, with the banks' money, into a position where it had almost half the Australian beer market. But more than that, it had achieved a virtual monopoly in Western Australia and Queensland, and had taken an iron grip on the drinkers of New South Wales. Given good management, good sense, and some concentration on the brewery business, there was little that could go wrong. Bond announced they would sell off a few assets, run down debts, and forget the deals. The other companies in Australia, he said, could relax: "We've got our hands full for a while. They can go back to sleep." The same promises were repeated in the 1986 annual report to shareholders, which announced that a programme of debt reduction was already under way. But good intentions were soon cast aside: before the ink was dry on the contracts, Bond started buying again.

In the eighteen months that followed the acquisition of Tooheys, Bond threw another $1500 million dollars worth of assets onto his pile, expanding his empire to include the Pittsburgh Brewing Company, Bond Media, various Hong Kong properties, British Satellite Broadcasting, Bond University and a host of other smaller projects besides. Meanwhile, another $1200 million was added to the group's debts as Bond Corporation discovered the joys of junk bonds, and helped itself to, among other things, a massive billion-dollar issue through the American junk-bond kings, Drexel Burnham.

But at the same time, something else was happening which spelt even greater danger to the future of the Bond empire. The earning power of the breweries was being put at risk by the way Bond's team was running the business. Some of the problems were apparently trivial, yet even they were damaging. In Queensland, Bond upset the locals to an extraordinary degree by ripping the old

Castlemaine sign off the famous Brisbane brewery and putting up a Bond Brewing sign instead. He then added insult to injury by doing the same thing on the XXXX cans, and including the letters WA (for Western Australia) as well. Queenslanders, being very sensitive about Castlemaine XXXX, were outraged: their beer had been hijacked.

Bond might well have got away with this slap to the face had he not upset Queensland's pub owners as well. Shortly after the Castlemaine takeover, and just before Christmas, the men who ran the pubs which now sold Bond's beer found that their free credit period on beer supplies had been cut without notice, from thirty days to seven. Not only did this move put them in some difficulty at an extremely busy time, by suddenly requiring them to find large cash payments, it also angered many pub owners by the arrogant way in which it was done. "It nearly sent a lot of people to the wall, including me," said Bernie Power, who owned a string of pubs. "We had done business with that company for fifty-odd years, and they did it without as much as a phone call or a letter."

The publicans were furious, and so was Bernie Power, who promptly decided to set up his own brewery. The banks laughed at him when he first asked them for money. But two years later, the increasingly fashionable Power's beer would have ten per cent of the Queensland market and be doubling capacity for a successful attack on New South Wales and the smile was on Powers' face. This rival's success would be one of the major factors dragging Bond down.

But as important a threat as Powers would become, Bond's problems in Queensland were

minor compared to the damage wrought by the way
Bond treated its publicans in New South Wales.
Bond executive Tony Oates told journalists after the
Tooheys takeover: "The first task will be to meet all
the people in each of the breweries and other opera-
tions and allow them to realise we are real people."
The Tooheys' leaseholders were soon saying that
"real bastards" was a bit nearer the mark.

CHAPTER 15

Burn the Bastards

Col Ritchie had been with Tooheys most of his working life. He had started in the trade back in the 1950s as manager of one of the brewery's Sydney pubs, and had then run a succession of hotels which sold the company's beer. They were a good outfit to work for, and when he went out on his own in the 1970s he had no hesitation in sticking with them. It had been a lot of money to find in those days, $220,000 for a short-term lease on the premises, but he had worked hard and ploughed the money back into the business. By 1985 he reckoned he could sell up for half-a-million dollars if the occasion arose. Then Bond took over Tooheys, and soon after, a letter dropped onto the doormat of Col's pub. It was clear and to the point: he had thirty days to quit the premises, and furthermore Tooheys would not be paying him compensation. He had sunk his life's work into the business, yet Mr Bond and his men now wanted to kick him out without a cent.

Col Ritchie wasn't the only one to be given a notice to quit: in fact, he received his marching orders for trying to defend other Tooheys' tenants already under threat. Nor was he the only one whose livelihood was endangered by the Bond takeover. Seven pub tenants in all were being kicked out with nothing, and many more were being invited to sign their life savings away on an instalment basis. Jim and Kath Elliott, for example, had scraped all their savings together in the early 1980s to buy a pub of their own. It had just the one bar, was neglected, and was not doing much trade, but at $105,000 it was all they could afford. They had sold their only asset, a block of land, and had borrowed money from the bank to do it. Now they had nothing to fall back on except the pub itself.

The first they had known of the changes was when a man from the brewery came round to take pictures of the place. "It's for the ledger", he said. "They just want a record of what they own." Then Jim had heard on the grapevine that something was afoot, and before he knew it, he was being summoned into Tooheys for a chat. Although they wanted him to sign a new lease to stay in the pub, and also wanted to increase his rent, that wasn't what worried him. Bond's men made it clear that at the end of ten years, if not earlier, Jim and Kath Elliott would come out of their pub with nothing. Aged sixty-five, they would slam the door on their life savings and walk away, penniless, into retirement. They had been with Tooheys, one way or another, for sixteen years.

It was not just the Elliotts and Col Ritchie whom Bond was threatening with financial oblivion.

This refusal to recognise the value of the business that the tenant had built up applied to anyone with a Tooheys' lease, or to roughly 130 publicans. All had spent hundreds of thousands of dollars to buy into their pubs (in the jargon, to purchase the "goodwill"), and all now faced the certainty that, if Bond won the fight, they would lose everything. They had bought their leases on the basis that they would have security of tenure, and with the firm belief that they would be able to sell out of the business, whenever they wanted, at a decent price. They had been told, it was true, that the brewery could, in theory, repossess their pubs without compensation, but they had been led to believe it meant nothing. Tooheys had never in its history evicted anyone, had always allowed its tenants to buy and sell their leases, and had even traded goodwill itself. What's more, the publicans knew that the arrangement suited the brewery. People wanted to sell Tooheys beer because the company treated its tenants so well. This was one of the reasons why Tooheys had climbed from a second-rank company in New South Wales to undisputed market leader.

But the leaseholders' reckoning had all been done before the America's Cup hero had walked into their lives. Bond now planned to play the game by his rules, and these were entirely different. He intended to take their businesses for himself without paying compensation of any sort. And his executives proceeded to go about it without the slightest compassion. One Tooheys tenant, who had taken early retirement from the railways, had sold his house and sunk all his pay-off into his pub, was told in an interview with the men from Bond Brewing that they wanted him out because they were going to sell the place. He asked them, "What about my interest in the business, I paid more than $400,000 for it?" only to be told that he had no interest, he owned nothing. "You mean, you're telling me I'm wiped out?" he asked. "That is correct," came the reply. "You made a commercial decision and you take the consequences."

The leaseholders could hardly believe it was happening. Nor could some of the old guard at Tooheys. It seemed to them to be stupidity on a grand scale to antagonise the people who pushed their products to the public. So, as the tenants clubbed together to form an action group, to fight for their financial lives, a number of top executives at Tooheys advised Bond Corporation to pull back. But Alan Bond would not listen.

He would later claim that the decision was out of his hands—that an associated company called Austotel, which bought the hotels from Tooheys after the takeover, was making the running. That was nonsense. While it was technically true that Bond Corporation owned only 26 per cent of Austotel, the power in the company, in practice, had to lie with Bond. It was simply not credible to suggest, given Bond's billion-dollar investment in Tooheys, that Bond would permit Austotel to do as it wished. And it was not true, in any case, that Austotel had set the policy: the attack on the leaseholders had begun in January 1986, five months before Austotel was even born.

There is also some anecdotal evidence to suggest that Bond was personally controlling operations, which makes sense given the way he ran the rest of his empire. At a fairly early stage in the proceedings, the key negotiators for the leaseholders were summoned to peace talks in Melbourne, where five hours of arguing with two of Bond's men eventually gave way to an agreement. Warren Weir and Ron Roberts, who were leading the fight for the publicans, say they shook hands on a settlement which would give the leaseholders compensation. But, as soon as the newspapers sniffed at it the next day, the Bond camp publicly denied it. It was hard to know what had happened, but when Ron Roberts rang the relevant Bond executive, John Booth (who had gone to Perth to report on the talks), he now found him: "irrational, angry, really distressed. He was acting as if he had had his arse chewed from one end of the street to the other. He was shouting at me, swearing at me, denying that the deal had ever taken place."

Roberts' conclusion was that Alan Bond had vetoed the deal because it was too generous. Warren Weir, for what it was worth, believed the same. The Bond men claimed, on the other hand, that the leaseholders had broken a pledge to keep their talks secret. But whichever way it was, there was every reason to suspect that Alan Bond was prepared to give nothing away. When Ron Roberts and Warren Weir had arrived for the Melbourne talks, they had waited in John Booth's office and listened as he finished a phone conversation with his boss. At the end of it, he had put the phone down and passed on his chairman's good wishes. "You know what Alan Bond's message is to you blokes?" Booth had asked the leaseholders' envoys. They had waited, agog. "Well, I'll tell you: Alan says Burn The Bastards."

When all attempts at a settlement failed, the Tooheys' tenants decided to dig in. They put together a fighting fund of nearly $2 million, or some $20,000 each from about a hundred leaseholders, and waited for Bond to try to evict them by force. And sure enough, that was what then happened. The big legal guns were wheeled up, and the two sides prepared to do battle in court. Once again, the old guard at Tooheys now warned Bond Corporation to hold off. They argued that a victory in court would still be a defeat, because the conflict would alienate the brewery's most important customers—the people who sold Tooheys' beer—and it would be disastrous for business. They might well have added that there would be an orgy of bad publicity to endure as well. This confrontation was as much a scriptwriter's dream as the America's Cup had been, and Bond was now on the wrong side. He would be cast as the big-business bully robbing the little man of everything he owned. And the caricature was pretty close to the truth. The money at stake was some $30 million. It was, at most, small beer to Bond's three-billion-dollar business empire. But for Bond's leaseholders, hard at work selling Bond's beer, it was everything. For some, like Reg Lynch, it was to be a matter of life and death.

Reg Lynch, according to those who knew him well, was an honest man: quiet, dependable, a bit of a socialist. He had had little formal education and a string of jobs that never took him very far. And yet now, as he reached his late fifties after a lifetime of working hard, he was comfortable for almost the first time. He and his wife Joan had bought the Pymble Hotel in Sydney's northern suburbs, and had finally made good. They had been fifteen years in the pub trade and, after running a couple of places out in the country, had moved to be near their two children who were at school in the city. They had wanted to buy a freehold on a pub, but they couldn't find one at the right price, so they had ended up with the next best thing, a Tooheys lease. They knew Tooheys well, and they liked the people who ran the show. It was an old-fashioned company, but according to Joan: "If you had any problems, there was always someone you could ring who would help you out. It was like being part of one big family."

The Pymble pub had been run down and neglected when they arrived, but with the help of the brewery, the Lynches had renovated it and made it a success. There was a large room at the back, with a balcony and views to the mountains: this room they made even larger and turned into a high-class restaurant, complete with French chef. Next, they were planning to create a cocktail bar to go with it. Business was booming, the customers liked them, sales were going up. Both of them were happy—they planned to make the place perfect. But then Bond had become Tooheys' new owner. Reg had read about it in the papers and it had worried him. Another Tooheys' tenant told him to relax—Bond had beer to sell, and he needed pubs to sell it in—but Reg worried nevertheless. Some friends of his had suffered in a takeover and he was afraid that he and Joan would come off badly too. Three months later, his worst fears were confirmed.

It was January or February 1986, there had been rumours in the trade that people were being called in to talk about their leases, but there had been nothing definite, certainly not as far as the Lynches were concerned. Then there had been a phone call. Joan went upstairs to find Reg sitting in a lounge chair, with his head in his hands. A friend had just telephoned the bad news: Bond was refusing to recognise the leaseholders' goodwill; he wanted to take pubs back for nothing. If he succeeded, the Lynches would be ruined. According to his wife, Reg was in a daze. "He just kept on saying: 'We've lost everything, we've lost everything, we've lost everything we ever worked for'." Joan tried to reason with him, saying there was no justice in it, there were too many involved, Bond couldn't get away with it. But Reg wouldn't listen.

From that day on, according to his family, Reg Lynch began to cut himself off: it was as if he had put a paper bag over his head to shut out the world. He was so worried, so unhappy that you couldn't reason with him. Till then he had been the life and soul of the party, the one who cracked the jokes; now he was always withdrawn and quiet. He had other burdens, it was true, which were weighing him down—he was recovering from major heart surgery just a few months before—but this really brought him down. He started to sleep more, sought help from his doctor, and was given Serapax to calm his nerves.

The leaseholders, meanwhile, had formed an action group to organise opposition to Bond's attack. And, although Reg was in no mood to fight, he and Joan joined in. Often, the two children went along to meetings too. With Josephine at university and Peter about to start, they should by rights have been studying but they felt they needed to be part of the battle. There was little encouragement to be had: no one seemed to have much idea what to do, but all had much at stake. "There were so many people there who had made a Tooheys' pub their last venture before retirement, so many who had mortgaged their houses, and thrown everything they had into the business." They had risked their all because a Tooheys lease was the best in the industry—it was secure, strong, a decent living. And now they were looking at losing the lot.

It was hard for Joan and the Lynches, or any of the other tenants, to keep on running the business, dragging themselves around for the eighteen hours a day that the pub demanded. They didn't know from one day to the next whether the business was still theirs to run. But for Reg it was hardest of all. Perhaps it was because he was supposed to be the breadwinner, the one who would fight on their behalf, perhaps it was made worse by the medication he was on. But the strain on him was building up. The family tried to help him snap out of it, but without success. Then, one Friday evening in May, Joan and the children noticed that he had slipped out of the hotel, taking the car with him. Later, even when they couldn't find him, they weren't too worried—he had been playing pool with some of the customers during the evening and had seemed more cheerful, as if at last he could see some hope. But next morning, when Reg still had not showed up, they naturally reported him missing. The police asked whether he was the type to take his own life. It hadn't even crossed their minds, they said. He was a family man, he wasn't the sort, they all agreed. No, it would be totally out of character.

That afternoon Reg Lynch was found. He had checked into a hotel room in Wilberforce, put a plastic bag over his head and drawn it tight. He had suffocated to death. But it was the worry that had killed him. At six the next morning, a journalist from one of the Sydney papers, the first of many, knocked on the door of the Pymble Hotel.

"Mrs Lynch," he asked, "would you like to make a statement about Bond Corporation?" She screamed at him. He ran. The lawyers would later agree to what is known as a "form of words". Joan was not allowed to say that the battle with Bond had killed Reg Lynch: it had been a "major contributory factor".

The Leaseholders' Action Group, however, had no doubts about why Reg had committed suicide, and it gave them renewed appetite for battle. There was now blood on their banner, and there would be more before the dragon was slain. But they had first to find their St George. The publicans had taken their case to several barristers before they found one who would even take up the sword. Two or three QCs had looked at the leases, glanced perhaps at the fearsome opposition, and concluded that it wasn't even worth the fight. But finally they had found a relatively junior QC who had agreed to go into combat on their behalf. And so, after more than a year of skirmishing, battle was eventually joined. The cavalcade of publicans wound into court, with Joan Lynch, and her two children, Jo and Peter, in the ranks to lend support.

It was an unfair match. In one corner, for the leaseholders, was their little-known QC, and his even lesser-known assistant. In the other, representing Bond and Tooheys, was a team of three, with two of Australia's top silks. In the public gallery was a motley assortment of publicans, some of whom had never been to Sydney before, let alone to the Supreme Court. And, centre stage, pouring scorn on the leaseholders' case as a dragon might pour forth fire, was the nation's leading advocate, Tom Hughes. A master of the raised eyebrow, the pitying look, the disbelieving sigh, Tom Hughes was scorching all before him. The leaseholders could not even get their evidence admitted. Every time Tom Hughes objected that it was not relevant to the case, the judge ruled in his favour. The court battle had barely started, and already it looked lost. But then the leaseholders made an important decision: they sidelined their original QC and hired another.

Their new champion, Frank McAlary, was not a little man by any manner of speaking—he owned a couple of cattle stations in the Kimberley, in north-western Australia, and his skills as an advocate earned him $5000 a day. But he was a little man at heart and he had seen a bit of life. As a young boy in the Depression, he used to go out at four o'clock every morning to set the rabbit traps and pick up his family's breakfast. At the age of twelve he was driving a team of Clydesdales, hauling wool trucks. And then ten or so years later he was a professional footballer. Now, in court, as you watched him listen to the proceedings, with an easy smile on his face, you could have been forgiven for thinking that he looked a bit slow, a bit short of the necessary. But when he got up to speak, he was mesmerising.

McAlary would later confess that he had fought two cases like this in almost thirty years at the bar, and had lost both of them. But on his first morning before the judge, he at least gave himself a chance to win the third. The judge had already ruled out evidence relating to the way Tooheys had treated its leaseholders and its pubs over the previous thirty or forty years, which was vital to their case. But McAlary persuaded him to reconsider. "Your Honour," said McAlary, not exactly in these words, perhaps, but as near as makes no difference: "if you hear the evidence that we wish to have admitted, and then rule against us, then justice will have been done. But if you were to rule against us without hearing the evidence we wish to put before you, then surely that would be a tragedy." The judge considered the argument and was forced to agree. Thus was the ground prepared for victory.

The battle came down to the letter of the lease, which gave Tooheys the right to kick out its tenants without paying goodwill, versus the practice in the industry over the previous twenty years or more. And once it was put in those terms, the tenants had every chance. Their case was that, before Bond had changed everything:

a) Tooheys had never evicted a tenant or refused to issue a lease.
b) Tooheys had always compensated the tenants for the value of their business on the twenty-one occasions since 1977 when it had repossessed a pub.
c) Tooheys had allowed 195 sales of leases where a substantial amount was paid for goodwill by the incoming tenant.
Furthermore, Tooheys had approved the contracts.

Bond's lawyers, on the other hand, had a letter to wave at the judge (which all Tooheys tenants had been required to sign), which stated that Tooheys had the right to take possession of the pubs when a lease was up, without paying compensation. It was quite explicit, and most (though not all) leasehold-ers had signed it. But the letter had never been given to the tenants to keep, had not been part of the lease agreement, and had, it was claimed, been concealed from tenants' legal advisers. A former Tooheys' property manager also gave evidence that tenants who were reluctant to sign the letter had been told that the letter "was merely a formality", that Tooheys would not act upon it, and that they shouldn't worry. Once again, there was an argument about whether the evidence was admissible, but eventually the judge ruled that it was.

It was not until August 1987, some eighteen months after the first clashes between Bond and the leaseholders, that judgement in the case was finally handed down. And even then the packed public gallery was kept waiting for the result. It was not a simple thumbs-up, or an "Okay, you won". As his Honour Mr Justice Waddell neared the end of his forty-seven pages of judgement, Kath Elliott still didn't know who was ahead; she leaned over to ask her husband what the judge meant, and Jim whis-pered back: "Don't cheer, but we just won." At the end, all the publicans in court were in tears. They had not won the right to stay in their pubs—Bond Brewing or Austotel could still throw them out when the lease came due—but they had been told they were entitled to compensation. They could not be kicked out onto the street with nothing.

The battle had ended, but the war was not over. After the judgement, the leaseholders' leaders and Bond's men met in Sydney to negotiate the terms on which publicans would be compensated if they did lose their pubs. According to Warren Weir and Ron Roberts, the meeting reached agreement that Bond would pay "market value" for their businesses; Warren Weir thought they had also agreed not to evict tenants unless they were drunk, behind with the rent, or running a brothel. But within two months, according to the leaseholders, Bond went back on the deal. Thirteen more tenants, including their most powerful public spokesman, Warren Weir, found themselves with notices to quit, on the grounds that Bond and Austotel wanted to manage the pubs themselves. And far from receiving an offer of market value, they say they were being offered as little as half. One tenant in Newcastle, for example, was offered $350,000 for a lease which two years earlier had cost him $395,000—two brokers had just valued it at $700,000. Another was offered substantially less than the amount Bond's own valuer had put on the property. As the uncertainty continued, the market value of the pubs was going down anyway, because new buyers could not be sure how much security they would have.

The war of attrition dragged on until the middle of 1989, and even then it was not exactly Bond who ended it. Bond Brewing became so short of cash that it was forced to withdraw the remaining notices to quit, because it could no longer afford to buy the tenants out. But, for many tenants, the uncertainty had continued until that point. For two years or more, those who were being thrown out didn't know where they would live, where the children would go to school, what sort of a house or a business they could afford. The strain broke marriages, harmed people's health, perhaps even pushed them nearer the grave. There had been a lot of pain, and none of the publicans and their families felt like winners.

Jim and Kath Elliott were luckier than some. They found a buyer for their little pub soon after the court case. They had decided to get out as quickly as they could, just as soon as they knew the business was theirs to sell. They didn't want Bond's sword hanging over their heads. Thus, one Monday in September 1988, they signed the papers to sell their place for $330,000—that's what the court case had meant to them. Three days later, on Thursday, Kath had a heart attack and died. She had suffered for many years from asthma. But Jim believes the stress of the battle with Bond had helped kill her.

Joan Lynch also sold up, against her wishes. The Bond takeover had destroyed her husband. Now, she said, they wanted to destroy her, by taking away her home and her business. Her "drinkers" gathered outside the pub and chanted "We want Joan, we want Joan." Two weeks later a front-end loader, coming down the hill outside the hotel, ran out of control and ploughed into the public bar. Some joked that Joan was driving. Joan misses her pub and she misses Reg. She has been left with a large hole in her life. Yet she bears Bond no hatred and little anger. She says: "I just feel sorry that he has to be like that; that he has to be so greedy. We should still be in the pub; Reg should be there too. It should never have happened."

CHAPTER 16

Nothing Succeeds Like Excess

The long-running battle between Bond and the publicans severely damaged sales of Tooheys' beers in the New South Wales market, as the old guard had predicted it would. The publicans saw no reason why they should sell Bond's beer while he robbed them of their life savings, so they pushed Fosters, VB and Resch's instead. And, as a consequence, Mr Bond's drinkers began to pour the competition's froth down their throats instead. In 1985, when Alan Bond had taken over Tooheys, the company's share of the New South Wales beer market had been over 60 per cent. By 1989 it had shrunk to 40 per cent or less—with the loss of millions of dollars in profits. But it wasn't just the cash flow that the war with the leaseholders had destroyed: it had tarnished Alan Bond's public image, especially when his ruthless treatment of the little man was seen alongside his own personal riches and extravagance.

Alan Bond's lifestyle was in almost all respects a catalogue of excess. He spent money in amounts that most of us would never even dream about, and he brought a similar abandon to his personal relationships. He seemed to live his life as though he were a child in a sweet shop—picking whatever he wanted off the shelves. Whether it was companies, cars, paintings or women, Alan Bond grabbed what he wanted, as it took his fancy. With a fortune that for most practical purposes knew no limits, there was almost nothing that he could not buy. He bulldozed his way through life, but whether he brought any genuine happiness to those around him, let alone himself, was a question he probably never asked. His male acquaintances, particularly those who operated in the same wheeler-dealer world, described him indulgently as a bit of a playboy. Women who observed him were often merely horrified by his behaviour.

The Australian public had received an early glimpse of the Bonds' extravagant lifestyle in 1985 at the much-publicised wedding of their eldest daughter, Susanne. Quite what the ceremony and reception had cost one could only guess, but a million dollars was probably not far off the mark. Four hundred guests had been flown into Perth from all over the world; St Patrick's Catholic Church in Fremantle refurbished from end to end at Eileen Bond's expense; and the bride and her attendants ferried to the aisle in a fleet of white cars, headed by a 1932 vintage Rolls Royce. There had been full morning dress, and pretty white veils; the wedding service had even been televised. Outside the church, the crowds had scrambled to get a better view of

Perth's first family. But to go with the undoubted touch of class there was also just a touch of crass.

Each of the guests had been summoned to the party by an invitation in a white leather wallet: inside was a gold medal, struck for the occasion, bearing a portrait of the bride and groom. To receive them after the wedding, a huge blue-striped marquee had been erected in the grounds of the Bonds' riverside mansion. Fifty metres long, lined with parachute silk, it stretched out on pontoons into the middle of the Swan River. It would have been so mundane, said Eileen Bond, to have put it over the tennis courts like everyone else in Perth. But that wasn't the only excitement which greeted the guests: when twilight fell, a spotlit band appeared, floating on the river, from where it was winched to the bank and moored alongside the revellers. Of course, everyone who was anyone in the west was there, including State Premier Brian Burke and his successor Peter Dowding, both of whom helped to down the $25,000 worth of Krug vintage champagne which the Bonds had laid on to quench the collective thirst.

One hadn't, of course, relied on local caterers: the chairs, the tables, the food, and ice-cream had all been trucked in from Melbourne, 3000 kilometres away. The flower arrangements, too, or the flower arranger at least, had made the same long and arduous journey. The hairdresser and make-up artist, meanwhile, had been flown in from Sydney. As for the dressmaker, or rather designer, he had come all the way from London. Bruce Oldfield had made the trip to fit the $60,000 wedding gown, with its four-and-a-half-metre train, and to make sure that there wasn't a stitch out of place. But he was also there to put the finishing touches to the thirty outfits he had made for the three female Bonds' comings and goings. Bruce Oldfield was The Royals' dress designer, beloved of London's high society, and Susanne was to be given the best possible send-off. After all, in dusty old Western Australia, this was almost a royal wedding. Certainly there was enough red carpet to make it so: three-hundred-and-fifty linear metres of it covered the floors of the marquee and formed paths across the lawns. Woven into it was a trumpet-blowing Cupid and the logo "Susanne and Armand".

In many ways, though, it was more like Dallas Down-Under, because the celebrations had hardly stopped before the arguments began. Susanne Bond had met her new husband through a shared love of show-jumping, yet they clearly had little in common. Armand was studying hard to be a doctor; Susanne, it seems, was more interested in partying. According to Armand's friends, Susanne always wanted to have fun, to rage till four in the morning, and Armand had always to work. But, for whatever reason, less than three years after their wedding, the couple separated, and a messy divorce action ensued. There was then a major legal row over their horses and houses, in which the bridegroom sued his wife for a million dollars, alleging mental cruelty.

The legal and personal rows surrounding the couple's break-up lasted for more than a year, when settlement was finally reached between the parties. By the time the battle was over, an interesting picture had emerged of what Alan would do to make his children happy. Susanne's various horses, of which there were half-a-dozen or more, appeared to have cost more than $2 million in total. Two of them had been bought through a mysterious Swiss banker and even more mysterious Jersey companies. Another, Apache, which cost $900,000, had been paid for by Bond Corporation International in Hong Kong.

But if Susanne and Armand's marriage was a disaster, Eileen and Alan Bond's was also hardly a rip-roaring success. In the 1980s there were a number of occasions on which they came close to divorce: Martin Rowley was asked several times to start preparing the papers, and more than once they reached the stage of working out a preliminary settlement. But money seemed to stand in the way: "Alan couldn't afford it," said one close acquaintance.

Alan may have toyed with the idea of not splitting his wealth in two, but there would have been little prospect of his getting away with it. Geoffrey Summerhayes who, as well as being Bond's architect, was a friend of the family, says he sat at the Bonds' breakfast table on two separate occasions in recent years when the marriage was about to break up, occasions when Alan was calculating the likely cost. Summerhayes helpfully pointed out that when his own marriage had broken up, they had split their possessions down the middle. "Alan just looked at me and said in front of Eileen: "Yes, but that was two pounds of fuck-all."

In any case, the couple had never proceeded to divorce, but remained married. As Eileen put it, they were "socially independent", or in other words, rarely together; and Alan, for his part, continued to have affairs. In the early 1980s he had become involved with the wife of a prominent business rival. Meanwhile, both in Sydney and abroad, there had been a number of semi-public liaisons. Eileen, at home in Perth, would hear the gossip and see photographs of Alan in the tabloid press, squiring beautiful women around town. Sometimes they would be her friends, but often they were not and she admitted that she suffered: "It is hurtful, yeah it is," she told an interviewer, "but I guess it will go on endlessly. As long as there's paparazzi around, it's going to happen." Or, in Alan's case, she might have said, as long as there are women.

One of Alan's mistresses was, by all accounts, a serious threat to the Bond's thirty-year marriage. Diana Bliss had been on the scene for almost ten years, and there was talk of her becoming the second Mrs Bond. Alan had supposedly met his Miss Bliss, the daughter of a Methodist minister, while she was a hostess at the Parmelia Hilton in Perth. Young, pretty and blonde, she was also intelligent, friendly and charming. No one had a bad word to say about her, except, perhaps, her rival. For a time she had lived in Perth, until, in the words of one Bond acquaintance, the West had become too hot for her. Thereafter, she had moved to Sydney, where she and Alan shared a rented flat in Wollstonecraft for a couple of years, and then a house in Paddington, for which Bond had paid.

Diana Bliss rarely came back to Perth, but on one occasion when she did, there was an extremely public row: during the 1987 America's Cup, Eileen Bond and a party of friends were lunching at the fashionable Mediterranean restaurant when Miss Bliss turned up with another group to have lunch. Eileen promptly summoned the manager and, according to observers, told him very loudly to "throw that bitch out". The manager politely but firmly declined—no easy task when Big Red was in full flight—and left Eileen to be pacified by her companions. But then, by some mishap, Mr Bond himself walked in, to have lunch with yet another party of people. With the scene set for an explosion, Miss Bliss lit the fuse by walking up to Alan to give him a welcoming kiss. Eileen thereupon blew her top: she marched over to Diana Bliss's table and started abusing one of her own friends who was sitting there—she then demanded at the top of her voice that, as a friend of Eileen's, she leave at once. The unfortunate woman burst into floods of tears as this tirade was turned upon her, and had to be escorted from the restaurant. Diana Bliss, meanwhile, was prevailed upon to leave.

There was another serious row on the subject of Miss Bliss not long afterwards, which was precipitated by the death of Alan Bond's mother. Kathleen, by all accounts, had never thought a great deal of Eileen, but had taken a shine to Diana Bliss, and had provided for her handsomely in her will. One can only speculate what the atmosphere must have been in the Bond household when the news was broken, but tense might be an understatement. Kathleen had left some of her jewellery to her daughter Geraldine. All the rest, which was all the jewellery given to her over the years by her son Alan, had been bequeathed in her will "to my friend, Diane Bliss". Eileen got nothing.

Quite how Eileen coped was not clear: she was loyal to her husband, her Catholic faith gave her strength; she might well have continued to love him. Meanwhile, she seemed to take refuge in having fun, and spending money, both of which she did in large measure. She was, as they say, a legend in her own lunchtime. As soon as Alan left town, the party would begin: her midday gatherings, at the Mediterranean or San Lorenzo, where she lunched three or four times a week, often merged into drinks and dinner, amid many bottles of French champagne. Sometimes they ran on into the small hours. Generously, she would often foot the bill for everyone's celebration.

As for spending money, it seemed she at least made Alan pay for his pleasures. She sported diamonds by the dozen: she had rings with stones the size of pigeon's eggs. Alan perhaps thought the expensive presents represented good value. They were, after all, cheaper than divorce, which could have involved giving up half a fortune, and losing control of the Bond empire. And there was plenty to lose.

In 1988, Alan Bond was ranked by Australia's *Business Review Weekly* as one of the nation's richest men, with a personal fortune of $350 million; it was commented that he would have had far more if some of his gold deals had succeeded. The magazine did not go into details, but a little enquiry revealed that there were a number of places where Bond stashed his money. There were companies like Shield Enterprises, for example, with an annual payout to the family of some $3 million a year; companies like Lapstone and Cairnvalley with one-off dividends several times larger than that and various discretionary trusts with assets which appeared to be at least $12 million. At the top of the heap was Dallhold, the biggest of them all, whose coffers contained the bulk of the Bond fortune.

It was always hard to assess how much Dallhold was worth, since the company was almost as weighed down by debt as was Bond's public

business empire. But, according to the accounts
Alan Bond sent his bankers, there was some $1600
million worth of gross assets in the company, and
some $700 million net—or what he said would be
left after all the debts had been paid. Dallhold's
primary wealth resided in its ownership of just over
half Bond Corporation, but there were also gold
mines worth around $480 million, a big nickel
project in Queensland, supposedly worth another
few hundred million, shares in Bond Media worth
some $50 million, plus more than 20,000 hectares of
prime Australian farmland, 100,000 sheep, three ten-
pin bowling centres, an assortment of residential
properties, some coastal land, an island, and a
whole swag of other private assets.

There was also the art. What international jet-
setting entrepreneur would be complete without it?
Bond had started buying in the 1970s, and had
amassed quite a collection, most of which was kept
in Dallhold's offices in a room shaped like a maple
leaf, fifty-one floors above the streets of Perth. There
was Webber's famous portrait of Captain James
Cook—whom Bond thought to be rather like
himself in that they were both bold, blunt and
adventurous, not to mention important to Australia.
And there was a gaggle of French impressionists: a
Gauguin, a Manet, a Pissarro and a Renoir, which
kept company with his most famous acquisition,
Irises, by Van Gogh—with whom Alan also identified, as a fellow creative genius not properly valued
by those around him. *Irises*, Alan Bond reckoned,
was the best of the lot: in fact, at US$54 million, he
was pretty convinced that it was the greatest painting in the world.

Some unkind friends of Bond's suggested that

Alan didn't really know much about art. Unkind critics went even further. There is an old tale, surely apocryphal, of how Bond had bought an Italian master in the early days for his house in Perth, and had found it was too big to fit on the wall. Bond, so it was said, had then cut the painting in two and put it on either side of the front door. There was also a more recent story, recounted by the Australian art critic, Robert Hughes, in *Time* magazine, which did seem to have the ring of truth about it. It suggested that Bond went after art in much the same way that rich hunters in the past had gone after big game:

> Like many another entrepreneur, Bond had never given much thought to art until he got rich. 'This Picasso, now,' he asked an Australian museum man over dinner in Sydney in the early 1980s, 'is he worth having?' But a major impressionist collection was what he hankered after. He knew this could not possibly come cheap. He didn't care. He was in short a dealer's dream: *Billionaris ignorans*, a species now almost extinct in the US but preserved, along with other ancient life-forms, in the Antipodes.

It was something of a mystery why Alan Bond would want to spend US$54 million on a painting, at the rate of almost US$100 million per square metre, even if it was the best bit of brushwork in the world. Doubtless it had something to do with the fact that Sotheby's and the banks were happy to lend him the money. No doubt it also reflected

Business is business. Bond and Chile's President Pinochet, August 1987. "You feel safe on the streets, and it's the best economy in Latin America," said Bond. *Reuter*.

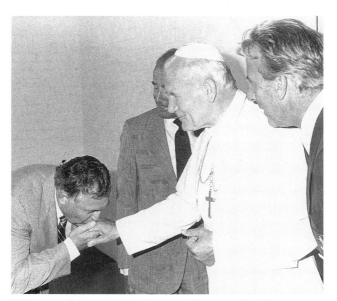

If God met Mammon … Alan Bond and Pope John Paul II, November 1986. *News Ltd*.

Susanne's wedding, 1985. The dress, from Royal designer Bruce Oldfield, cost $60,000. St Patrick's church in Fremantle was refurbished for the occasion. *News Ltd.*

Alan and Eileen. Together, after a fashion. *John Fairfax & Sons Ltd.*

Big Red. Having
fun. *News Ltd.*

Eileen with eldest
daughter Susanne.
News Ltd.

Diana Bliss, "an
old friend of my
mother".
*Australian
Consolidated
Press.*

Old pals act. Alan Bond and Laurie Connell, two of Australia's richest men, days before the October 1987 stock market crash. Connell's Rothwells merchant bank finally collapsed in 1988, having lost at least $400 million. *News Ltd*.

Bond with Van Gogh's *Irises*, the world's most expensive painting. Bond bought it in November 1987, two weeks after the stock market crash, for US$54 million, or almost US$100 million per square metre. It was sold in 1990. *News Ltd*.

Captain Bond and Prime Minister Hawke at the launch of Bond's *Endeavour* Project in 1987. "There's a lot of sloppy talk going around this country", said Hawke, "that there should be no place in the concerns of a federal Labor government for the Alan Bonds of this world. I want to repudiate that nonsense unequivocally.' *News Ltd.*

Glympton Park, Oxfordshire, England. An eighteenth-century house, with 2000 acres of farmland, and gardens credited to Capability Brown. Bond bought the estate for £14 million in October 1988, and sold it in early 1990. He visited it maybe six times, and never lived there. *Times Newspapers Ltd.*

Glympton's feudal village, complete with church, post office, and eighty-one inhabitants, came as part of the deal. Its peace was shattered by job losses and the threat of wage cuts and evictions. *News Ltd.*

The beginning of the end? The Rothwells' rescue of October 1987 cost Bond hundreds of millions of dollars. A disconsolate Laurie Connell sits in the background as Bond fields questions from the press. *News Ltd*.

Where did it all go wrong? Bond listens to angry European investors at the Bond Corporation annual general meeting, December 1989. *News Ltd*.

When the going gets tough, the tough go sailing. Alan Bond and friends on the march to *Drumbeat* for the Southern Cross challenge series in Sydney, December 1989. *News Ltd.*

Debts? No worries. Two billion dollars short of the money needed to pay creditors, but Alan's still laughing. *News Ltd.*

Sailing to victory in the 1989 Sydney-Hobart yacht race in the 26-metre, $3 million *Drumbeat*. Onshore, Bond's bankers were pulling the plug. *News Ltd.*

Alan's girlfriend Tracey tells him the bad news as he steps ashore in Hobart, Friday 29 December 1989: receivers have been appointed to Bond Brewing. *News Ltd.*

Alan's desire both to be and to have the best. According to Geoff Summerhayes, Alan talked often in the 1970s about how much his pieces were worth. "He'd never actually mention a price but he would hint at it. He would explain why they cost a fortune." He was at that time, apparently, no connoisseur: he would buy antiques and think them drab, so would have them stripped and varnished to jazz them up. Once, according to Summerhayes, he had bought a pair of life-sized bronze statues, which had acquired a delicate green sheen with age. Alan "thought they looked old so he had them sprayed with that glitzy orangey-bronze paint."

Art expert or not, the incredible extravagance of Bond's collection did not greatly endear him to the ordinary Australian or, indeed, to the ordinary Englishman. For, just a month before Alan was telling the world's press about the beauty of his world-record breaking Van Gogh, Bond's agent on the other side of the world had been imposing wage cuts of twenty pounds a week on his British farm workers, on the grounds that they were paid too much.

Alan Bond's personal and corporate residences in the United Kingdom by late 1988 already included two mews houses in Belgravia, two far larger houses in Kensington, and a ten-bedroomed, moated Elizabethan manor, Upp Hall, in Hertfordshire, which came complete with pheasant shoot and 1000 acres (405 hectares). But he hadn't, clearly, found quite what he wanted. He was thinking of retirement, he said, and he had hoped for something grander. And then the Cotswold estate of Glympton had come up for sale.

According to West Oxfordshire District Council's

conservation officer, the house at Glympton was just "a pretty ordinary Grade II listed building", but if you saw it, you would find that description hard to believe. It was in fact a lovely eighteenth-century house, built of honey-coloured stone and set in exquisite gardens falling away to a small river. There were two huge cedar trees by the front door, and vast beeches, sycamores and horse chestnuts throughout the rest of the gardens which in autumn gave it the most wonderful gold and orangey hues. There was also 167 acres (68 hectares) of rolling parkland and a small lake, reputedly landscaped by Capability Brown.

Glympton had come on the market because the previous owner, Eric Towler, had died, and the son who planned to take it over had shortly afterwards been killed in a polo accident. There had been rich men crawling all over it during the five weeks that the house was up for sale, whizzing to and fro in their helicopters and private jets. It was, said the agent, "that sort of house". British newspaper tycoon Robert Maxwell had shown some interest, so too had the king of Virgin Records, Richard Branson. Even Prince Charles had toyed with the idea of buying it, but his purchase had been ruled out because it would have been a security nightmare for his minders: there was a public footpath past the back door of the house.

Without bothering even to look at Glympton himself, Bond had summoned a Lincolnshire landowner, Nicholas Turner, whom he knew through a friend, to meet him in the south of France, where Bond was relaxing on his motor yacht, *Southern Cross III*. There, Turner had been told to do the necessary, which he duly did: the asking price was £11 million, but Bond had paid nearly £14 million so as to be certain to secure it. Not content with having just the Georgian house and 2000 acres (809 hectares) of prime Oxfordshire farmland, Bond had bought the village as well—lock, stock and barrel. He could hardly have avoided it: twenty-one houses, eighty-one inhabitants, the farm and the house were one job lot. For Glympton was one of the last outposts of feudalism. And Alan was now the squire.

When it was first made public that Bond was the buyer, the press and TV cameras immediately laid siege. With the expectation of a meet-the-people tour from Alan and Eileen, the normally empty village street was packed: you couldn't move for the cars and press thronging about. But after that first show of interest, the initial excitement subsided, and there seemed every chance that the world's journalists would not bother Glympton again. On Bond's behalf, a statement was issued to say that nothing would change: there would be as little disruption to staff and tenants as possible. And so a quiet and comfortable future seemed assured. But as things rarely turned out like that with Bond, there was trouble—before anyone had even tugged a forelock.

Twenty-five days after Bond became the owner, Nicholas Turner, now "Managing Director, Dallhold Estates UK", announced that the pig farm would shut, economies would be made elsewhere, and a total of ten jobs would be lost. The remaining eleven workers would take a £20 pay cut from their £140-a-week wage, or go the same way. They would also accept a reduction in their lunch break from one hour to thirty minutes. Some of Glympton's tenants, meanwhile, were being given their marching orders, for, in Glympton, as in good old feudal England, the cottages were "tied" to the work. Once you lost your job, you lost your home as well.

There must have been many a squire in the past who had slimmed down his workforce and evicted a few tenants without the whole of the world getting to know about it. But feudalism went out before the tabloid press came in. And few landlords provided such good copy as the "signwriter from Ealing" or the "corpulent corporate from Down Under", as the British press delighted in calling him. Now in the village and in the newspapers there was uproar: the TV crews and journalists thronged in again, to be told in broad Oxfordshire tones that one worker had been "nearly knocked sideways" by the news. He was losing his job after eleven years, and his home into the bargain. So were several of the others, who had spent half their working lives on the estate. Even without the beat-up, even without Dallhold's broken promises, one had to admit that it did not show Mr Bond in the best of lights. Here was a multi-millionaire throwing people on the streets.

Within a week, or a fortnight at most, Eileen Bond was saying that she had been "horrified" to read what had happened. The first she had known about it, she said, was from seeing the Australian papers. A few days later, she and Alan were there on the spot at Glympton to smooth the feathers and set it all to rights: the wage cuts were restored, the lunch hour reinstated, the tenants told they could stay. But the job cuts remained. True to form, the Bonds even won friends among the villagers in the manner of the reconciliation. There were not, after

all, many feudal British landowners who shook
hands with the locals, clapped them on the back and
behaved like ordinary people. The Bonds, some
villagers noted approvingly, had no airs and graces,
just lots of money.

For the next six months in Glympton, the verdict
was favourable. Much-needed improvements were
made in the village—walls repaired, chimneys
rebuilt, cottages renovated—and work was started
on the estate. The lake was dredged and enlarged, a
£350,000 redecoration job begun on the interior of
the house. But the honeymoon did not last: cottages
fell empty; the village fete and the fireworks party
were cancelled; and most of all, the landlord stayed
away. Bond had declared that he was planning to
come back to England to settle because Australia
did not appreciate him. But he showed no signs of
doing so. In the year after he bought the estate,
Bond appeared there half-a-dozen times at most.
Before long, the renovations had ground to a halt,
the improvements to the village had stopped and
Glympton House had become virtually uninhabit-
able. The interior had been gutted, the doors were
stacked in the stable, and Bond had run out of
money. He had paid $30 million for the ultimate in
weekend cottages, and it seemed that without his
ever using it, it would be soon be up for sale again.

Glympton, however, was not the only purchase
Bond had made in 1988: it had been an expensive
year for his private companies. He had paid $2.2
million for an extra half-acre of land next to his
house in Perth to extend the drive and garden. He
had also bought another large waterfront block just
down the road in Dalkeith for $9 million, where his
chum Laurie Connell had flattened seven perfectly

good houses to make way for a super mansion, and then got into difficulties. He had also bought the lodge on Rottnest Island, just off Fremantle, for around $4 million, which he planned to refurbish and run as a hotel. Then he had acquired a half share in the fashionable Mediterranean restaurant where he liked to lunch (also bought from Connell), and Cockatoo Island in the Indian Ocean, which he and Eileen planned to make into a holiday resort. Shortly afterwards, he would be taking delivery of a new toy—a $400,000 Bentley Turbo R. One imagined it would replace one of the two similar vehicles that already sat in his drive with the personalised plates AB 083 and EB 083, a gift from the West Australian taxpayer for bringing back the America's Cup.

There had also, in this great spending spree, been the schooner *Jessica*, which would be renamed *XXXX*, after the beer. At a cost of $7.8 million, she was probably the most magnificent sailing ship in the world. A three-masted gaff topsail schooner, built of steel and teak, her masts were just small enough to fit under Sydney Harbour Bridge. She had a magnificent nine-metre-wide saloon with an open fire in a marble fireplace, and most of the trappings of a small stately home. There were four double cabins, all with ensuite bathrooms and personal library. There was also a trophy room, and wood panelling throughout. It was, as one visitor to the boat observed, the nearest one could come to the luxury that the Morgans and the Vanderbilts once enjoyed. With two huge motor yachts already, and at least one very large racing yacht, Alan hardly needed *XXXX* as well, but it was not in any case for his personal use. It belonged to the public part of his empire, specifically to Bond Brewing Holdings who would use it for corporate entertaining. It would, said Bond's managers, more than pay its way in publicity.

The publicity, however, did not increase the group's beer sales, which continued their decline. Nor did it improve Alan Bond's image: it seemed to be just another example of conspicuous consumption—yet another extravagant, expensive toy.

CHAPTER 17

Tax, What Tax?

When *Irises* and the other famous Bond paintings went on tour in 1989, the opening of the exhibition was greeted in city after city by hundreds of angry protesters. It was the nearest the art world had ever come to riot. Much of the venom was directed at Bond Corporation's involvement in Chile, and Alan Bond's personal endorsement of the Pinochet Government (which was related, no doubt, to his desire to do business there). But some of the anger fixed on a target far closer to home and to Australians' hearts—Bond's record in paying taxes, or more precisely, in not paying them.

There are few things people like less than the taxman, but a rich tax dodger is one of them. And when it came to huge amounts of money and tiny amounts of tax, Alan Bond was the master. Bond, typically, did not see it in quite this way: Bond Corporation's annual report claimed repeatedly that the group was one of Australia's top ten taxpayers, making payments to the government of some $800 million dollars every year. But the argument was nonsense. Almost the only tax that Bond and his companies ever handed over to the government was the excise tax on beer, which was paid by the drinkers who sat in his pubs and pushed money to him over the counter. When it came to real tax—the tax on Bond's profits, or on the money going into his pocket—Bond and Bond Corporation ranked as the arch tax avoider. Yet on more than one occasion he had the nerve to tell the government that they should cut welfare payments, because the nation couldn't afford it.

Quite how Bond avoided paying his dues was not always clear, but the fact that he and his companies escaped tax on an absolutely massive scale was indisputable. As an example, Alan Bond's main private company, Dallhold, paid no tax at all in 1988, yet it had earned a profit of $48 million. Bond was even claiming that the taxman owed *him* $8000. The previous year, Dallhold had not done quite so well, but it had still achieved a record that the man in the street would have found dazzling—it had earned a profit of $8 million and paid less than half-a-million dollars in tax. Dallhold's accounts contained intriguing clues to suggest that the company might also be trying to claim tax relief on Alan Bond's paintings. Bond's art was in Dallhold's books as "plant and equipment"; it was being paid for on a finance lease, whose payments normally attract tax relief; and it was being depreciated in value. These pointed to the fact that Bond was seeking the Aussie wage-earner's help to pay for Manet's *La Promenade* and the other multi-million dollar acquisitions.

But Dallhold was not alone in the tax-avoidance stakes: the other main family company, Shield Enterprises, was up to the same game. Shield had paid tax of just $13,000 in 1987 on a profit of $2 million. The following year, 1988, it had paid no tax at all, yet had earned a profit of $2.6 million. It was conceivable that some tax had been paid further up the line; conceivable, too, that it had not. The taxman, it appeared, was chasing Shield for more than $1 million tax and penalties.

The pattern in Bond's public companies was no different. In the seven years from 1982 to 1988, Bond Corporation had paid the taxman a total of $20 million in tax. Yet in the same period, if its accounts were to be believed, it had earned some $700 million in profit. It had paid income tax, therefore, at the rate of three cents in the dollar, which compared with a top rate of fifty-six cents for ordinary, employed Australians, and a rate of around thirty cents in the dollar, paid on average by the top 150 Australian companies. There was no other big company over the distance that could match Bond's record in slipping away from the taxman's grasp.

Bond Corporation's defence of its tax-paying performance was first of all to state baldly, and misleadingly, that it paid more tax than anyone else. Then it fell back on the position that Bond created jobs for thousands of Australians—which wasn't quite true either, since Bond typically bought businesses rather than built them. And finally, Alan and his executives retreated to the line that Bond Corporation gave generously to the community—in terms of allowing the paintings to tour, or in sponsoring sport, or in the much-publicised *Endeavour* project. In 1988 Bond Corporation was making great show of building a replica of the ship in which Captain Cook had discovered Australia. At a cost of $12 million, Bond was giving Australia its biggest and best Bicentennial gift. But even here the taxpayer was paying 40 per cent. Bond had in fact threatened Canberra with ditching the project if it couldn't get the tax deduction.

There was nothing wrong with Bond sponsoring sport, or with giving the *Endeavour* to Australia: the latter was a venture of considerable historic and educational value. But it doubtless also had a promotional pay-off to the company. And, alongside the tax that Bond was avoiding, its cost was tiny. It was certainly no substitute for paying the taxman his dues. And it was somewhat galling that Bond seemed to expect the average taxpayer to thank him for the gift.

Nor was it just income tax that Bond hated to pay. He had managed to avoid several million dollars of stamp duty in 1985 when Bond Corporation had taken over the Tooheys brewing empire. And he and his three fellow directors had even avoided stamp duty when they made their killing on the Palace Hotel in 1980. Bond's lawyers had found a variety of loopholes in the stamp duty net: oral contracts (which created no document that could be stamped), trust arrangements (which avoided any transfer of title), and shuffling the shares through Darwin (where tax was not levied), but the final effect had been always the same: they had avoided thousands, if not millions of dollars in tax.

In the case of the Tooheys' deal, the state of New South Wales, in particular, had lost out. On the 125 hotels in that state which had changed hands, Bond

Corporation had paid a total of $430 in stamp duty—which was less than would normally have been payable on the purchase of one average suburban house. The New South Wales Finance Minister, Bob Debus, had not been pleased by the discovery, to put it mildly, and had launched a scathing attack in Parliament. Bond Corporation, he said, had resorted to "trickery, sly lurks and devious schemes". Bond's advisers, meanwhile, had "subverted their professional talents". Legally, said Debus, there was no doubt the scheme passed, but "morally it had cheated the Australian taxpayer of between $8 million and $9 million". Debus then tackled the philosophy of such schemes, with some eloquence.

> There are apologists for this type of tax avoidance. It is sometimes characterised as the right of every taxpayer. I have even heard it suggested as an obligation of a company director to shareholders. That is arrant nonsense: in every sense but strict legality, it is nothing but a fraud practised against the community. Tax laws, like every other law of the land, should apply equally to all citizens. The amount one contributes to public services, such as education and health, should not depend on one's ability to buy a tailor-made tax avoidance scheme concocted by big-ticket lawyers, accountants and merchant bankers. I now give notice that from the time of this announcement, the use of these avoidance practices designed to escape the payment of stamp duty will be illegal.

Far from being ashamed by the revelations, Alan
Bond was indignant, as only he could be. It was
outrageous, he said, that he had been attacked in
this way. Bond Corporation didn't avoid its taxes:
on the contrary, it paid more tax than anyone else in
Australia. What *was* wrong was the way in which he
had been attacked under the cover of parliamentary
privilege.

In Queensland, Bond had tried to get away with
the same tricks, but the authorities had been
sharper. There, the State Treasury had got wind of
Bond's tax avoidance scheme before the deed had
been done, and had taken the direct approach to
sorting it out. The Under-Secretary of the Treasury
had rung the Premier, Sir Joh Bjelke-Petersen, who
was ceremonially opening a grain terminal. As Sir
Joh told the Australian Broadcasting Tribunal, in the
course of being questioned about large payments to
him by Bond to settle a libel suit, he had immediately got on the phone to Bond Corporation:

> I rang Western Australia before I went into
> the opening of the terminal and spoke to a Mr
> Beckwith, Peter Beckwith, and I said to him
> that if this was about to take place we would
> view it very, very seriously and we would
> protest very strongly, because we felt that
> being in Queensland we were entitled to the
> stamp duty, and that was a very, very large
> amount of money, as you can imagine.
> *Q*: What was the outcome of that?
> Well, the outcome of it was that he indicated
> to me that they would do the right thing, as
> he said they always did, and they did do just

> that, transacted in Queensland and paid a
> very big amount of stamp duty.

On that occasion, Bond indeed did pay the duty. But
eight months later, when Bond Corporation sold
the pubs into an associated company, Austotel,
Queensland's tax was sidestepped successfully.
Unknown to Sir Joh, Bond Corporation this time did
"the right thing" for itself, rather than for the
taxpayer. The stamp duty saga, however, was just a
sideshow in Bond's tax avoidance performance. The
main act took place in the area of his companies'
profits—in income tax or corporation tax—where
far larger sums were at stake.

There are many ways in Australia or the UK by
which companies can lighten their tax burden.
There are legitimate and desirable allowances for
such things as capital expenditure, investment in
machinery, exploration costs and the like. But
Bond's tax-avoidance methods did not confine
themselves to these. As a general principle, Bond
Corporation attempted to shift its profits to places
where tax was not payable, and to shift its expenses
to where tax relief could be claimed. A team of six
tax advisers in Australia, and one each in the United
Kingdom and the USA, devoted their working lives
to the task. Money for Bond's international deals
was typically borrowed in Australia, where there
was a tax liability from the breweries, and profits
were made in the Channel Islands or other more
exotic tax havens. The dealing profits were thus
made tax-free while the Australian taxpayer put up
part of the cost of the finance.

There are numerous examples of how easily it

was done. But the most blatant was also one of the first. In April 1986 Bond bought and sold a business in the space of one week. It was the Screen Entertainment division of Thorn EMI: the company was based in Britain, the deal was negotiated in London, a profit of $45 million was made. Yet Bond didn't pay a penny of British tax on the deal. Nor did the group pay tax in Australia. It got away with the money, scot-free.

It wasn't, however, the tax dodge that brought Bond notoriety in Britain over the deal. Alan was seen by the British film industry as a saviour when he bought Screen Entertainment from Thorn. Yet four days later, when he sold out to the predator he was supposed to have been protecting them all from, he was branded the betrayer. The anguish arose because Screen Entertainment's assets included the old Elstree Studios, where the last flame of British film-making still flickered. Elstree was the home of Lion, and a proud, if somewhat ancient, film-making tradition. Cannon Films, on the other hand, whom Bond sold out to, was a producer of R-rated schlockers, heavy on the sex and shootings. It was also Hollywood-based, and run by two Israeli cousins, Menahem Golan and Yoram Globus, who could hardly be relied upon to keep the Union Jack flying.

When Thorn EMI had first put its Screen Entertainment division up for sale, there had been much wailing and gnashing of teeth in the British film industry about the suggestion that Cannon might buy it. So Thorn had agreed to let the company's management, led by Gary Dartnall, have a crack at buying the company. Dartnall, a cheerful man, given to wearing colourful braces, promptly found a bank in the City of London who agreed to lend him most of the money, but soon found that he could not borrow all the £100 million which Thorn was asking. Then, one day, after a piece in the *Financial Times* suggested that the management buy-out might collapse for lack of cash, the phone had rung in Dartnall's office and his secretary had come through to say: "There's a Mr Bond from Australia on the phone."

The two men met the same afternoon, and Dartnall both liked Bond and was impressed. Bond explained to Dartnall that he was keen to help on the deal because he wanted product for his TV network in Australia (Screen Entertainment also owned EMI's library of 2000 films). And by the evening they had become partners. Bond agreed to put up the 10 per cent deposit, or £10 million, which Dartnall needed to get to first base, and promised then to pitch in a further £35 million if the deal went through. Bond, in exchange, would pick up 45 per cent of the company. And the Israeli cousins would be kept at bay.

Bond and Dartnall then went to Thorn and clinched the deal. Thorn's Managing Director, Colin Southgate, was apparently dithering about whether to sell, saying there were lots of people round town in hotels just waiting to pay more. But Bond, typically, had no time for it. He upped the bidding by £10 million, and gave Southgate fifteen minutes to make up his mind. "If I don't hear from you by then," said Bond, "I'm going to get on a plane and go back to Australia." Ten minutes later Southgate rang down to Dartnall's office to say that the deal was on.

Several months passed while they tried to find

the money for the deal. But, for one reason or another, the finance could not be raised. Dartnall asked Thorn for more time to get the cash, but Bond was keen to go ahead on his own. Knowing that he had Cannon, a ready buyer, waiting in the wings, he would only need to borrow the money for a matter of days.

Dartnall was surprised and disappointed that their partnership had fallen apart, while others were relieved because it ended the uncertainty. As their new owner, Alan Bond then gathered the staff together at a London restaurant, and told them they had no need to worry. "Everyone felt pretty good," says Dartnall, "that Alan was going to run the company and grow the business, and that he had the resources to do it." But the good feelings didn't last. Four days later, to everyone's amazement, the business was sold on to the Israelis—the very people that Bond had supposedly kept at bay. Dartnall, meanwhile, had gone off on holiday to recover from the strain of it all: "I was on a Greek island just getting into a dinghy and this guy says have you heard the news, Cannon has bought Thorn EMI from Bond. I said, you've got to be joking, and he said, no, we've just had it over the wires. I nearly fell out of the boat." After four gruelling months working with Bond Corporation to save the business, Dartnall's efforts had all been ditched. "I must say I felt pretty numb. I came late to being an entrepreneur and I guess I was pretty naive. But I just couldn't believe it."

As so often in Bond's career, there was an outcry at Bond's manoeuvring, but also a certain amount of chuckling. One had to admit it was clever. Bond had paid £125 million for Screen at the beginning of the week and sold it four days later to Cannon for, he claimed, £50 million more. But the British film industry was not amused. Nor were the directors of Thorn, who had been made to look stupid. And nor was the British taxman.

Bond had structured the deal so that the British taxpayer would not get a penny. The purchase and sale of Screen Entertainment had been handled through a shelf company in Jersey which had been set up for the purpose, and it was here that the profits had ended up. Bond's accounts showed that Bond Corporation had cleared some $45 million on the deal—all of which had been taken in the Channel Islands, tax free. But that was only half the story. Back in Perth, a Bond subsidiary called Bond Entertainment Pty Ltd, which had been activated to finance the deal, had incurred interest charges that would cut Bond's tax bill in Australia by $3 million.

That same year, 1986, held another good example of how it all worked, this time with the Bond Tower in Hong Kong (which was then under construction). Bond Corporation found itself short of money to complete the building and sold a half-share in the project, at a profit, to Japanese developer EIE. There was no capital gains tax in Hong Kong, but there was a risk that the Hong Kong taxman might rule the profit to have come from *trading* in property—since Bond had bought and sold half the site in a matter of months—and demand income tax on it. Bond's advisers, however, had already planned for such an event: they had placed ownership of the tower in a subsidiary called Kerrison, based ten thousand kilometres away in Jersey, and had put Kerrison into the hands of another Jersey company, Savay Investments. All that Bond needed to do, then, to sell the Hong Kong property was to have Savay sell half of its Kerrison shares to the Japanese buyer. That way, the building technically changed hands in Jersey, and the profit of HK$128 million could be taken there—tax-free. In this way, the British, the Australian, and the Hong Kong taxman were all kept at bay.

But deals like the Bond Tower and Screen Entertainment were insignificant compared with what was to come. By 1988, after a little bit of practice, Bond had the game of tax avoidance down to a fine art. That year, Bond Corporation reported worldwide profits of $274 million, and yet rang up a credit with the taxman of almost $1 million.

The secret of Bond's remarkable success this time lay out in the middle of the Pacific Ocean, roughly halfway between the USA and Australia, on a string of tiny volcanic rocks called the Cook Islands. Spattered across two million square kilometres of ocean, with a total population of just 18,000 people and 3000 goats, the Cooks were about as far as you could get from the cut and thrust of international business. There were palm trees, sandy beaches, sparkling blue water, a few tourists, and little to do except relax. But if you had tax to avoid, they were hard to beat. Not only did offshore companies pay no tax of any sort, they were also allowed to operate with complete freedom: they did not have to file accounts, appoint auditors, or even reveal who were their shareholders. They were protected, too, from prying taxmen and journalists by a veil of secrecy: it was impossible as an outsider to check whether a company was registered there. And prison sentences awaited anyone who divulged confidential information about a company's activities.

Antipodean and Asian tax avoiders thus flocked there to "do business". None of these was larger or more obvious than Australia's Bond Corporation. While others at least used the Cooks with some discretion, Bond by 1988 did it quite blatantly: Bond Corporation's annual accounts for that year, published in Australia, revealed that 96 per cent of its declared profits, or some $270 million, had been made in the Cook Islands. Naturally, Bond Corporation had paid no tax at all on these earnings.

The puzzling thing to the simple-minded was that Bond Corporation clearly didn't do business there in any meaningful sense. There was no public sign of Bond's presence, nor was there any listing in the Bond Corporation annual report of executives or activities located in the Cooks. It was, in fact, one of the few places in the world where you couldn't buy Bond's beer, where you didn't see XXXX ads on the television, and where you didn't have a Bond blimp buzzing around over your head. But the Cook Islands, in any case, weren't a place where you could do much business—their gross national product was barely one fiftieth of Bond's worldwide sales, the main town a one-street affair along the beachfront, and the harbour just a small jetty where the supply ship from New Zealand occasionally pitched up. The islanders, meanwhile, had never even heard of him.

Bond's office on the main island of Rarotonga was also something of a puzzle. To judge by the profit figures, this was the world headquarters of Bond Corporation, the international nerve centre. Yet when you saw it, it looked more like a provincial accountant's office. Bond's forty Cook Islands companies lived on the first floor of a small white house owned by the local telephone people, Cable & Wireless. Inside were half-a-dozen fax machines, a few typewriters, and a couple of solicitors from New Zealand. Hardly anything appeared to happen there. If you stood outside, the only noises you could hear was the sometime thump of a coconut hitting the ground, or the buzz of an engine as the occasional South Sea Islander rode past on his motor scooter.

In early 1989, in an attempt to find out how Bond used the Cook Islands to avoid paying tax, a team from ABC TV's *Four Corners* paid Bond's headquarters a visit. The man we found, at the Cook Islands' Trust company, was an embarrassed New Zealander by the name of Trevor Clarke. A director of many, if not most, of Bond's Cook Islands' companies, the casually-dressed Mr Clarke was sporting a pink-print shirt and a golden tan, and was apparently in charge of the profit-making magic. When asked whether he would mind answering a few questions, Mr Clarke said he did not. One could see, as soon as the interview started, that he realised it was a mistake. It was not that he told us any secrets: his answers revealed next to nothing at all. But his manner gave the whole ridiculous game away. When asked about what Bond's companies actually did in the Cook Islands, his cheek began to twitch nervously and he started to stumble. A nervous grin remained fixed on his face, but his eyes showed that he was not enjoying himself. The exchange went like this:

Q: How does Bond make his profits here? I mean, you can't see Bond Corporation in the

Cook Islands, at least, I can't.

A: Well, I don't think I can answer that question you (pause) you're seeking some commercial information that's not appropriate that I discuss that.

Q: But how, broadly? I mean, $250 million in an island with 9000 people, where Bond Corporation isn't present, it seems bizarre.

A: (laughs, pauses again) I don't think I'm in a position to discuss that with you either.

Q: Has Alan Bond ever been to the Cook Islands?

A: Not to my knowledge, not him personally.

The answer, of course, was that Bond's companies didn't do business there at all. Trevor Clarke and his Cook Islands' Trust Corporation acted only as a postbox for Bond's business deals, which were being carried on elsewhere. In a way that wasn't the question. What one wanted to know was how was it possible to keep all this money from the taxman, and where had the profits come from in the first place.

The answers were not easy to uncover, because the Cook Islands' secrecy laws made it impossible even to find out whether the companies existed, let alone what they did. But Bond Corporation's annual report listed various Cook Island companies and reported what money they had made. It was possible therefore to discover that Cashel Securities had made nearly $46 million, that Orpington had made $21 million, or that Sphinx Holdings had made $74 million. And from there, with a certain amount of digging and a bit of luck, one could see where some of the companies had earned their money.

As a rule, the money was coming from the purchase and sale of shares, companies or property around the world. The transactions were merely routed through the Cook Islands, in the same way that the sale of Screen Entertainment and Kerrison had been routed through Jersey. And in just the same way, it was therefore possible to "make" the profits in a place where they would be out of reach of the British, American or Italian taxman. As Bond Corporation's taxation manager, Graeme Pepper, would admit when questioned by a Parliamentary committee investigating tax avoidance, the notion of Bond "doing business" in the Cook Islands was little more than a sham.

Q: Do you pay any tax in the Cook Islands based on the business you do there?
A: Not to my knowledge
Q: But they (the companies) are not necessarily all doing business in the Cook Islands?
A: Correct.
Q: Are any of them?
A: It is a question of what is doing business.
Q: Indeed.
Q: Where were the profits derived?
A: In relation to the Cook Islands companies?
Q: Yes.
A: In a number of places.
Q: Can you tell us where?
A: I do not have full details of all of them, but in transactions done overseas.
Q: None in Australia?
A: In what way?

Q: None of the profits in the Cook Islands have been derived from operations in Australia?
A: Not to my knowledge.

From the Australian Parliament's point of view, the fact that none of the profits came out of Australia was obviously the prime concern. But it merely meant that the taxman in the United States or the United Kingdom was losing out instead. And, in any case, Pepper's account was wrong or, to put it politely, incomplete. There was a transaction that involved profits which would have been taxable in Australia: in December 1987 Bond claimed to have sold the Sydney Hilton at a profit of some $80 million. And all of that had been taken offshore. It was the same technique that had been used with the sale of Bond's Hong Kong Tower: the Hilton Hotel was owned by an Australian company, Iwak; Iwak in turn was owned by a Cook Islands company, Mossbark; and Mossbark in its turn was owned by another Cook Islands company, Lawson Holdings. When Bond sold the hotel, it did not do anything crude like sell the property: Lawson Holdings sold the shares in Mossbark so that the transaction took place in the Cook Islands, and the profit could be taken there tax-free. Needless to say, they did not boast about this in their annual report to shareholders.

On ABC TV's *Four Corners* programme in 1989, I asked Bond Corporation's Finance Director, Tony Oates, about the Hilton transaction and why Bond had paid no tax on it. He had first told me that the Cook Islands dealt only with "international" operations.

Q: You have just said that it is only the international operations we are talking about. What about the sale of the Sydney Hilton?

A: That was an operation that was owned by a Cook Islands company.

Q: But it's not international, is it? The Sydney Hilton is in Sydney as far as I remember.

A: It is absolutely, but in about 99.9 per cent of cases the operations are international.

Q: That is $80 million profit, one third of the profit you made in the Cook Islands, on an Australian asset.

A: That is right. That is absolutely right.

Q: That is not an international transaction, is it?

A: It is actually because the purchaser was an international company.

Q: But why did you not pay tax on that? It is an Australian company, that is you, selling an Australian asset?

A: Well, you are making the assumption, which I think is quite wrong, that Australian tax would have been payable in any event.

Q: Capital gains?

A: Then it may not attract Australian tax.

Q: And that is chargeable at 49 per cent at the time you sold it.

A: That may not be correct either, because it depends when you acquired the asset.

Q: You acquired the asset in July 1987 from AMP.

A: In which case we have done something which we believe is appropriate in that kind of operation. Now, again.

Q: But tax would be payable, so don't put

that argument to me.

A: Tax may be payable, tax may be payable.

Q: And you have avoided it by sending the transaction offshore. Are you happy with that? Are you happy with a "good corporate citizen" like Bond Corporation doing a transaction like that?

A: I am pleased you recognise we are a good corporate citizen. We believe we are. We believe that what we do and what we will continue to do in Australia is what we believe is right in the administration of our business.

And damn the rest of you, he might have added.

But the question was how did Bond get away with it? Surely the law was not such an ass that it made such things perfectly legal? Sadly, in a sentence, it probably was. But the transactions were not often challenged in any case, because the taxman rarely found out about them. The secrecy of the Cook Islands and the offshore registration of the companies made it extremely hard for the British or Italian taxman to know that they might have missed out. And the same secrecy made it almost impossible for the taxmen to win a court case, even if they did get suspicious.

The law relating to profits made offshore on Australian assets also did not help. To succeed in any attempt to charge tax on a transaction like the Hilton sale, it was necessary for the taxman to prove that the Cook Islands company was in fact controlled from Australia. Provided the paperwork could show that the Cook Islands directors had "taken" all the decisions (after suitable advice, of course), it was almost impossible for the taxman to prove his case. There was (and still is) a powerful anti-avoidance provision in the Tax Acts which could be used against "artificial" transactions, and might well have succeeded against deals like the Sydney Hilton, but the Australian taxman had inexplicably never sought to use it. As Parliamentary investigations revealed, during the early 1980s, the Australian tax system had been particularly incompetent when it came to chasing tax avoiders. Inaction was par for the course.

But there was another, broader, reason why Bond and his companies' scheme succeeded. One of the general rules of the world is that if you have enough money just about anything is possible, and this certainly held for Bond and his tax affairs. He had the advice of the best lawyers and tax accountants, both within and outside Bond Corporation: his tax chief, Graeme Pepper, for example, had been one of the high fliers at the Australian Taxation Office, while another adviser had been in the same organisation's important "legislation interpretation" section. The Bond team and their highly-paid fellows in the big law firms and accountancy practices might well therefore have been smarter than Canberra's poorly-rewarded public servants. They represented the pick of the public crop—the ones who had been bought out by the private sector as soon as they knew how the tax laws worked.

It was then a combination of ingredients which made up the recipe that allowed Bond to pay so little tax: secrecy in the tax havens, poor laws in Australia, and hot-shot advisers who had few moral scruples about the way in which their talents were used. (There was also another, which we shall come to later, involving the quality of Bond's profits.) Perhaps, however, the balance has now changed: the taxman is investigating Bond's Cook Islands transactions and the rest of Bond Corporation's tax affairs in a detailed audit. Meanwhile, new tax laws in 1990 will make it impossible for anyone to legally use havens like the Cooks as a refuge from Australian tax. Profits "earned" there will be taxed in Australia, irrespective of where they came from, and where they are going to. "We will not tolerate," said Federal Treasurer, Paul Keating, introducing the legislation in 1988, "any action which rips off the rest of the community."

The sad fact, however, was that he and the Labor Government had in the past done exactly that. By deregulating financial markets in 1984 and allowing the free movement of money in and out of Australia, *they* had made Bond's use of tax havens possible. Six years later they would still be talking about how to close the loopholes.

CHAPTER 18

October 1987–
The Rothwells Disaster

On Tuesday 20 October 1987 Australia awoke to forecasts of financial disaster. People turned on their radios or opened their morning papers to discover that there had been a bloodbath on the London and New York stock markets overnight. US$700,000 million had been wiped off share prices on Wall Street as the market went into free fall. The Tokyo market was reacting in panic, they were told, even as the bulletins were being broadcast; and Australian markets were bound to follow suit. There had been nothing like it since the horror days of October 1929 when the Manhattan sky had been thick with defenestrating brokers. And this time the market fall was even larger, the risks of Armageddon apparently much greater. Everyone knew what had happened to the world almost sixty years before: it had sunk into the Great Depression, into years of misery, massive unemployment, and widespread corporate collapse. It was hardly surprising then that in Australia that October morning there was a feeling that history was being made. Both there and on the other side of the world there was fear of what the morrow would bring.

The dreadful predictions of economic catastrophe did not, of course, come true. But for Australia's high-flying entrepreneurs the October Crash spelt disaster just the same. Before the fateful day they were the darlings of the stock market and could do no wrong. After it, they could suddenly do nothing right. In the timid Old World which the crash restored, they were seen all at once from a starker, more cautious perspective and their shares were hammered as a result: Robert Holmes à Court's Bell Group, for example, lost almost 90 per cent of its value. Laurie Connell's Rothwells merchant bank fared even worse—it threatened to collapse altogether.

The tremors that shook Laurie Connell's Rothwells started on the morning after Wall Street's collapse. As the first search for victims of the stock market crash began, rumours spread in Perth that Rothwells was short of cash, and immediately its funds began to flee. Depositors rushed to get their money out: first to the tune of $50 million, then $100 million, and by the end of the week $250 million, whereupon Rothwells' own bankers put up the shutters and refused to honour the company's cheques. One hundred depositors packing into Rothwells' lobby on the 23rd floor of Perth's Allendale Square found doors barring their entrance and the tills closed. Security guards were hired to keep the mob in order while, inside, the bank's anguished directors debated what to do.

The public perception of Rothwells, fanned by Laurie Connell and his friends in the Western Australian Government, was that the bank was a significant force in the Australian financial community. And the published accounts supported that picture: its profits had grown steadily from $700,000 in 1982 to $16 million in 1987, while its assets had multiplied from around $50 million to more than $700 million a few months before the crash. Its reputation was that of a dynamic, successful outfit at the cutting edge of Australian finance. What's more, it was run by the much-lauded Mr Connell, who was known to be one of the richest, if not the richest man in Australia. Although known somewhat scathingly in Perth as Last Resort Laurie because he funded projects that others wouldn't touch, Connell was a glamorous figure as far as the nation's press was concerned: he might have been common, but he knew how to make a buck. So even if journalists from the eastern states made fun of his sweaty armpits and his mismatched alligator-skin shoes, no one seriously enquired where his supposed personal fortune of $300 million or $400 million had come from. The overwhelming verdict of the admiring scribes was that this tough little bus-driver's son must be a financial genius.

Unfortunately, the reality was entirely different. Although Rothwells generated new cash on a massive scale—at times at the rate of $1 million every week—it did so by the simple device of paying depositors better interest rates than anyone else in the market. And far from using that money well, almost as fast as the money came in the front door, Alan Bond's mate Laurie Connell shovelled it out the back. In the six short years, 1982 to 1988, in which the Rothwells star streaked across the financial firmament, Laurie Connell's "bank" ran up around $900 million in borrowings from the public. And in those same six years, Mr Connell contrived to lose more than two-thirds of it, or some $620 million. Far from being a genius, he was at best a hopeless incompetent. A large part of the vanishing millions disappeared into Laurie Connell's private companies, where the money was either lost or spent. Alternatively, the cash was lent to other companies who did the job just as effectively. Some of it went straight into Laurie's pocket, to fund his extravagant lifestyle: he bought the biggest racehorse string in Australia, a private racetrack and training facilities, a $27 million private jet, fast cars, vast yachts, huge properties, and rivers of Dom Perignon. With hundreds of millions of other people's dollars at his disposal, it was no surprise that he was able to live like Australia's richest man.

By June 1987, Laurie and his satellite companies had already worked their way through more than $320 million of Rothwells' depositors' funds—$320 million that would be lost for good—and the reckoning could clearly not be long delayed. As the Western Australian Premier, Brian Burke, privately observed to Connell during the first attempt to rescue the bank, Laurie was an "accident waiting to happen". The stock market crash merely provided the trigger.

It was not till Thursday 22 October, that Laurie Connell first heard that Rothwells was in trouble. It was only then that the four other directors, who were in Perth watching the drama unfold, contacted Laurie in Sydney where he was busy giving advice to others—notably Warwick Fairfax, budding tycoon and newspaper heir. The directors told Connell that they wanted to throw in the towel and call in the receivers, but Laurie would have none of it. They would fight to keep Rothwells afloat; Connell's mates would rally round; Alan Bond and the government would come to Rothwells' rescue.

That weekend, all flights led to Perth: one of the Bond jets hopped over from Sydney with a team from Bond's bankers, Wardley Australia, on board; then came Brian Yuill, principal of Spedley Securities, which had money with Rothwells and close ties of friendship to Connell and Bond; and finally, Alan Bond himself jetted in. Bond had been sailing his 12-metre on the Costa Smeralda and had then been buying property in Rome, but had dropped everything when he heard the news. Now he threw himself into rescuing Rothwells with a vigour which some would later find puzzling. Perhaps it was out of loyalty, perhaps out of fear that Bond Corporation could be next if Rothwells were allowed to go. But whatever it was, Bond immediately took charge.

No sooner had Bond arrived in the Rothwells office than he seated himself behind Laurie Connell's desk, asked for the story so far, and began to direct operations. Connell, who was used to dominating any meeting at which he was present, sank into the background like a naughty little boy. When the bankers from Wardley raised doubts about the risk of underwriting any rescue, it was Bond who twice took them aside to promise them that they would come out all right. When the Liberal Opposition leaders were called in to be lobbied for their support, it was at Bond's house that they met, and Bond who was in charge.

When David Parker, the state's Deputy Premier, was asked for a government guarantee it was Bond who did the talking, Bond who called the shots, and Bond who was in control.

Alan Bond liked nothing more than to make deals and to be the centre of attention. And the Rothwells rescue mission brought him both. He planned to pull his mate Connell out of the mire by getting the top names of corporate Australia into harness. But to persuade these august persons to join the team, Bond first needed the security of a guarantee from the Western Australian Government: without that, Rothwells' nervous bankers would not put up a crucial $150 million that the rescue relied on. Bond and his men told the Premier and his Deputy that the guarantee was most unlikely to be called: Rothwells would have to lose a couple of hundred million dollars before the government was put at risk; on the other hand, without government backing, the rescue was bound to fail. Burke and his senior ministers went off to chew it over, while Bond and his executives set about raising the money.

That weekend they bashed the telephones with the men from Wardleys in the biggest corporate whip-round Australia had ever seen. In the space of an afternoon and evening, $150 million was pledged to keep Rothwells from going under. The rescuers read like a Business Who's Who of Australia—Kerry Packer, Robert Holmes à Court, John Elliott, and Larry Adler all agreed to throw a lifeline; Brian Yuill and Alan Bond also held out a hand: not least because they had money already at risk on the Rothwells wagon. And Connell too was persuaded to promise $70 million of his personal fortune. Seeing that Connell was putting his money in (when it was argued he could walk away scot-free) Burke dragged the Western Australian taxpayers into the party. Whereupon the National Australia Bank came up with its $150 million to keep Rothwells' worried depositors at bay.

The following Monday, 26 October, it was Alan Bond who announced triumphantly that a $370 million rescue package had been put into place. Banking was about confidence, Bond was moved to say, and he had now restored it. Rothwells, Bond's good news continued, was now as safe as houses: it had been the victim of the stock market crash, its problems had arisen because people had panicked. The future was now secure, and so was the financial system: Bond and Premier Burke both agreed that they had saved it from collapse. If the government and Bond had not stepped in, they argued, there was no knowing what could have happened. After all, if a sound, respectable, thriving merchant bank like Rothwells could go down the gurgler, who was safe?

It was, indeed, a glorious moment—not least because Bond was happy for once to be the rescuer and not the victim. But the triumph was short-lived, for Messrs Burke and Bond had misread the script: this was not the end of the play, it was merely the close of Act One, and events from here on would not turn out so merrily. The rescue had put barely enough cash into Rothwells to cover its existing problems, and in the year that followed, the money would very quickly run out. A second and a third rescue attempt would be necessary and neither would save Rothwells from ultimate collapse. The squandering of cash before October 1987 had already been too great. The black hole was too deep to be filled.

Rothwells' insoluble problem was that it had to pay interest of more than $100 million a year to its loyal depositors, but there was virtually no income coming in to meet the bill: a large proportion of Rothwells' so-called assets had either already been spent by Laurie Connell, or were now tied up in companies which themselves had no funds. It was thus inevitable that cash would continue to haemorrhage from the company at an alarming rate. But there was an added complication which hastened the day of judgement: far from contributing $70 million in new money to the rescue, Laurie Connell, within a matter of weeks, had taken another $40 million out.

The slow and painful collapse of Rothwells eventually took more than a year, and involved increasingly complex attempts to avoid the inevitable disaster. But in essence, there were two key problems which could never satisfactorily be solved. The first was the need for yet more money—a need that became clear only weeks after the initial rescue. The second was the problem of covering up losses that Rothwells had already made. To keep the merchant bank in business, something had to be done about $350 million of Rothwells' debts which had already gone bad. If the auditors examined these various debts in preparing the balance sheet for 30 June 1988, they would almost certainly demand that a large proportion of the loans be written off as lost, which would be enough to bring the bank down. So the debts had to be got rid of.

For a short time, and a short time only, the problem of raising enough cash to keep Rothwells going was solved by Bond Corporation and the State Government Insurance Commission getting their hands on some money—they seized control of Robert Holmes à Court's Bell Group, which conveniently had several hundred million dollars in the vaults. But the $350 million of debts needed some fancier footwork: if these were to be removed from the books, someone had to pay the money back, but no one on earth would be crazy enough to pay $350 million for a bunch of bad debts with a realisable value approaching zero. Not even the man whose bank had incurred them in the first place, Laurie Connell. He, in any case, had no more chance of raising that sort of money than he did of being knighted for services to industry.

There was, however, a brilliant solution to the problem: some years earlier, Laurie Connell had been given a mandate by the government to develop a petrochemical plant at Kwinana, south of Perth. If the government and Bond were to stump up the money to "buy" this petrochemical plant back for $350 million, then Connell could use the funds to buy the bad debts and get them out of Rothwells' books. Whereupon the $350 million could be recycled into repaying Bond Corporation and the National Australia Bank, whose $150 million loan had been government-guaranteed.

The attractions of this extraordinarily complicated deal were immense. Not only would Rothwells float safely past the 30 June balance sheet date, but the government could meet its $150 million guarantee to the NAB while pretending to taxpayers that it had never been called. Bond Corporation, meanwhile, which had essentially already lost some $220 million by pumping it into Rothwells, could transform this lost money into something that might eventually bring a return: a petrochemical plant whose profitability would in the future be guaranteed by the government. It was an extremely elegant solution and, apparently, an arrangement in which no one could lose.

But there was of course someone who would foot the bill, and that was the great body of West Australian taxpayers. Not only was their government forking out $200 million to buy something they had given away in the first place, and which was worth practically nothing, it was also now promising financial guarantees to Bond Corporation, to ensure that the petrochemical project would be profitable, which could cost many millions more. The government had therefore exchanged one embarrassing liability for another—a fact soon abundantly clear to the public. But the greatest problem of all was that Rothwells had still not been saved. The juggling had put in hardly any new cash and Rothwells, by late 1988, was once again out of money.

When Laurie Connell's merchant bank finally met its inevitable end in October 1988, after yet another attempt at rescue had foundered for lack of cash, the investigators moved in. And trouble for Bond and the government then started in earnest. For not only did the forensic experts reveal the way in which Rothwells had lost its millions, they also exposed the increasingly desperate manner in which Bond and the government had tried to cover up the mess. The tangled web which Bond and the government had woven around Rothwells would eventually ensnare them both in violent public rows and legal action; it would also bring the downfall of Western Australia's Premier, Peter Dowding; what's more it would ultimately cost Bond Corporation some $300 million which it could ill afford to lose. Yet even now, before all that, it had an important impact on how Bond was perceived. It did not escape notice, as the excesses of Laurie Connell were revealed, that the tough little financial genius had oft been described as Bond's best friend.

The demise of Rothwells was important for another reason—it was the harbinger of doom, the first star to fall in the great Australian corporate collapse. Before the 1980s were over, those cut down by the rise in interest rates or poisoned by the spreading fallout from the October Crash would include almost every entrepreneur on the Australian scene, and a fair number of property companies to boot. By 1990, and much earlier for some, Ariadne was gone, so were Equiticorp, Spedley Securities, Tricontinental, Girvan, Hooker Corporation, Qintex, Westmex, Rothwells, Parry Corporation, and a host of smaller fry besides. Indeed, as the carnage spread and the whizz kids fell, only one genuine Australian entrepreneur of any stature was left standing.

In stockbrokers' offices around the nation, in the days following the 1987 Crash, the name of Bond Corporation had been high on almost everyone's list of likely casualties. Bond's empire had rarely been financially secure in its twenty-five year history; the big institutional investors had always steered clear, and as always it appeared to be dangerously over-borrowed. Yet Bond Corporation not only survived that immediate aftermath of the crash, it profited from it. As the governments of Australia, the USA and Britain flooded their financial systems with cash to keep their economies afloat, interest rates fell around the world and an extraordinary property boom swept through. Bond Corporation promptly went on a spree of buying and developing, and appeared to make a fortune. By October 1988, a year after the crash, Bond Corporation seemed not only to be alive and kicking, it appeared to be stronger, richer and more aggressive than ever. Alan Bond, too, was bubbling with confidence, convinced that his empire was immortal.

Bond's overconfidence, however, was ultimately his downfall, because the crash had changed the world, and Bond had failed to notice. He continued to buy, to borrow, to expand and to deal, just as he had done before the stock market's fall. And for a time, he rose on the flood. But when the property boom finally burst and the banks began to call in their loans, Bond was left high and dry. Just as the climate of the Earth had once changed to extinguish the dinosaur, so, slowly but surely, the financial climate after October 1987 now dried up to destroy the habitat of creatures like Alan Bond. During the 1980s the entrepreneurs had towered over Australia. Now, slowly but surely they all fell to the earth whence they had come.

Bond's initial reaction to the crash, just three weeks after it had happened, and two weeks after the Rothwells rescue, was to enlarge his painting collection, by spending US$54 million of the banks' money on Van Gogh's *Irises*. Two weeks later, he demonstrated further confidence in the future of his empire by distributing some largesse to Bond Corporation's six top executives. Bond gave each of them a pair of golden handcuffs, worth $30 million in total, designed to tie them to the company for the next four to five years. Peter Beckwith, the group's managing director, was himself being promised a third of the total, which would help pay for his vast new neo-classical mansion in Dalkeith's Jutland Parade. The shareholders at the Annual General Meeting were less than thrilled by the plan—even though Bond Corporation at this time was apparently profitable—but Alan Bond's personal shareholding railroaded it through.

Then on the business battlefront, Bond went into action, pushing the frontiers of his empire ever outwards. In the year to June 1988, Bond Corporation more than doubled its size, gobbling up $5000 million of other people's assets. Bond's net debt mountain in the same time grew by $3000 million. And while some of the biggest buys, like Heileman, were made before the October Crash, almost as many were made afterwards: Chifley Square in Sydney, for example, was picked up in early 1988 for $300 million, the St Georges Hospital site in London, in May 1988, for $74 million, Merlin Petroleum for $125 million, the Chile Telephone Company for US$300 million, while shareholdings in Petro Energy and Waltons Bond were tidied up for an outlay of another $100 million. Meanwhile, another $800 million was spent in mid-1988 on the biggest of them all, Bell Resources and Bell Group. To be fair to Bond, he expected to get Bell far cheaper, and it was a serious problem that he had not. But in fairness to the National Companies and Securities Commission, who scuppered the deal, there was every reason why Bond should pay the full price.

In the early months of 1988, when it had become clear that the Rothwells rescue needed more funds to avoid a collapse, Bond's eyes had focused on Robert Holmes à Court's Bell Resources. Sitting there in its coffers in Perth, by great good fortune, was $1200 million in cash and saleable assets, ready for the taking. The money was locked deep in Robert Holmes à Court's business empire, it was true, but the Emperor was keen to sell up: his plans had been wrecked by the crash; his pride was bruised; he wanted out. So Bond set about securing Holmes à Court's controlling shareholding in Bell Group, which would give Bond Corporation access to the cash. During March and April 1988, Alan Bond battered Holmes à Court's door down and made Holmes à Court an offer he could hardly refuse: $2.70 a share, against the $1.50 that the shares were selling for in the market—almost double the ruling price. It seemed an exceedingly generous deal, especially since Stock Exchange rules would require Bond to make a full bid for the company if he acquired more than 20 per cent of Bell Group's shares—and he was planning to purchase twice that amount. But Alan Bond had a plan to get round this inconvenient rule.

By splitting Holmes à Court's parcel of shares into two, Bond and the Western Australian Government could together gain control of the company without triggering a full bid. They could each limit their purchase to 19.9 per cent of the shares, yet take control of the Bell Group board. Then they could get the key to the Bell Resources safe and unlock the $1200 million in cash. The beauty of the scheme for the government had been that there would then be plenty of funds to keep Rothwells afloat; the beauty of the scheme for Bond was that there would be hundreds of millions left over to fund his own activities. But, most of all, the brilliance of it was that the money could be seized with the minimum of outlay—Bond Corporation would get its hands on the $1200 million by spending just $175 million to buy Holmes à Court's shares. The bet would thus pay out at seven to one.

There were just a couple of snags: apart from the Australian Stock Exchange rule which triggered a takeover bid once anyone owned 20 per cent of the shares, there was another inconvenience, enshrined in company law, that made it an offence for parties to act in concert. And it was patently obvious that Bond and the State Government Insurance Commission had done just that. A further problem appeared: the minority shareholders in Bell Resources, led by the Australian Mutual Provident Society and its investment manager Leigh Hall, were horrified at the prospect of Bond getting his hands on their money—his record in Bond Corporation did not encourage them to believe he would spend it well. A row now ensued, the National Companies and Securities Commission intervened, and the deal was laid bare.

As the investigators discovered, Bond and the SGIC, who claimed to have acted independently, had followed each other in and out of Robert Holmes à Court's house, had talked to each other constantly and had concluded their purchase on the same day. The NCSC made public their opinion that a concert party had taken place, and to avoid messy legal action, a commercial settlement was then agreed. Bond was required to make an offer of $2.70 a share for all the shares in Bell Group (apart from those held by the SGIC, where an accommodation was reached), and his outlay on the Bell deal was thus multiplied more than fourfold. At $175 million, it had been a bargain; at $800 million it was almost a headache.

The Bell setback was critical to Bond, for its purchase on the cheap had been designed to solve a host of problems that his empire now faced. After the great spending spree of 1987-88 Bond Corporation now had gargantuan debts—some $10,000 million dollars if Dallhold was lumped in as well—and the property bust was only months away. Interest rates had already risen dramatically, and were set to go higher, bringing Bond's prospective interest bill to $300 million more than it had been the previous year. But to complicate matters even further, the breweries were not doing well. When Bond had taken over Castlemaine Tooheys in 1985, he had been toe-to-toe with Carlton & United at 45 per cent of the Australian beer market. Now, thanks to the rows over XXXX in Queensland, the rise of Power's beer, and the fight with the Tooheys' lease-holders, Bond Brewing had only 40 per cent of the market, and was discounting heavily even to keep sales that high. In terms of lost profit, millions of dollars that should have been flowing into the Bond coffers now failed to appear. Had Bond been just a brewing company, that would not have mattered unduly because profits of a sort were still being made. But the money was needed by the rest of the Bond group for its survival.

Unfortunately for Bond, the problems did not end there: a whole host of the things he had splurged his bankers' money on were in trouble. For one, the Channel Nine Network, which had cost more than $1000 million at the beginning of 1987, was not even paying the interest on the funds that had been borrowed against it. Meanwhile, other operations were consuming cash at a great rate: in Britain, Airship Industries was losing millions,

British Satellite Broadcasting was soaking up hundreds of millions, and an investment in Allied Lyons was tying up $500 million more that was not earning its keep. On top of that, there was the $300 million which had been poured into the great Rothwells' void and countless properties on which the interest clock was ticking, but the rent clock had stopped.

The worst troubles lay in Bond's American breweries. Two weeks before the October Crash, Bond had splashed out $1500 million (net) on the failing US brewing company G. Heileman. It had more sales than the whole Australian market put together, and had been bought only after "painstaking research" and eight months planning. But it was a major disaster all the same. Heileman had lost maybe $150 million in the year since Bond acquired it, and its fortunes seemed to be declining inexorably. Sales had fallen 10 per cent in 1988 and would show a further decline of 14 per cent in the first quarter of 1989. Beer analysts in the United States judged the company to be a lost cause: they pointed out glumly that in American history, beer brands with falling market share had rarely, if ever, been turned round. Meanwhile, they reckoned it to be worth half what Bond had paid. Instead of contributing to the group's cash flow, Heileman was in fact proving to be a major drain.

At the end of 1988, Bond's financial empire was thus stretched to the limit. Like Napoleon, another great chaser of dreams before him, Alan Bond was also fighting on too many fronts. He had expanded too far, bitten off too much. Though apparently at the peak of his power, he was in fact at his most vulnerable. To get his borrowings and his finances under control, Bond now needed a quick and decisive victory, or he would have to retreat. But it seemed that retreat was not a word in Bond's vocabulary, for he now chose the opposite course: he picked a fight with the UK company Lonrho and its passionate and dangerous defender, Tiny Rowland. He might as well have invaded Russia with winter coming on—as Napoleon had done—for all the good it would do him.

CHAPTER 19

A Tiny Problem

In October 1988, British businessman Tiny Rowland told a journalist on London's *Observer* newspaper, which he owned, that he suspected Alan Bond to be in deep financial trouble. He then added, with delightful irony: "I would of course do what I can to help."

Nine months later, Alan Bond would be contemplating the imminent collapse of his corporate empire, and trying to work out why the world no longer loved him. He would not have to look far for an answer. If there was one person whom he could blame for his downfall, it would be the man who had promised publicly to help him out, Roland "Tiny" Rowland. For in October 1988, Alan Bond made the greatest mistake of his spectacular corporate career: he attempted a hostile takeover of the UK public company Lonrho. An unglamorous company, little-loved by the City, Lonrho had one thing in its favour: it had been built from scratch by Rowland who had vowed never to let it go. He had once said of his beloved creation: "By God, it has got one thing and that is it has got a protector, and that's me. In other words, anybody who wants to kill that company has got to have a machine gun, mortars, guns, all sorts of ammunition because I am going to protect it to the bitter end."

Former railway porter, Mercedes car dealer and farmer, Tiny Rowland had always been somewhat on the fringes of polite society. Born in a British internment camp in India in December 1917 of a German father and an Anglo-Dutch mother, he had been christened Roland Walter Furhop. Most of his childhood had been spent in Germany, where he was briefly a member of the Hitler Youth. At the age of seventeen he had emigrated to England only to be interned again during WW II as an undesirable enemy alien. Much of the rest of his life Rowland had spent in Africa—where other people's prejudices and one's own past were less important than in the drawing rooms and banking halls of England. There he had been recruited to run a tinpot outfit called the London and Rhodesian Mining & Land Company, or Lonrho for short, which in the space of a decade he had built into a huge multinational organisation with mines and estates across the continent, to go with its oil and gas interests, printing and engineering businesses, and luxury hotels around the world. Some of his methods on the way, however, had earned him the title: "the unacceptable and unpleasant face of capitalism", conferred on him without ceremony by Britain's Prime Minister Ted Heath.

At the age of seventy-one, Tiny Rowland retained

a certain attractiveness. He was tall, with greying hair and a permanent suntan—derived no doubt from his continuing jaunts round Africa. He was also well dressed, good looking and indisputably charming. But at the same time, as Bond might have discovered by looking at Tiny's history, he was secretive, obsessive and extremely dangerous. Described by one acquaintance as "always on the lookout for enemies", he was not a man to tangle with. He would not so much defeat his enemies as destroy them, and on occasion he had threatened to do the same to his friends. His most intimate companion during the 1960s and early 1970s had been Princess Alexandra's husband, Angus Ogilvy, to whom Rowland owed his initial selection for the Lonrho job. The two men and their families had for a time lived next door to each other in London's Park Lane, and taken breakfast together on the terrace. But Ogilvy had then crossed Rowland. The falling-out had occurred in 1973 when Rowland was being threatened with removal from the Lonrho board after certain "irregularities" were discovered. Ogilvy, who was personally implicated in the scandal, having received large secret fees from Lonrho through a Bahamas trust account, had come under pressure from Buckingham Palace to disentangle himself, and had refused to support Rowland against his attackers. His great friend Tiny had then written him what one could hardly describe as a charming or understanding letter. "I am," wrote Rowland, "going to crucify you and your family."

Had Alan Bond studied the course of this particular battle in 1973 between Tiny and his foes, he might well have had the sense not to challenge the man. Plenty in England around that time had made a mental note never to take Rowland on in a fight. For, apart from his ability to denigrate his opponents, he had demonstrated in this battle that he could command fantastic personal loyalty both among Lonrho's shareholders and its customers. He also had an extraordinary rapport with a number of African leaders who were crucial to Lonrho's continued prosperity. Kenneth Kaunda, the President of Zambia, for example, declared publicly that Lonrho would never do business in Zambia again if Rowland's opponents succeeded in sacking him. Rowland's faithful army of shareholders meanwhile ensured that Kaunda did not need to carry out his threat—they backed Rowland against his would-be deposers, and the rebels were routed.

There was good reason, on the strength of this battle alone, for Bond to steer well clear of Tiny and his beloved company, but the 1973 row paled into insignificance beside the five-year battle that Rowland had waged with the Al Fayed brothers and the British Government for control of Harrods. In the mid 1980s Rowland had sold some shares in House of Fraser, the company that owned Harrods, to the Al Fayeds, intending to buy them back later when he made a bid for the company. The Al Fayeds had instead proceeded with a takeover bid themselves. Rowland was not only convinced that the Al Fayeds had betrayed him, he was adamant that successive Conservative Government ministers had conspired to do him down. Whether Rowland was right hardly mattered as far as the implications for Bond were concerned: what did was that Tiny had demonstrated yet again how dangerous he could be. For, from 1985, Rowland had with unceasing energy, devoted his life, the resources of Lonrho, the time of

Britain's courts, and the columns of his newspaper, the *Observer*, to damning the Al Fayeds and their supporters. And he had done a magnificent job. He had once again showed his special talent for blackening people's names, and the lengths to which he would go to bring down his enemies. All in all, one did not need the hindsight of 1990 to know that tangling with Tiny was as safe as kissing cobras.

Why Alan Bond thought he could charm the snake where others had been bitten one can only surmise—it would appear to have been either arrogance or incompetence. But it seems the decision to go for Lonrho was both impulsive and Alan Bond's alone. The person who most often stood up to Bond in his executive team, managing director Peter Beckwith, was dangerously ill; and the other two in the triumvirate, Peter Mitchell and Tony Oates, were run off their feet trying to rule the empire without him. They seem to have taken little interest in the Lonrho venture despite its enormous importance to the group. In the words of John Richardson, Bond's chief executive in London, on oath in court:

> I do not think anyone other than Alan Bond wanted to purchase the shares in Lonrho, and I think that the attitude of the senior people around, bearing in mind Peter Beckwith, the managing director, was quite ill with a heart attack and was not in the office from the beginning of October to some time in January, was that this is one of Mr Bond's deals and he can get on with it.

Bond, in assessing the target by himself, may well have reasoned that Lonrho was vulnerable because Tiny had so few friends in the City of London. The Establishment not only shunned the man, it thought little of his company, so it seemed likely that, when it came to a battle, few would rise to Lonrho's defence.

But perhaps the huge rewards also made Bond take his eye off his opponent. This was to be Bond's biggest deal ever, and lined up behind it was an even larger one. The plan was outlined by Alan Bond to his three top executives in secret session in Hawaii, in September 1988, and it went like this: if Bond Corporation could pick up Lonrho at a reasonable price, which should be easy since few liked the shares, there would be a profit of at least £1000 million to be made by selling the assets. With that cash in the tuckerbag, Bond would then have enough ammunition for an attack on Britain's largest brewer Allied Lyons, in which Bond already had a small strategic stake. Bond Corporation, by taking over Allied, could then catapult itself into the position of the world's number two in beer, and with the cash that its new breweries would produce, secure the future of the Bond business empire.

Conquest of Britain's largest brewer would also be a fitting moment for Alan Bond, the prodigal son, to return home. In Australia, he was now complaining, people were not sophisticated enough to appreciate what he and Bond Corporation had achieved. In Britain, he was sure, people would give him his due. He would return in triumph to the country he had left thirty-eight years before, and go back to his roots. It would not be to Federal Road, of course: the new Squire Bond would settle at Glympton along with his Lady. But before it could be brought to fruition, the master plan faced one small problem— all six foot three inches of him.

Bond first met Tiny Rowland in the Mediterranean in mid-1988, sometime during the northern summer. Whether by accident or design, the two had become neighbours in the harbour at Antibes in the South of France—on Billionaires' Row, where the largest and most vulgar motor yachts in the Mediterranean are moored. On Rowland's 164-foot yacht *Hansa* Tiny was relaxing with his wife and a couple of friends. Next door, on *Southern Cross III*—a mere 162 feet—Alan Bond was enjoying himself, according to Rowland, with a party of twenty-five to thirty people. Inevitably, in and around the jetty, their paths soon crossed, and before long Rowland was on board the *Southern Cross III*, and Bond on board the *Hansa* for drinks and a chat. They met thus on four or five occasions, but what they discussed is a matter of dispute. Bond said on oath in a London courtroom in 1989 that he talked in detail about buying Rowland's 15 per cent stake in Lonrho. Rowland, for his part, says this is nonsense: "Good God, no. He knew he wouldn't get anywhere doing that. Bond talked about himself, that's all he ever talked about. About how many bottles of beer his breweries produced, how big his goldmines were and what his empire was worth."

At the time, the two men clearly got on well. Rowland, for his part, says he liked Bond: there was obviously something of a father-son relationship about it. Apparently, there were even "bear hugs", no doubt initiated by the younger man. But at the next meeting in late September, at Rowland's English country home in Hertfordshire, things did not go so smoothly. According to Rowland, Bond telephoned on a Friday night and insisted that they meet, whereupon Rowland invited him down for lunch. Bond duly turned up with an "old friend of his mother", Miss Diana Bliss, more usually identified as Alan's long-time mistress. On this occasion, there was discussion about several joint ventures suggested by Bond—including the idea that Lonrho buy a share in Dallhold's Greenvale Nickel project—but the subject of shares also came up. In the course of the lunch, according to Rowland, Bond took Mrs Rowland aside and said to her that Tiny was getting on a bit and perhaps it would be a good idea if Bond took over the reins instead. Finally, the conversation turned to the question of Asher Edelman, a corporate raider who had acquired a small stake in Lonrho and looked dangerous. Bond asked whether he should buy shares in Lonrho to help keep Edelman at bay. Rowland says he told Bond that that would not be necessary, and says Bond then agreed to make no purchases without first getting the go-ahead.

Two days later, amid great secrecy, the raid began. On 26 September 1988 Bond instructed his London chief executive John Richardson to acquire a 4.9 per cent stake in the company—the most that he could buy without notifying the authorities that he was a shareholder. The following week the hush-hush Hawaii meeting was told by Bond that they would go for more. Alan Bond himself then lined up an American adviser, Barry Lepley, at Ocean Securities, to buy him a big parcel of shares, on which the ultimate outlay would be $735 million. It was vital that Rowland did not find out that his company had become a takeover target, vital too that others in the stock market didn't know, because they would instantly push up the price. People were thus informed on a need-to-know basis (or, as it turned out, were frequently *not* informed). The operation acquired a code-name: Project Bligh. The target was Bounty.

It was not till two weeks later that Lonrho first realised something was afoot: on 10 October a substantial shareholder notice was lodged with the London Stock Exchange revealing that Barlane Nominees, a company registered with American bankers Merrill Lynch, had built up a stake of more than 5 per cent in the company. The backers of Barlane were a mystery, but British company law allowed one to unmask them, and Lonrho promptly fired off a Section 212 notice to reveal their true identity. The answer came back sometime later bearing the name of Hurstmere, a Cook Islands-registered company, operating out of the first floor of a small white house in Rarotonga. Hurstmere, they were perhaps not surprised to discover, was a wholly-owned subsidiary of Bond Corporation.

Given Rowland's nature and his past form, one would hardly have expected him to sit quietly while Bond stole Lonrho from beneath him. But Tiny's own explanation of why he set out to crush the man is hilariously petty. In the harbour at Antibes on Billionaire's Row some sixteen yachts were moored, and Rowland's, being the biggest, had pride of place against the quay. Next door to Rowland was Robert Maxwell the newspaper magnate, then there was Gerald Ronson the British property tycoon, and out on the end of the string was Alan Bond and his *Southern Cross III*. As Rowland tells the story, after Bond had revealed himself as Lonrho's largest shareholder, Tiny was phoned from the South of France by his captain on the *Hansa* with a message that Mr Bond's captain wanted to know when the *Hansa* was going to be moved so that Bond could put his boat up against the quay—the implication being that as largest shareholder Bond should take over the parking space. Rowland was furious, the mooring was his: "It was so embarrassing. It's such a small community down there, everyone must have heard about it. It was then that I decided to destroy him."

By mid-October, Bond had built up a 20 per cent stake in his target company, as much as one could hold without making a full bid. And the fight began. His intention appeared to be to mount a proper takeover but, as with Bell, it was possible that he would try to gain control of the board, and thus the Lonrho chequebook, without going to the expense of buying everybody else's shares. Rowland and Bond together now commanded more than 35 per cent of the Lonrho stock, which, with Rowland's following, would be enough to take control of the company. But Alan Bond would first need Tiny's assistance and co-operation. On 20 October, he faxed Lonrho a letter containing this message:

Dear Tiny,

By now you will have been informed that we have acquired some shares in your company.

As a shareholder, and with a keen interest in your company, I wondered if it would be

> possible to meet with you in London at, say, 4.00 p.m. on Tuesday 1 November 1988. If this time is not suitable to you any time on that day would be acceptable.
>
> I trust you and your family are well.
>
>
> Kindest regards
>
>
> Alan

Lonrho waited until 1 November to reply, at which point the chairman wrote to say that 4.00 p.m. was not possible, but that Bond should put proposals in the form of a letter. Once again, then, Alan put pen to paper, saying inter alia:

> I would very much like to explain the background to our recent purchases of shares in Lonrho. Also, as your largest shareholder, I think it would be useful for both of us to follow up on our meeting of 24 September and to discuss how we might agree to take things forward to our mutual benefit and that of our respective shareholders.

Rowland himself then wrote a reply which was published on the front page of the business section of his own *Observer* newspaper, under the heading: Rowland Couldn't Give A XXXX. It was eloquent, waspish, and set the tone for future attacks, for it focused on Bond's financial weakness. It went, in part, like this:

Dear Alan,

No discourtesy is meant but it would be ridiculous to pretend that the Bond Corporation is anything other than a very acquisitive company which has rapidly become a large shareholder in Lonrho. It brings an end to informality.

The scale and initial secrecy of your share purchases indicate the hope of bidding for the whole, but you should inform your bankers that the Lonrho board will effectively oppose any offer which is regarded as unrealistic. We have looked at your accounts in depth and at the style and extent of funding. We don't think that the Bond Corporation can bring anything to Lonrho other than a need to sell our valuable assets to service your very large debts.

I'm sure it was an accidental implication of your letter that you and I should seek some personal mutual benefit—you don't know me very well, but you know I work for Lonrho.

Very kind regards, Yours Sincerely,

Tiny XXXX

Rowland was always favourite to win the public jousting, not least because he had his own newspaper on side. But the outcome of the real battle was more likely to depend on whether Bond Corporation could raise the £2000 million it needed to make a full takeover bid for the company. After all, there would almost certainly be some price at which even Rowland's loyal band of shareholders would take the shilling and join the opposing force. So it was to money-raising that Bond executives, Tony Oates and John Richardson, now put their efforts.

The initial shares had been bought on credit without any finance being in place, but while that was eventually remedied in November, filling a £2000 million war-chest proved far more difficult. There was no question that Bond Corporation was prepared to pay for its borrowings: prospective lenders would be lining up for fees of up to £7 million, and looking at a rate of 3 per cent over London Interbank Rate which, on a £2000 million loan, would produce an annual profit of £60 million. But bankers like Amex, Merrill Lynch, Banque Paribas, Rothschild and Shearson Lehmann, all of whom were canvassed at some stage, were hesitant nevertheless. Negotiations bogged down, and as Bond's executives tried to convince the bankers they should lend the money, Lonrho tried equally hard to persuade them that they shouldn't.

If one was minded to underestimate Lonrho, a visit to their offices in London's Cheapside might serve to confirm one's prejudice. To the Australian corporate raider it must have seemed like the British Establishment in all its outdated splendour. It was not so much the maps of Africa on all the walls, or the talk of breakfast in Nairobi, catching the night plane to Khartoum, and settling the details with the Chief—though it must be said these things gave Lonrho a certain imperial flavour. It was more the decor and decorum of the place that struck visitors. The sixth floor at Cheapside, where Lonrho's top management reside, had the quiet and comfortable atmosphere of a 1950s gentlemen's club or a Chelsea mansion flat: there were deep-piled carpets the colour of pea soup, on which sat deep-buttoned leather armchairs; the walls were panelled in wood. Behind old-fashioned wooden desks sat old-fashioned-looking gentlemen in old-fashioned dark pin-striped suits, which appeared to have been made to measure some years before and have since become slightly crumpled. Club ties were the order of the day. In the bookcase in the boardroom, there were volumes on salmon fishing, shooting and the like, and certainly nothing on junk bonds, leverage and discounted cash flow. There was, in other words, a less than dynamic atmosphere about it all. But appearances can be deceptive, for the defence that Lonrho now launched against Bond was quite brilliant.

Rowland's tactics were straightforward. Since the main issue was whether Bond would be able to raise the funds for an attack on Lonrho, it was decided to frighten the bankers by highlighting the financial weakness of Bond's empire. Lonrho's initial assessment had already told them that Bond was overburdened with debt and chronically short of cash. Now they set about a far more detailed investigation of the accounts. They collected a room full of press cuttings, logging and analysing each one; they then set their offices and contacts around the world to gathering documents relating to Bond Corporation's deals and finances. And with those in hand they began to pick the accounts apart and examine the figures in detail. Lonrho's own team, led by finance director Terry Robinson, did the bulk of the work. But merchant bankers, accountants and Bond's old rival, Robert Holmes à Court, all pitched in. The latter's contribution was to lend Lonrho the services of his personal assistant, Steve Johnston: he and Holmes à Court brought valuable information about the state of Bell, which Bond had taken over earlier in the year, and gave Lonrho a window into the state of Bond Corporation itself.

On the face of it, trying to destroy Bond's financial credibility was not a promising approach. The public perception of Bond was that he was at his peak. *Australian Business* had just assessed his personal net worth at $400 million, making him one of the richest of Australia's rich. He was in the process of buying Glympton, had picked up a host of other baubles, and was about to be revealed (a year after the event) as the purchaser of *Irises*. And as for his business empire, the rumours about him going bust had, for once, gone quiet. To the surprise of many, he had not fallen victim to the October Crash as others had done. Indeed, in its annual accounts for the year to June 1988, Bond Corporation had just brought in a record operating profit of $400 million, substantially more than its previous best. It was also boasting of "recession-proof cash flows and quality assets", and the message from the chairman, Alan Bond, was that his empire was stronger than ever. Brokers' reports from County Natwest, Morgan Stanley and Merrill Lynch among others told a similar tale: the shares were a good buy, the market was underrating the stock, Bond was rock solid. Some of the Australian press went even further: Bruce Stannard, an old acquaintance of Bond, who would later complain about inaccurate and biased reporting of Australia's business heroes, was moved in August 1988 to write in Australia's *Bulletin* magazine:

> Bond is not about to tumble. On the contrary, with the Holmes à Court empire and a portfolio of vast cashflow enterprises now (all but??) carefully locked in place, the indications are that Bond is founding a financial dynasty no less comprehensive and powerful than those carved out last century by the classic figures of American capitalism.

It did not take Lonrho long to produce a rather different picture. In mid-November, Terry Robinson's team came out with a 93-page analysis of the Bond Group, including the master private company Dallhold, which amounted to a blistering attack on Bond's accounting practices. According to Lonrho the accounts were essentially a lie: millions of dollars of advertising expenses had not been charged as expenses but had been put into the books as an asset, with the result that profits had been grossly overstated; notional foreign exchange gains, which had not yet been realised (and might never be) had been counted as profits from the normal run of business, while similar large losses had been treated in the opposite way; assets had not been revalued where market prices had fallen, thousands of millions of dollars were tied up in intangible assets that were of doubtful value—future tax benefits that might never be usable, licences that might be taken away, exploration expenditure that might never pay dividends, and masses of "goodwill".

But much more eye-catching than the pages of argument and supporting calculations was the verdict and the catchphrase that went with it: Bond, according to Lonrho, was the South Sea Bubble of Debt. Far from being on top of the world, the group, according to Lonrho, was technically insolvent—in other words, bust—and surviving only through the extraordinary support of its bankers, to whom the empire owed some $14,000 million gross. Were Bond and Dallhold to be split up and sold off, said Lonrho, there would be nothing left at the end except a pile of debts $3000 million high. Meanwhile, the problem was getting ever worse: cash was flowing out of the company at the rate of $500 million a year. And as for Bond's 1988 "profits" of $400 million, those, said Lonrho were a complete fiction: a truer version of events was that the group had made a $300 million loss.

The reaction from Alan Bond was that Lonrho's document was "amateurish and superficial" not worthy even of a reply. But privately, he was livid about the detail it contained, for someone had obviously gained access to inside information about the state of the company. Managing director Peter Beckwith, once he had recovered from his heart attack, let it be known that the analysis was "bullshit" and "billions out". But the document had already done its work: even if no one could follow the technical analysis that supported its conclusions, they understood full well what the allegations were, and they knew that Bond either would not or could not rebut them. At the very least, the seed of doubt about Bond's financial strength was now sown.

As the press had a field day with Lonrho's unchallenged suggestions that Bond was bust, negotiations with the bankers bogged down even further, and a long war of attrition between Bond and Lonrho began. This, for Bond, was defeat in itself: he had desperately needed a quick victory from his sortie into Lonrho so that he could turn his energies to other battles which were vital to his empire. The campaign was costing $2 million a week in interest and tying up another $700 million of funds that Bond Corporation sorely needed. There was also now the growing probability that the bankers would not put up the £2000 million Bond needed for a bid, and thus the danger that he would be locked into Lonrho for good. There would hardly be a rush of volunteers to buy Bond's shares and take over the fight with Tiny, so the stock would most likely have to be dumped at a substantial loss if it could be sold at all.

Even more significant was that Lonrho's financial analysis had undermined the foundations of the whole Bond empire. Bond Corporation was built entirely on debt, and while there was, as yet, no danger that Bond's existing bankers would pull their money out or demand repayment, banking was about confidence, as Bond had so often remarked. And confidence in Bond had suddenly been shaken. The key question that now needed to be answered was whether Lonrho's analysis was correct: for if it was even half right, Bond was in serious trouble. The empire's whole survival had suddenly been called into question.

CHAPTER 20

Dodgy Profits

Back in Australia, as the Lonrho stand-off continued, Bond's survival and reputation were being threatened by another battle, this time over the future of Bond's media empire. At the beginning of 1987 Bond had outlaid more than $1000 million to buy Kerry Packer's Channel Nine TV stations. The investment had proved a disaster in that the network was now both losing money and worth far less than Bond had paid for it. But, as 1989 began, an enquiry by the Australian Broadcasting Tribunal threatened to make matters considerably worse by declaring Alan Bond to be not a fit and proper person to hold a broadcasting licence. If the ABT were to bring down such a verdict, Bond would be forced to sell his Australian TV stations at a rock-bottom price. And given the problems elsewhere in Bond Corporation, the write-off of several hundred million dollars could be a crippling blow.

The ABT's enquiry related mainly to events in 1985 and 1986, before the Packer takeover had even taken place. Bond had purchased Brisbane's QTQ9 television station in Queensland, and had promptly paid $400,000 to settle an old defamation action brought by the state's Premier, the notorious and colourful Sir Joh Bjelke-Petersen. The station's *Today Tonight* show had ruffled the old man's feathers in 1983 by suggesting that Sir Joh had used his official position to procure a large loan for his son. An initial enquiry by the ABT in 1987 had concluded that the settlement was justified. But Alan Bond had then caused the whole affair to be reopened. Gazing into the deep blue eyes of Ms Jana Wendt on his own network's *A Current Affair* he had been moved to admit that the $400,000 pay-out had been made to Queensland's Premier because: "Sir Joh left no doubt that if we were going to continue to do business successfully in Queensland then he expected the matter to be resolved." Commercially, the decision to pay up made sense: $400,000 was nothing to Bond Corporation alongside its billion-dollar business interests in the state, and Sir Joh ruled Queensland as if it were his personal fiefdom. But TV licence holders were supposed to operate fearlessly in the pursuit of truth. Bribing premiers to keep them sweet, which was conceivably what Bond had done, was not meant to be on the agenda. And so the ABT's enquiry had recommenced.

The nub of the prosecution case, if it could be so termed, was that Bond had paid the Premier far more money than was warranted to settle the action. No defamation payment in Queensland had ever exceeded $40,000, and Bond had been told by lawyers for his insurers that he would win the case anyway. Even if Sir Joh were to secure victory in court, which the lawyers deemed unlikely, Bond was advised that damages would not be greater than $50,000. The case had lain dormant for two years, and the most that had been heard from Sir Joh's solicitors was an offer to settle for $30,000. Then Alan Bond had come on the scene, and had paid the Premier more than ten times that amount. It seemed clear that the only reason why he had done so was that it was the Premier who was asking for the money. Alan Bond had even admitted as much on his own network.

As the evidence to the ABT revealed, Sir Joh had at first demanded $1 million. Bond and Joh had then negotiated privately and had shaken hands on a figure of $400,000. One could argue the propriety of the payment, but it did not help Bond's case that he had concealed it. Not only had he kept the pay-out secret from the non-executive directors of QTQ9, his new TV station, but he had failed to inform the Australian Broadcasting Tribunal, even though his lawyers had told him he must. Even more to the point, the ever-resourceful Mr Bond had tried to persuade Sir Joh to accept a scheme whereby the size of the payment could be hidden. One of Bond's suggestions was that the payment should be made overseas where it would be far more difficult to trace: they could "make a big deal" on something that Sir Joh owned, which Bond could buy for an inflated price. Another was that they could call most of the payment a "loan"—one of that nice kind that did not have to be paid back.

Sir Joh had written to Bond after meeting with him, to set out what he had been offered:

You informed me that you now wish the sum of $400,000 to be paid rather differently from what is required by our agreement. You told me that you wish to pay me an initial payment of $50,000, with the balance of $350,000 being lent to me with no obligation to repay, or being the price of property which I would sell to you. I understand this proposal has been made because you will have difficulties with your insurers if you adhere to our agreement.

Sir Joh went on to say that he would have none of these arrangements and wanted cash on the table. But, two days later, the secretary of Bond's private company Dallhold had written back on Bond's behalf to explain why Alan wanted the payment covered up. It was clearly not just the insurers he was worried about.

Mr Bond...is not prepared to put both parties in a position where they will be exposed to allegations of improper conduct.
The advice we have received expresses grave concern and indicates that the proposed method of payment is fraught with danger.

The danger was quite clearly that if people like the ABT investigated they would find exactly what the ABT was now finding—that Bond had been told he could settle for $50,000, but had thought it prudent to slip the Premier an extra $350,000 to protect his other business interests.

The large sweetener to Sir Joh, if that's what the ABT decided it was, would probably be enough on its own to lose Bond his Channel Nine licences. But there was a second skeleton in Alan Bond's TV cabinet, which he was having difficulty in explaining away. It had come to the ABT's attention, through reports of another enquiry (by the National Companies and Securities Commission), that Alan Bond had threatened to use his Channel Nine TV staff to dig up dirt on a business opponent. The threat had been made to Leigh Hall, the investment manager of one of Australia's most-respected institutions, the Australian Mutual Provident Society.

The row between Bond and Leigh Hall had blown up in May 1988 when the AMP was standing between Bond and a large bag of money. Bond and Western Australia's State Government Insurance Commission (SGIC) were trying to get their hands on the cash reserves of Bell Resources, without making an offer to all shareholders. The AMP, as a shareholder left out of this cosy Western Australian deal, and faced with the prospect that its money might be squandered, had publicly demanded either that Bell's cash be returned to shareholders or that a proper takeover bid be made. Either demand threatened to prise Bond's grip off hundreds of millions of dollars which he needed for his business empire. And, according to Leigh Hall, Alan Bond was furious at the prospect. He rang Hall in Sydney and angrily abused him over the telephone, saying that if Hall did not back off, he would have his TV staff expose the AMP. Hall had immediately made notes of the conversation, and sent a memo to his colleagues. He was a credible and persuasive witness, and the Tribunal did not hesitate to accept his evidence.

By early 1989 as the hearings of the ABT dragged inexorably towards a conclusion, it was becoming increasingly clear that Bond would ultimately lose. There was some comfort for Bond in that the ABT had no history of doing anything difficult or dangerous: it was regarded as a toothless tiger. But the Tribunal's members did not like Bond or what he had done, and they now seemed determined to make a name for themselves. In March 1989, the ABT gave Bond early warning of what it "might" find against him: which was tantamount to revealing what it had already decided. Within a couple of months it seemed almost certain they would bring down findings of fact (as they later did)—that Bond had lied to the Tribunal, had attempted to conceal the $400,000 payment to Sir Joh, and had threatened Leigh Hall with exposure by his TV staff. The only question that then remained was whether the ABT would have the nerve to rule that Bond and his companies were unfit and improper persons to hold TV licences. If they did, the Broadcasting Act gave the Tribunal little choice but to take Bond's licences away. And, against the background of Bond's growing financial distress, that decision might well be enough to sink Bond Corporation.

By March 1989 it was already clear that Bond's bankers had rejected the £2000 million takeover of Lonrho, and Bond was staring at the prospect of a large capital loss. But if the bankers were now worried about throwing new debt onto the pile, there was still no suggestion from Bond's existing backers that they were worried. Nor was there any confirmation of Lonrho's conclusion that Bond was bust. A few Australian analysts had asked the question: Is Bond in Trouble? but most had answered with confidence that he was not. Bond's profits looked good, they argued, and the bankers were still happy, so things could not be too bad. Then, in March, two things happened to change that view: Australian Ratings, whose business it is to assess companies' credit worthiness, ran the ruler over Bond and downgraded the empire to a rating of B—which put Bond Corporation in the bottom two per cent of Australian companies. Next, ABC TV's *Four Corners*, after investigating Bond's business dealings for some months, produced a programme which demonstrated that half of Bond's "profits" weren't profits at all: they had been invented to keep bankers and shareholders happy.

Four Corners focused on two deals which between them had produced more than $150 million of Bond Corporation's 1988 net profits. The first was the "sale" of the Sydney Hilton, the second was a similar "sale" of some land in Rome. In both cases, the deals had been struck around the end of 1987, and the profit had ended up in companies in the Cook Islands. There, the profit was not liable for tax—which was important if no real money had been made. But, there too, with the Cook Islands' secrecy laws to protect them, full details of the transactions were impossible to obtain.

The Sydney Hilton sale was most puzzling in that no one seemed to know who had bought it. Even the management of Hilton Hotels Australia, who occupied the building, had no idea who the new owner was. They still paid rent to the same Bond company, Iwak, and still dealt with Bond Corporation's property division over renovations to the hotel, all of which led them to the conclusion that Bond had not sold the building at all. Hilton had a caveat on the property which required that Bond tell them of any transfer of title, but they had not been informed of any such transfer, and a check with the Titles Office revealed that the Bond company, Iwak, still owned it. The managing agents, Colliers, meanwhile said their lips were sealed, but no, they didn't know who had bought it, and yes, it was interesting wasn't it.

It was a serious matter if the sale had not been completed, for Bond Corporation had claimed an $80 million profit on the Hilton "sale", which was roughly a quarter of the group's profit for 1988. But there was yet more evidence that the hotel had not been sold. Bond's annual report to shareholders, two hundred pages thick, suggested that the $80 million profit had ended up in a Cook Islands company called Lawson Holdings. Lawson Holdings had apparently effected the Hilton sale by selling another Cook Islands company called Mossbark together with its Australian subsidiary, Iwak, the company that actually owned the Hilton building. But if this complex transaction had genuinely taken place, then Iwak would now have a new owner. And, according to Iwak's records, it did not: the company was still a subsidiary of Bond Corporation in March 1989, fifteen months after the supposed "sale" had been completed. Looking at Iwak's accounts, it was also clear that Bond Corporation had borrowed money against a mortgage on the Hilton building. This mortgage had been taken out by Iwak on 9 December 1987, when Bond was already supposedly selling the hotel, and was still outstanding fifteen months later.

The profit of $80 million had clearly been neither made nor received; of that there was not the slightest doubt. So *Four Corners* then asked Bond's finance director, Tony Oates, for an explanation:

> *Q*: Can I ask you a question? Who did you sell the Sydney Hilton to?
> *A*: An overseas corporation.
> *Q*: Who?
> *A*: I can't tell you.
> *Q*: Why not?
> *A*: Because I am not free to tell you, but it was sold to an international corporation operating in the business of owning international hotels.
> *Q*: Have you been paid for it?
> *A*: Partially.
> *Q*: How is it that Hilton are not aware that the building has been sold, or they don't know who it has been sold to, and Colliers the managing agents are also not aware who it has been sold to?
> *A*: Well, I am surprised you say that. Firstly, as I am sure you are aware, it is not unusual, particularly in property transactions of a major size, to have a deferred settlement. Secondly, I'm surprised that Hilton say that because, in fact, they are well aware who the owner is. Maybe you didn't ask the right person in Hilton. As to the agent, I can't answer that question. I mean, I just don't know. But it is well known by the management of the Hilton who the owner is.

Four Corners then double-checked with Hilton's management to be told again: "We absolutely have not been notified of any sale, and we do not know who owns it." Six months later, in September 1989, the story would be exactly the same, both at Hilton Australia and at the London head office of the parent company, Ladbrokes, who would still deny that any deal had taken place.

Immediately after the *Four Corners* programme, Bond identified a Singaporean businessman, Ong Beng Seng, as the phantom buyer. But Ong did not in fact complete the deal until November 1989, eight months after the broadcast, and two years after the "sale" had supposedly taken place. He would then pay less money than Bond had originally claimed to sell it for; he would deliver only part of the purchase price. And, most of all to the point, he would borrow all the money for the transaction from a Bond Group company. He would not put up a cent of it himself. So much for the near-$80 million "profit" claimed in December 1987.

But the Hilton mystery was only the half of it. The 1988 Bond accounts showed an even more doubtful deal, again producing a large profit in the Cook Islands, and again where neither the taxman nor anyone else could get a look at it. The deal involved 280 hectares of real estate on the autostrada just outside Rome, which Bond had bought in October 1987. Bond had imaginative plans to develop the site: there would be hypermarkets, hotels, a couple of golf courses and fancy houses, all based around Europe's largest distribution and warehousing centre. Huge trucks would drop off their loads for repacking into smaller trucks which would then deliver them into Rome's narrow streets. But even in 1989 the development was still at the dream stage: there were planning procedures to be negotiated and miles of red tape to be cut before any money would be flowing in. There was also opposition from locals and politicians which could conceivably prevent it from happening.

Bond claimed to have made $74 million profit within weeks of buying this Rome property. On paper, what he had done looked brilliant—Bond Corporation had bought the Porta di Roma project for $50 million one day, and then sold half of it two months later for $110 million, or more than double. But its very cleverness aroused suspicion. The property had supposedly quadrupled in value almost overnight. And, once again, the question that no one could answer was: Who had Bond sold it to? Who had paid this marvellous price?

Bond Corporation's 1988 accounts certainly did not reveal the buyer's identity, and nor did the accounts of Bond's Hong Kong company, Bond Corporation International. But when both sets of accounts were used to piece the jigsaw together, an extremely interesting picture emerged. Bond Corporation had sold the property, but Bond Corporation International had the option to buy it back before March 1989 and, what is more, might actually have an obligation to repurchase it. In other words, the deal was both reversible and quite likely to be reversed. And on that basis, a profit should certainly not have been recorded, because either the buyer or the seller could untie the deal at any moment (and thus rub out the "profit"). But the interesting question was why such a strange deal should have been made.

For three months, *Four Corners* tried to discover

the identity of the buyer, but without success. Then, fortuitously, they sent a team to Hong Kong at a time when Bond Corporation International was offering to buy out its minority shareholders. As part of this offer, Bond's Hong Kong company had been ordered by a Hong Kong court to make all material documents available for inspection. And there, on the list of documents that shareholders might inspect, were three that laid out the details of the Rome property transaction.

The first thing the documents revealed was that the "buyer" of the Rome land for $110 million was a Canberra-registered company called Kitool, whose net assets were just $2. The second was that "put and call" options were attached to the sale: Kitool had the right to sell the Rome property back to Bond for the price it had paid, plus all costs, fees, taxes and interest; Bond Corporation International, meanwhile, had a similar right to buy the property back at the original price. The third revelation was that Kitool appeared to be a front for an Australian company called Bisley—which was controlled by Alan Bond's and Laurie Connell's old friend, Brian Yuill. Bisley, according to the Hong Kong documents, had been paid a fee of no less than $20 million by Bond Corporation International for introducing the bogus buyer.

Looking at these documents there appeared to be no chance that Kitool, a company with just $2 to its name, could possibly complete the transaction; it was almost certain that the "sale" would ultimately have to be reversed. Far from making a profit of $74 million by selling the Rome property, as Bond's accounts had claimed, it therefore appeared that Bond shareholders had in fact lost $20 million.

It was a staggeringly bad deal for them, and they had also been grossly misled.

The first question was why had Bond done it—who wanted fake profits? But that was easily answered: the deal had been cooked up in December 1987, just two months after the October Crash. Bankers, shareholders and others were worried at the time about the health of companies like Bond, particularly since Rothwells had just needed rescuing. The $74 million profit from "selling" Rome to the obliging Mr Yuill was vital because it allowed Bond to report that everything was fine: profits had more than doubled when compared with the same period the previous year, the bankers could relax.

But the second question was how on earth Bond had got the transaction past his auditors. Here, the waters were much muddier, but in September 1988, Bond had engaged in a second series of transactions over the Rome property which had shuffled the put and call options into an "unrelated" company. These transactions had clearly satisfied the auditors that Bond had genuinely sold the property and that a profit could be claimed, but whether they should have done was another matter: *Four Corners* was assured by two top accountants, one an academic, Professor Bob Walker, the other one of Australia's top practitioners, Stuart Grant of Peat Marwick, that the "profit" should still not have been recorded in the 1988 accounts. And Bond Corporation's action after the programme went to air, which was to promise to wipe out the profit by booking a $74 million loss in the next accounting period, only served to reinforce that view. Bond's story, that the "sale" had fallen through because "unnecessary and inaccurate publicity" had made Kitool pull out, was hard to believe. Looking at Kitool's $2 worth of net assets it seemed abundantly clear that the "sale" had been a sham all along.

The Rome deal gave a dramatic insight into the quality of Bond Corporation's profits and the way that Alan Bond did business. But it also spotlighted the methods of Bond's old mate Brian Yuill. It had been Yuill's job to raise the $30 million which Kitool put up as a deposit to "buy" the Rome property, and he had been forced to employ a number of companies in his empire as borrowers. One of them, Tulloch Lodge, was well-known to the Australian racing public as the company that ran the stables of Sydney's leading racehorse trainer, Tommy Smith. Tulloch Lodge had been launched on the Australian Stock Exchange with a detailed prospectus which promised that its funds would be invested in blood-stock. But now shareholders unwittingly found they had lent $11 million to a shelf company, Kitool, to buy an overpriced piece of real estate on the other side of the world. Their $11 million, lent to a company whose total net worth was just $2, meant they had absolutely no security if things went awry.

One might ask how Brian Yuill had persuaded Tulloch Lodge's directors that this was a good idea. But the answer was that he hadn't: his fellow directors at Tulloch Lodge knew absolutely nothing about it. According to the company's board minutes, three of the Tulloch Lodge's directors had agreed in two separate meetings to borrow $13 million from the Bank of New Zealand and to lend $11 million of it on to Kitool. But the meetings had in fact never taken place. While the directors were supposedly authorising the $11 million loan to buy

Bond's Rome property, one director was skiing in
Thredbo, one was on his farm in Cootamundra, one
was sticking needles up horses' backsides, and one
was overseas. The only director in Sydney was the
ample figure of Brian Yuill, who was presumably
sitting in three seats at once. Indeed, the first his
fellow directors at Tulloch Lodge would hear about
the $11 million loan to Kitool was when they were
contacted one evening by *Four Corners*. Even then,
two of them thought that they were victims of a
practical joke; they were adamant that Tulloch
Lodge did not have $11 million, and were sure that,
if the money had been lent, the directors would
have been told. They clearly did not know how
Bond's friend Mr Yuill did business.

Brian Yuill and Tulloch Lodge, however, were just
a sideshow to the main drama. Far more important
were the reactions to the *Four Corners* revelations: on
almost every front these were a disaster for Bond.
The day after the programme, the Australian
Institute of Chartered Accountants announced an
investigation; so too did the Australian Stock
Exchange (although it was at first satisfied with the
most unsatisfactory replies to its enquiries); and so
too did the National Companies and Securities
Commission, which later claimed that it had been
investigating anyway. The newspapers went on to
fill their business pages for weeks with the strange
story of the Rome land deal and the mystery of
the Hilton "sale", while the financial columnists
pronounced that Bond had some fast explaining to
do, if he wanted to restore confidence.

The stock market, however, gave Bond a much
better reception: far from greeting the *Four Corners*
report with a wave of selling, the market pushed up

the price of Bond's shares. Bond's supporters suggested that the programme had said nothing new, that the ABC had been paid by Lonrho, and that the buoyancy of the share price demonstrated the real strength of Bond's finances. But the truth was rather different. Bond's shares were rising in price because someone was buying, and that someone was Alan Bond. The turnover figures for the month from 13 March when the *Four Corners* programme went to air, showed that fifteen million shares were traded on the Australian market. Quite conceivably Bond's friends were among the buyers, but Bond's private company, Dallhold, itself bought two-thirds of them. At a cost of $15 million to himself, or more probably his bankers, Bond was desperately trying to bolster confidence in his sagging empire. But even Bond's large-scale buying could not neutralise the next blow.

When Bond Corporation announced on 31 March 1989 that it was reversing its $74 million Rome profit, because the $2 company Kitool had found itself unaccountably short of cash, faith suddenly evaporated. Bond had never been highly-rated by the stock market because the company's profits were regarded as being of low quality—made on deals which might not be repeatable. Now there was a realisation that the profits might not be there at all, because the deals had not even been properly concluded the one time. Suddenly there came the dawning that perhaps Lonrho was right; perhaps the accounts could not be trusted; perhaps Bond really was insolvent.

Citing the *Four Corners* programme and the Lonrho analysis, Australian Ratings now downgraded Bond once again to CCC—the lowest rating for any Australian company and a clear warning to creditors that their money was at risk. No company had ever descended to such depths and risen again: corporations rated CCC had all either sunk into liquidation or disintegration. Shortly after, Baring Securities published a report pronouncing Bond's shares to be worth *minus* $5.65 each.

From here on began a horror period for Alan Bond and his companies. The next few months would see his share price collapse, and the Australian Broadcasting Tribunal declare him to be unfit to hold a television broadcasting licence. There would also be a growing public perception that Bond was finished. In May, *Australian Business* splashed on its front cover the dramatic headline: "The End of Bond Corp?" It was surely now not far away.

CHAPTER 21

A Billion-Dollar Killing

When the accounts of Bond's subsidiary, Bell Resources, were published in May 1989, the severity of Bond's financial problems suddenly became clear. The financial statements revealed that the Bond Group had raided Bell's coffers of some $800 million. Ten days later, Bond was forced to admit that it had helped itself to another $400 million of the company's money. Bell's unfortunate shareholders, locked into a situation where Bond had seized their chequebook, would be lucky if they ever saw any of their money again.

Technically, Bond's action appeared to be legal, in that the money had been borrowed at commercial rates of interest with the full approval of the Bell Resources board. But Bell's minority shareholders had neither been informed nor consulted, and the Bell board that had authorised the loan was made up entirely of Bond Group executives—Peter

Mitchell, Tony Oates and Alan Bond himself. There was thus considerable doubt about whose interests they had considered when they took the money. The second matter of concern for Bell shareholders, only discovered much later, was that their security for the loan was grossly inadequate: there were virtually no assets to rely on if the money was spent. The third, which was the most serious of all, was that, only six months after it had been taken, Bell's $1200 million had already disappeared into Bond's black hole.

Bond Corporation in fact now had no cash to make even the most minor of payments. On the first of May, Bond Corporation was due to pay a $34 million dividend to its shareholders, and all round the country people waited for the cheque to drop through their letter box. But they waited in vain, for the cheque never came. Ten days later, after shareholder complaints, the Australian Stock Exchange made enquiries, only to receive the incredible reply that Bond's managing director Peter Beckwith had decided the dividend should be paid at the end of the month, but had forgotten to tell anybody else. Given the extreme state of chaos that ruled in Bond Corporation, where, according to a British court judgement from Justice Browne-Wilkinson, no one except the four top executives had a clue what was going on, the excuse was just about plausible. But some days later, lightning struck again. Bell Resources, which was run by Bond, missed its dividend: Bond's excuse this time was that the computer had broken down.

In Hong Kong, by mid-1989, Bond Corporation was busy liquidating assets and pumping funds back home as fast as it could—another unmistakable sign of a chronic cash shortage. No sooner had a buyer been signed up for Bond's huge Hong Kong tower block in May than Bond was borrowing against the contract and despatching a "special dividend" back to the parent company in Perth. Bond's explanation for this unusual procedure was that it would be good for shareholders to get their money quickly, but it was far more likely that his own interests were the prime motive.

By now, cash was pouring out of the Bond empire at the rate of $2 million a day, and nothing could stop the flood. The only way that Bond Corporation could generate funds was to sell properties or companies for more than was borrowed against them, but everything in the empire was hocked to the limit. To complicate matters, the property boom had suddenly gone bust and prices had collapsed, so even if buildings and sites could be sold, hardly any cash would be produced. Hence had arisen the need for the raid on Bell Resources—the $1200 million had been the only thing that had kept the Bond Group alive so long.

Alan Bond had tried to get at the cash in Bell Resources from the moment he bought into Bell in May 1988. But for several months his hands were tied because he and his executives did not have control of the board. Bond had tried several times to persuade Bell Resources' general manager, Alan Newman (who was Holmes à Court's right-hand man), to steer cash in the direction of Bond Corporation, but Newman, with the full support of his board, had constantly refused, because he was horrified by what Bond wanted to do with the money. Among the schemes that Alan Bond had suggested was that Bell's cash should be deposited with his friend Brian Yuill's Spedley Securities—

a company that crashed in 1989, owing $1400 million.
There were also proposals for Bell to buy a variety of
Bond's shares and properties so that money could be
injected into Bond Corporation. And at one point,
Alan Bond even tried to bulldoze Bell into buying
his old mate Laurie Connell's Falcon business jet.

At $27 million, the plane was going to cost Bell
shareholders $4 million more than a new one—
perhaps because Laurie had had the interior gold-
plated, but also because there were interest bills
outstanding. Even more disturbing, the cheque was
to be made payable to Bond's private company
Dallhold, which seemed to Alan Newman to be
most improper. Newman therefore refused the deal,
on the grounds that Bell had a plane already, and
certainly did not need another one at that price. All
then went quiet. But on 29 June 1988, the day before
Dallhold needed to balance its books, and demonstrate to the auditors that all its money was in the
bank, Dallhold's finance director rang to say that he
was expecting a cheque for $27 million. When met
with incredulity and denials, Bond's man replied:
"Yes I am, Alan Bond told me it was coming." A
flurry of phone calls then ensued, in which
Dallhold's managing director, Michael Cross,
contacted the treasurer of Bell Resources and
allegedly said: "It's desperate. I need that cheque for
$27 million tomorrow."

As Newman and his board refused to part with
the money on this and all subsequent occasions,
Bond's executives then came up with a more radical
solution. In August 1988 they proposed that Bond
Corporation and Bell Resources be merged into one
company, so that Bond could get direct access to
Bell's sorely-needed cash. But this plan too came up

against at least one insurmountable obstacle in the form of Bond's own interests. The proposed reconstruction would have shrunk Alan Bond's personal holding in Bond Corporation to only 20 per cent, and forced him to give up control. And Alan, not surprisingly, refused. It was, perhaps, a measure of the Bond executives' desperation that they had suggested it in the first place.

The problems were resolved shortly after, however, in that control of the Bell Resources board was passed to Bond Corporation and the keys to Bell's safe placed in Bond's hands. Bell's poor minority shareholders now found their cash being handed over by the bucketful: Laurie Connell's lavish jet was acquired by Bell; so were two houses in Kensington's Cottesmore Gardens, where Alan Bond lived when he was in London; so was *Southern Cross III*, Alan Bond's $33 million Mediterranean-based runabout, and a ragbag of other assets. But even then Bond Corporation's hunger had not been satisfied, so eventually more money was "borrowed". Between October and December 1988, Bell's bank accounts were swept clean, and $700 million paid over to other companies in the Bond empire.

It is not difficult to understand why Bell's minority shareholders were never asked for their permission: the choice for them would have been between the absolute safety of a bank, where their funds could earn $170 million interest a year, and the dangers of lending it unsecured to an outfit with $10,000 million worth of debts, on its way to a rating of CCC. Alan Bond and his fellow directors had therefore helped themselves. Except for a slight difference in scale, it was like raiding the Christmas

Club and promising to pay it back later. But this was hardly petty cash, for the IOU would soon add up to $1200 million: $1200 million that the Bond Group would not be able to pay back.

Once the existence of this huge "loan" was made public, the stage was set for Bond's grand finale. In the months that followed, every plan for Alan Bond's escape would turn on whether he and his band of magicians could make the debt disappear. It seemed to be facing an impossible task: cash was still flooding out of the group, even without repaying the money to Bell, and liquidation of everything Bond Corporation owned would leave a $2000 million mountain of debt. Logic therefore suggested that the end had arrived. But Alan Bond would have none of it: he had not got to the top of the pile by panicking in a crisis. And now, in true style, he came up with a scheme. It was like 1975 all over again.

Bond's plan was to get rid of the debt to Bell, and a few others debts besides, by selling his Australian and American breweries to Bell Resources for $3500 million. No money would in fact change hands, because Bell Resources would take over $2300 million of the breweries' borrowings and settle the rest of the purchase price with the $1200 million that it had already "lent", but two of Bond's problems would nevertheless disappear. At the cost of giving up only half the breweries (since Bell Resources would still be half owned by Bond), Alan Bond's empire would repay the problem $1200 million, and also unload some of its massive debts onto Bell, which would then have to pay the interest.

There were, however, a number of snags to this deal, including one major one: the breweries were not worth anywhere near $3500 million. What's more, they weren't producing enough cash even to pay the interest on their existing debts of $2300 million, let alone to justify Bell parting with a whole lot more money to acquire them. Bell's unfortunate minority shareholders, who had seen their Christmas box raided, were therefore being asked to wave goodbye to their share of $1200 million by paying vastly over the odds for one of Bond's assets. It was all rather akin to the old pea-and-thimble trick. But, sadly for Bond, those shareholders of Bell knew it, as did the Australian Stock Exchange and the National Companies and Securities Commission. That Bond fell foul of the last body was a particularly unfortunate development; the NCSC already had strong views on the propriety of some of Mr Bond's business dealings.

Privately, some of the top people at the NCSC considered Alan Bond to be the biggest menace on the Australian corporate scene, a powerful accusation indeed, given that Brian Yuill and Laurie Connell were also contenders for the title. What is more, the NCSC was at that moment investigating Alan Bond in relation to another matter.

As part of its habitual Bond-watch, the NCSC had been monitoring people who bought shares in companies that Bond was making a move on. And one name kept coming up on its computers. There had been nothing particularly suspicious about Miss Bliss (beyond that the NCSC had found the name hard to believe) until she had suddenly struck lucky. By guile or good fortune she had bought half a million shares in an outfit called Petro Energy just before Bond Corporation had made a cash bid for the company. When the takeover offer had quite naturally sent her shares rocketing in price, Miss

Bliss had promptly sold her stake and picked up a tidy profit of $30,000. Miss Bliss may simply have been shrewd with her investment, but the NCSC's interest was aroused because she had done the deal through a broker whom the authorities already had their eyes on. The NCSC's investigators had therefore retrieved Miss Bliss's address from the broker's records, and checked who owned the house where she lived, whereupon they had found, to their immense surprise, that it was jointly owned by Diana Gwenyth Bliss and a fellow "investor" called Alan Bond. Mr Bond's signature on the title documents matched that in the Bond Corporation accounts and, sure enough, when the NCSC had made enquiries at the address, they had found that Alan Bond of Bond Corporation was a regular visitor.

When later questioned on his own network's *60 Minutes* programme, Alan Bond's explanation of his relationship with the delightful Diana was that Miss Bliss was an old friend of his mother—an answer which produced peals of mirth in several quarters, although in fact it was partly true. But as anyone who knew Bond personally could have testified, and as *60 Minutes* was surely aware (even before Bond objected strenuously to the interview being broadcast), Diana Bliss had long been Alan's mistress. They had bought their Victorian terrace house, aptly named "The Nest", in Sydney's fashionable Paddington back in 1986, when Bond had apparently produced the money for the purchase. But before that, they had shared a flat on the other side of Sydney Harbour. Despite Alan's protestations, there was no doubt that they were lovers, or that Alan treated her generously—he showered her with expensive jewellery, had bought her a

Mercedes Benz, and had signed over his half-share in the Paddington property, enabling Miss Bliss to make a profit of almost half a million dollars. But nor, on the other hand, was there a scrap of evidence that the couple were guilty of insider dealing.

As the NCSC soon discovered, if it did not already know, convicting either Miss Bliss or Mr Bond for insider dealing was an extremely tall order. It would not only need to prove that Diana Bliss had used inside information to make a profit on her shares, but would also have to prove that Alan Bond had given her the information about Petro Energy *intending* that a profit should be made. And, since they had no documentary evidence that anything like that had taken place, they were relying on a confession. Needless to say, Alan Bond vigorously denied the charges; and when Diana Bliss was questioned in Sydney by the NCSC, she apparently said nothing, or next to nothing, on legal advice. There the matter had ended, but with relations between Bond and the NCSC still sourer than before. Bond's private views of the NCSC were by now probably unprintable, but even his public ones were forthright enough.

> They make judgements outside the law. They make appalling statements on confidential matters. Everybody knows that the NCSC leaks like a sieve. It breaks all the requirements of confidentiality. One of these days someone is going to hang one on their nose over this lack of confidentiality.

It was with this background that the NCSC discovered that Bond had taken the $1200 million from Bell without full shareholders' consent; with this also that it was about to oversee Bond's proposed brewery sale for some $1000 million more than the breweries were worth. After some dithering, the NCSC decided to get tough. To demonstrate to the world that $3500 million was a fair price for the assets, Bond Corporation was required by the NCSC and the Stock Exchange to produce five years' audited accounts for both the Australian and the American breweries, together with two independent estimates of what the breweries were worth. The decision whether or not to buy the breweries would be in the hands of Bell's minority shareholders. Bond Corporation, which had a great interest in getting their approval, would not be allowed to vote.

Bond and his team baulked and complained for a month, arguing that all these reports would take ages, cost a fortune and be misleading anyway. They then threatened to take legal action, to drop the sale or to go ahead regardless. But when the NCSC and the Stock Exchange stood firm, Bond finally gave in and agreed to comply. The financial press promptly pronounced that the brewery sale was a dead duck because any reports would show that the breweries weren't worth what Bond wanted for them. Bond had to go back to the drawing board.

The next solution offered, in August 1989, was even more ingenious than the first. Since essentially the shareholders of Bell Resources were blocking the deal because they would not agree to pay $1000 million more for the breweries than they were worth, the obvious solution was to buy them out. If there were no longer any minority shareholders, there would no longer be any opposition to the deal; the brewery sale could then go ahead at any price. Bond therefore proposed that Bell's shareholders be bought out at $1.60 a share, or roughly twice the market price. This only left the business of how Bond would raise the necessary $400 million. Given that few banks in the world wanted to lend him anything, and given that no bank in the world would lend $1.60 to buy shares worth 80 cents, that scenario might have its problems. But Bond had already considered that. He had found someone who wanted the breweries badly—or, more precisely, who wanted Bond to keep them. Bond's biggest rival.

Carlton & United Breweries, which was controlled by the would-be Liberal Prime Minister of Australia, John Elliott, was extremely happy competing against Bond in the beer market. It had been beating Bond soundly, even when times were fairly good for Alan and his team. And with Bond now starved of cash, it foresaw an even easier life. What Australia's beer-market leader did not want was to be up against a major brewer like the USA's Anheuser-Busch, Japan's Kirin, or the UK's Allied Breweries, who might play a much harder game. So there now followed the touching sight of Carlton coming to Bond's rescue, with its chief John Elliott attempting to put together a consortium that would provide the money to take out Bell's minority share-holders. Even more heart-wrenching was John Elliott's plea that Bond had been much maligned, that he really was a Great Australian, and that people should get off his back.

Unfortunately, it was not long before snags appeared in this deal as well. The Trade Practices

Commission was bound to block any scheme that included Carlton owning part of its only Australian rival—seemingly an inevitable consequence of Elliott helping to fund the breweries' sale. So Version Two of Bond's escape plan appeared to have little more chance of success than Version One. But, undaunted, Bond duly came up with Version Three. On the face of it, this one was a much better gambit, even if it was infinitely more complicated. It introduced a new buyer to the game in the form of the New Zealand brewer Lion Nathan, and a yet more ingenious solution. The brewery price of $3500 million would stay, but, as in Version Two, Bell's shareholders would all be bought out at $1.60 a share, and so wouldn't object to paying over the odds. Lion Nathan, meanwhile, would pick up half the breweries from Bell at a considerable discount. And here came the sting: Lion Nathan would "earn" its discount by putting up funds for Bond Corporation to buy out its debtors.

Bond's ingenious escape plan now depended on persuading various European and American bankers and investors to settle for half what the Bond empire owed them. There was some $1200 million worth of convertible bonds around the world which had been issued by Bell Resources and Bond Brewing. The bonds were trading in the market at around 40 per cent of their face value, for the simple reason that many people expected Alan Bond's empire to go bust before they were due for repayment. And Bond now planned to make their holders what he thought was an irresistible offer: settle for 50 cents in the dollar now or watch Bond Corporation sink beneath the waves and get nothing at all. It was an offer remarkable for its cheek, because Bond Corporation was planning to renege on its debts. In Europe, it was greeted with derision and anger; some suggested it would give all Australian companies a bad name in the world's financial markets for years to come. But no one need have worried, for not only did Lion Nathan not appear to have the necessary funds to complete the deal, the NCSC was not happy, and nor was the Western Australian State Government Insurance Commission (who indirectly owned shares in Bell Resources but were not being bought out). And that was just the start of the problems: the incredible complexity of the transactions, and the way in which each of the steps relied on all the others, simply made success most improbable. This duck now looked as dead as any of the others.

But even if life were breathed into the corpse, it still seemed unlikely that the deal could work the miracle Bond needed. The Lion Nathan agreement envisaged deferring purchase of the American breweries (at $1000 million of the $3500 million) for a year so there would no longer be enough to repay the $1200 million Bond had taken from Bell. Nor would there be much of value left in the rump of Bond Corporation. Since the breweries basically provided the cash that paid Bond's huge interest bill (or in fact no longer paid it), the Bond empire without the breweries would be in far greater trouble than before; there would be virtually nothing but debts. It therefore began to look as though the collapse was exceedingly close, and all that Bond could do was delay it.

But delay it he would. There would eventually be half-a-dozen versions of the Great Brewery Sale, and half-a-dozen extensions to the deadline. While this deal was still a possibility, Bond would not be forced to repay the missing $1200 million, because Bell's shareholders would always be about to be asked whether they wanted their money back or whether they wanted to buy the breweries instead. In this way, Bond had bought himself time, and with time, anything could happen. He might even wriggle off the hook.

CHAPTER 22

The Black Hole

On 10 October 1989 Bond Corporation's shares plunged to an eleven-year low of 23 cents—their lowest value since the dark days of 1978. The Australian Stock Exchange intervened to stop the rout, banning any further short-selling of the shares, but that did not prevent the carnage. The market was suddenly gripped by the fear that Bond Corporation would be delisted if the company's preliminary figures for 1989, which were already overdue, were not published by 23 October. Delisting of the shares would not only trigger default clauses in several of Bond's loan agreements, it could also bring about the complete collapse of the Bond Group if the bankers called in their loans. The next day in London, on Wednesday 11 October, there were strong rumours that the Bond empire would go bust on the morrow. But Thursday came and went, and Bond was still standing.

The accounts were delayed, according to Alan Bond, because the NCSC had tied up his top executives and Bond Group's accountants with constant enquiries. But this was merely the excuse: as Alan Bond knew full well, the real reason why the results were so late was that a pitched battle was taking place in Perth between Bond Corporation and its auditors, Arthur Andersen. Other unofficial valuers had already reached the conclusion that the Bond empire was worthless and had questioned its solvency. Now, if Bond was to survive, it had to persuade its auditors to take a more optimistic view.

That was proving difficult: in the first place the facts inevitably pointed to the conclusion that Bond was as good as gone; in the second, there was a compelling reason why Arthur Andersen should give the figures a cold hard stare. In September 1974, during a similar credit squeeze and property market collapse, when Bond himself had so nearly gone under, a finance company called Cambridge Credit had crashed with debts of $180 million. Yet just two weeks before the company's demise, the accounts had proclaimed an increase in profits and talked confidently of the future. Remarkably, Cambridge Credit's auditors, Fell & Starkey, had at the time given the accounts a clean bill of health, despite the appalling trouble the company was in. In the aftermath of the crash, Cambridge Credit's angry creditors had taken the auditors to court, sued them for negligence and won $145 million in damages.

For almost three years, Fell & Starkey's thirty partners had faced the prospect of ruin: it seemed clear that they would be forced to sell their houses and everything else they owned to pay the bill. And even those who had been on holiday at the time and had played no part in the Cambridge Credit audit had shared the common fate for, as partners, they were deemed to be jointly liable. Then, to their immense relief they had been spared: the Appeal Court had overturned the award, and a much smaller negotiated settlement of $19.5 million had been reached—which was a sum quite probably covered by their insurers.

Fell & Starkey's partners had been reprieved after several years under sentence. But with their narrow escape as a precedent, Arthur Andersen was certainly not going to let itself be blinded by Bond's Blizzard of Hope. Indeed, the auditors had already flown in a team equipped with special snow glasses.

The huge international accounting firm of Arthur Andersen employs five directors whom it can send at a moment's notice anywhere in the world, to give advice in difficult situations. Normally, one per continent is enough to iron out even the toughest problems, but the Bond audit had attracted three of these troubleshooters, who had flown in to Perth to thrash out the issues and give a helping hand. Their man in Perth, Terry Underwood, was himself tough and experienced, one of the firm's top audit partners. But he and his partners now had plenty to worry about, because the firm's audit of Bond's 1988 accounts had arguably blotted their copybook already. There were several "profits" in those 1988 accounts of a rather dubious nature, such as the ones derived from the "sale" of the Sydney Hilton, the "sale" of the Rome land, and the remarkably similar "sale" of Perth's Emu Brewery site, which came in total to some $200 million. There was also a considerable amount of expenditure that had not been charged as an expense but had been deferred, and arguably should not have been.

Certainly, the Institute of Chartered Accountants in Australia had been less than impressed with Arthur Andersen's work. Following the *Four Corners* report, the Institute had asked a "senior non-practising accountant" to investigate whether Bond's 1988 accounts complied with Australian accounting standards; his conclusion was that they did not. Even more worrying, perhaps, was the fact that the NCSC was making threatening noises—it had also investigated Bond's figures for 1988 and now questioned whether they had shown a "true and fair view" of the company's financial situation. The opinion of the NCSC's investigators was that the accounts were both false and misleading.

The NCSC had by this time called in the men from Arthur Andersen for a chat and told them in no uncertain terms that the 1989 accounts should be done a great deal better. This reading of the Riot Act obviously had an effect, as not only did Arthur Andersen strengthen its audit team for the new battle with Bond, but it now went about its task with great rigour. When the results eventually appeared, it was an utterly different picture from the previous year. The only good news for Bond supporters was that the figures made it to the Stock Exchange before the October deadline expired: thus, default and disaster were for a time avoided. But the rest of the news was all bad, as the results themselves were quite awful.

Not only did they show that Bond Corporation had made a loss in the year to June 1989 of $980 million—by far the biggest in Australian corporate history—but they revealed a doubling of Bond's

annual gross interest bill to around $1000 million.
Even more to the point, they implied that Bond
Corporation had a negative net worth of more than
$100 million, which was to say that if everything
were sold off, there would still be $100 million in
debts. The future of Bond and Bond Corporation
was thus now hanging by a thread, and the reaction
of the stock markets could be critical. A plunge in
the share price when the markets opened up for
business could be enough to send Bond and his
companies crashing into the abyss. The logic of
Bond's implied $100 million deficiency was that the
company's shares were worthless.

But at least there were two days for things to cool
down. Bond had cleverly announced the catas-
trophic loss late on Friday 20 October, after the
Australian stock markets had closed for business, in
the hope that panic would thereby be avoided. And
with a whole weekend to build his defences, Alan
Bond now played the media to his advantage. He
invited two of Australia's more influential journalists in for an exclusive interview, whereby he would
tell the waiting world that everything was going to
be fine.

It was a stunning interview for what it revealed
about Alan Bond and his ability to believe his own
sales talk; it was stunning too because of the way in
which the journalists, from the *Sydney Morning
Herald*, glossed over Bond's financial predicament.
Bond was essentially given an opportunity to
expound his fanciful version of the future, and to do
so almost unchallenged. His message was that he
would survive this little local difficulty and push on
to even better things:

The man you find bouncing round an office high above the Perth skyline is apparently fit, vibrant and brimming with optimism. Rather than slumping into self-pity the irrepressible Alan Bond wants to talk about billion-dollar deals five, or even ten years down the track.

Not only is he far from finished, he says, but in a few years his companies will be bigger and better than ever. Will Bondy survive? That is probably the most-asked question in Australian financial circles today. Well, he is convinced he will, and so are the writers of this article.

Quite how the authors had come to that conclusion was hard to see. They apparently had not asked Mr Bond whether his companies were still solvent or whether the banks would now call in their loans. Nor, it seemed, had they enquired whether his over-paid executives should be asked by shareholders to pay for the disaster with their jobs. But perhaps the unreality of Bond's view of his prospects had unsettled them, for Alan Bond certainly seemed to have no concept of the mess his empire was in. He was prepared to concede that there might be lean times ahead and that the Bond Corporation would be slimmer in the future, but he was sure that the boring business of dieting would not last more than a few months. And after that, he was happy to tell them, it would all be back to normal:

Alan Bond is above all a salesman, and he soon leaps away to his sample bag. Suddenly, the Perth office is transformed into Ali Baba's cave, his audience is swept away on a magical mystery tour of Italy, Hungary, South America, and up to the clouds to the coming television satellite battle with Rupert Murdoch in the skies above Britain. His listeners find themselves entranced by the glittering cavalcade of deals laid out before them. Would you buy a used car from this man? Most of us would pay up without even checking if it had four wheels. Just how the banks came to lend him all that money is very plain. The master salesman became a master borrower by building a world glittering with magic and glamour in drab banking chambers on four continents.

Accompanying the breathless prose was an heroic picture of Alan and his managing director, Peter Beckwith, staring like Roman statues into a prosperous future. It was as if they had just carved out a triumphant $1000 million profit for Bond Corporation, instead of staggering to a $1000 million loss. Never mind that it was hopeless gush, it was through such pictures and prose that the whole adoring myth about Alan Bond had been created in the first place.

Bond followed his success with the *Sydney Morning Herald* with television interviews for Channel Nine's *Business Sunday*, and the Monday morning talk shows, where he repeated his patter that Bond Corporation might be suffering a temporary setback but that a billion down the drain was really nothing to worry about. And clearly his bravado must have impressed somebody for, come Monday 10 a.m., when the markets opened, Bond's share price stayed rock steady. It was true that there were no longer any institutional investors left in Bond to dump the shares, and true also that the Stock Exchange had outlawed short-selling of Bond's paper, the effect of which was to prevent any action there. But it was a mystery why the Mums and Dads did not get out now. Either someone was in there buying for Bond again to keep the price up or, more likely, their faith in Alan Bond just knew no bounds.

Although another share-price collapse had been avoided, Bond's troubles were not yet over. There was another deadline to meet, just a week away, by which time the final audited accounts were supposed to be filed with the Stock Exchange. More importantly, there was the question of whether the $980 million loss marked the full extent of the damage. Bond and Beckwith had been confidently telling interviewers that all the bad news had now been published, that all the losses had been "taken on the chin". But it was clear that the real punches were still to come. It was almost certain that the auditors were now asking for massive write-downs of Bond's overvalued assets—the loss-making American breweries, for example—to bring things into line with what they would fetch in the market. If the auditors now played really tough, as it seemed they would, the Bond Group would not just have a negative net worth of $100 million, it would be nearer $2000 million short of what it needed to repay its bankers. The solvency of the whole Bond empire would then have to be called into question.

And, sure enough, it was. When the Bond Group

accounts were finally published in mid-November, the auditors declared that the Bond Group was surviving only by courtesy of its bankers, whose continued support would be needed if the group were to pull through. They then went even further: there was a reconstruction programme under way, said the auditors, which Bond's directors believed would solve the problems. But for their part, the auditors were not convinced it would. There was therefore "some doubt" that the Bond Group would be able to continue as a going concern. Some doubt, in other words, that it could last much longer. But that was not the end of it.

The auditors of a company are required by law to state whether the accounts give a "true and fair view" of the company's finances, or in other words, to certify that you can trust the picture painted therein. The "auditors' report" is normally just a formality and usually dispensed with in a couple of lines. But in Bond's case, the qualifications stretched to four pages and set out the longest list of financial health warnings anyone had ever seen. At the end of it all, the auditors concluded that they could *not* certify that the accounts showed a true and fair view: there was far too much uncertainty about the value of Bond's assets and about its ability to carry on.

In laymen's terms, the audit report said that some $2000 million of Bond's assets were of questionable value. There was doubt, for example, over whether *any* of the $250 million that Bond Corporation had invested in the doomed petrochemical plant could be recovered—even though the directors had said it would be. There was doubt whether Bond could escape paying $170 million to Western Australia's State Government Insurance Commission to compensate the SGIC for losses on its Bell Group shares—even though the Bond directors said that court action would let them off. There was doubt whether the Emu Brewery site could be sold for $200 million (half that figure seemed more likely), even though the directors said it could. And on it went: there were doubts about Bond's broadcasting licences being worth $1000 million, and even greater doubts about the value of the American breweries, where $600 million appeared to have gone for good. There was even uncertainty about Heileman's ability to continue in business—since it was losing money and would not be able to pay its loan instalments in 1990.

All in all, it was a litany of doom and gloom, and after reading it no one could say they hadn't been warned—which was probably the effect the accountants had aimed at. But there was even more to come. Bond had told people in June that the empire had halved its debts. Yet the balance sheet now showed them to be more than $8500 million, far larger even than the previous year. More to the point, it showed that $3600 million of those debts were now due for repayment within twelve months, yet Bond Corporation was still losing money. One can get a rough indication that a company is insolvent when its current liabilities exceed its current assets. In the case of the Bond Group, the difference was $1400 million. Subtracting the empire's immediate debts from the money it could lay its hands on, it was that far in the red.

Despite all this, Alan Bond did not appear to be worried. He seemed certain that he could bluff his way through yet again. On the day that the preliminary results had been published, Alan had been having lunch in the Mediterranean restaurant, where more Dom Perignon is consumed than in any other establishment in Australia. According to fellow diners, Bond was on top form, treating his company's disastrous figures as a terrific joke, telling all and sundry to read the next day's papers to find out that his losses were the biggest in Australian history.

That night he and his new friend Tracey, a twenty-six year old air hostess, had gone off to Racquets nightclub in Perth, and partied till the small hours. As one of Tracey's friends had remarked: surely Alan couldn't be bust—he had just bought his young girlfriend a house and a new mink coat.

CHAPTER 23

The Banks
Bite Back

To rework an old saying: if you borrow $10,000 from the bank and can't pay it back, you have a problem; if you borrow $10,000 million from the bank and you can't pay it back, your name is Alan Bond and well, you can guess the rest of it. Towards the end of 1989, a host of Australian, American and Asian banks who had lent millions of dollars to Bond's public and private companies faced massive problems in getting their money out. Making sure they got all of it back would prove to be even more difficult. The banks had largely themselves to blame for their plight, for they had bought Bond's promises, sometimes not once, but twice. "I don't know how many times I heard bankers say in the 1970s that they would never lend to that man Bond again as long as they lived," says one financier, recalling 1975, "but there were plenty of them, and lots of them broke their vows."

The bankers had lent their billions on a ragbag of assets whose earnings would not pay the interest bill and whose realisable value was considerably less than Bond had borrowed against them. Now they were left holding vast amounts of Bond debt, often without adequate security, and sometimes with no security at all: in some cases they had even lent twice against the same asset. As they now contemplated their multi-million dollar losses, one could only ask what they thought they had all been playing at. But perhaps they were wondering the same thing themselves.

There is no doubt that a major cause of the banks' recklessness had been plain greed. High fees, fat profits and foolish optimism had combined to make the bankers a soft touch. But it owed something, too, to the deregulation of Australia's financial markets which had taken place in 1984. Not only had deregulation scrapped most of the controls that held irresponsible lending in check, but it had doubled the number of banks in the market so that after 1984, three dozen banks were fighting for business adequate to feed only half that number. In such a cut-throat climate, two things had happened: the banks had been forced to become less fussy about whom they lent to, and the style of their lending had been dictated by the most rapacious among them. Just as a petrol station has to cut prices if the garage over the road knocks a few cents off a litre, so the big banks had been forced to match the terms that their rivals were offering. The old conservative financing practices had thus been replaced by Negative Pledge, or Non-Recourse Lending. As a consequence, come late 1989, loans to Bond were often unsecured (so that there was nothing the banks could seize and sell), or "quarantined" from the assets in the rest of the group. Now, with Bond in deep trouble, the banks often had rights only to the *income* produced by the assets they had lent against. And since Bond was in strife, that income, almost by definition, was insufficient to pay their bills.

As salvation for the banks could come only if the Bond empire sold its assets at a decent price, the bankers now tried their best to keep quiet about Bond's financial problems. All were bravely saying there was no problem and things were fine: "We are comfortable with our exposure," went the jargon. But in private they were trying their hardest to get Bond to give them their money back. Already, the banks had given notice that they would not roll over their debts when they came due and, as a result, virtually everything in Bond Corp was under the hammer. Bond Tower in Hong Kong had already gone, Bond headquarters in Perth was going, the new Bond building in Sydney was going too if a buyer could be found. The toys were also up for sale: the schooner *XXXX* and *Southern Cross III* were both up for grabs, as was the English country estate at Glympton (finally sold at a huge loss). Even Van Gogh's *Irises* was on offer.

According to Bond's directors, an orderly liquidation of the Bond Group was already under way, so the banks did not need to take action. But in reality Bond had no intention of selling up everything. He had presented a survival plan to his bankers which would leave him with half of Bond Media, half the Chile Telephone Company, half the Australian breweries, all of Heileman, and all of Bell Publishing. In Alan Bond's ever-optimistic view, he had only to complete the brewery sale and there would be blue skies ahead: his corporate planning department had produced a huge volume of figures and calculations with a host of red and green glossy graphs that pointed inexorably skywards. The future for a restructured Bond Corporation, according to this version, would see huge profits, healthy cash flows, a rising stock price and an asset value of $4.50 to underpin each share.

Bond's picture of the future, however, had been painted by the fairies; the valuations of Bond Media and Heileman were outrageously generous; the cash flow and market share from the breweries already hopelessly below target; and it was all built on hope in any case. To get there, Bond would, among other things, need to persuade the holders of some $1500 million of convertible bonds to settle for half their money or less, and then would have to charm his bankers into lending a new $800 million on the brewing joint venture. The future could thus only be reached via the goodwill of Bond's bankers and, as a more sensitive person would have realised, there was no future—the bankers had had enough of Alan Bond and his antics.

By October 1989, the chairman of National Australia Bank, Nobby Clarke, had told Alan Bond to his face that the NAB had completely lost confidence in Bond Corporation. And this was no small problem, because Nobby Clarke headed a syndicate of sixteen bankers who had lent $800 million to Bond Brewing. These banks had good reason to be fed up, for Bond had broken their loan agreements. They had suspected as early as May 1989 that such was the case, and had started to ask detailed questions of Bond's executives about the whereabouts of some $200 million. But two months of argument had failed to bring satisfaction, and had led to the bankers putting their own accountant in to investigate the company.

Six weeks later, the banks' representative, David Crawford, was reporting that Bond Brewing had been raided for cash by other companies in the Bond empire. Millions of dollars had been "upstreamed" or "sidestreamed"—which, in simple language, meant passed over to Bond Corporation and other Bond Group subsidiaries. According to the sworn evidence of a senior NAB executive, during 1989 the bank accounts of Bond Brewing had been frequently swept clean, and surplus cash had been fed into Bond Group's central treasury. Money had been removed from Bond Brewing, in just the same way as it had earlier been lifted from Bell Resources: as Justice Browne-Wilkinson had observed in London's High Court in July 1989, finding cash in the Bond Group appeared to be a matter of "putting your hand into whatever till was available". According to the bankers, at least $160 million had on this occasion been taken from Bond Brewing. There were other breaches too, including the mortgaging of assets to other lenders—but the missing money was the worst infringement.

Though angry, the bankers had at first agreed not to declare a default or demand their money back—provided Bond promised not to breach the agreements again, and provided that he started repaying the funds. They had insisted, too, that David Crawford be allowed in to monitor the company on a day-to-day basis and to make further investigations. But only two weeks after this settlement in mid-November, a further report from Crawford changed the bankers' minds. The first message it contained was that Bond Brewing had lost market share and would probably be unable to pay all the interest due to the syndicate over the coming year; the second was that the breaches were more serious even than the bankers had thought, in that many of the millions (such as $40 million pledged on the notorious Emu Brewery deal), were almost certainly lost.

There was also one breach that made the bankers quite furious: Crawford's investigations revealed that the "cash" in Bond Brewing's balance sheet included $119 million owed to the company by Singapore businessman Ong Beng Seng, the phantom buyer of the Sydney Hilton. Ong had finally completed the purchase of the famous hotel two years after Alan Bond had announced its sale, but had clearly driven a hard bargain—almost all the funds that Ong had paid for the Hilton, and quite possibly the whole lot, had been provided by Bond to enable him to go ahead with the deal. Bond Brewing now had $119 million of its money lent to the mysterious Mr Ong, who apparently had no duty to repay the loan until he had sold the hotel to somebody else. Meanwhile, despite the hotel's sale, Bond Brewing was paying for the Hilton to be refurbished and even paying the mortgage every month. It was a scandalous state of affairs, especially since Bond Brewing only ranked third in the queue for any eventual payout from the Hilton's disposal, so there would quite probably not be enough for the debt to be repaid. But as if all that were not enough, the funds had been lent via the Cook Islands where a fee of $16 million appeared to have stopped off at the European Pacific Banking Group—which was another name for the white house in Rarotonga and the embarrassed New Zealander, Trevor Clarke.

Quite what, or perhaps who, the $16 million was for
was not immediately clear. But the real story of what
was going on was opaque. It was, as Justice Beach
would observe in the Victorian Supreme Court, an
extraordinarily complex tale:

> The Ong transaction is one of the more myste-
> rious transactions I have been called upon to
> investigate during the course of my legal
> career. In some respects it has been like deal-
> ing simultaneously with a slippery eel and a
> very large and active octopus. I fear that a full
> investigation of the transaction or multiplicity
> of transactions will ultimately take some
> unfortunate member of the judiciary a consid-
> erable period of time.

The banks, however, did not need to grasp the
precise details of Mr Ong and the $119 million to
know that they didn't like the deal at all, or to be
convinced that Bond executives had deceived them.
They now decided they would like their money
back once and for all. On 7 December 1989, the
syndicate took the first step towards calling its $800
million loan, by issuing a notice of breaches that
Bond would have to rectify within fifteen days or
face immediate default. On 12 December, they
issued another notice listing more violations of the
agreement, and then a third on 13 December. Then,
having set the time bomb, they sat back to wait.
Now only loss of nerve by the bankers or money
from Bond could prevent the explosion, and Bond
had long ago run out of funds. Doubtless he was

praying for a miracle sale of the breweries, but it was seven months now since the first sale had supposedly been tied up. The clock was ticking away. On the stock market, Bond's shares were now so low that you could buy the whole of Bond Corporation for less than the price of a famous Van Gogh painting.

In the meantime, other Bond creditors were already racing to do the bankers' job for them. John Spalvins' Adsteam group had bought a large parcel of Bell Resources shares in 1988, only to see $1200 million removed from the company and Bell's share price collapse. Now, after months of negotiations, Spalvins was fed up with waiting for return of his money or for Bond to offer a satisfactory alternative. He was also worried that cash was still being siphoned out of Bell—which indeed it was, to the tune of another $300 million since June 1989—and so petitioned for a receiver to be appointed to protect Bell's assets. The court case duly began in Perth, and Bond's dirty linen, including details of how Bell's money had been taken, was hung out for all to see. Perhaps realising the jig was up, Bond quickly stopped dancing and agreed to settle: Spalvins and Bond would split control of the Bell board between them, and in exchange, the receivership action would be dropped.

But the threat to Bond was still not removed. The National Companies and Securities Commission was concerned that Bond and Spalvins could make deals that would disadvantage other Bell Resources shareholders, and promptly announced it would petition for the receiver instead. Once again, the parties went into a huddle and a new compromise was reached. Under the threat of NCSC action,

Bond now lost control of the Bell Resources board. Three new independent directors were appointed who would act in the interests of all Bell shareholders, thus making it much harder for Bond to shuffle off the breweries for more money than they were worth. It would also be harder now for any last-minute escape plan to work.

There was soon a guide to how the new Bell board would proceed. At the company's annual general meeting only a week later, the new directors dissociated themselves from the "totally unacceptable" state of affairs that Bell's accounts revealed and promised investigations into the whereabouts of the money that had been taken. They also warned that legal action would be taken to recover it, if necessary. They held out little hope of the $1200 million being repaid. And, as the new chairman Geoff Hill pointed out, you did not need to be Einstein to realise that total loss would be devastating to shareholders since it amounted to all the funds in the company. It was an angry meeting that this new team addressed, and there was no doubt who had roused the shareholders' ire. A proposal to re-elect Bond's man Peter Mitchell to the board met overwhelming opposition from the floor, even though the Bond block vote then proceeded to push it through. And Alan Bond himself was continually attacked. He had told them that their $1200 million was safe, that the company was on the threshold of an exciting new era, that prudence, wisdom and optimism would guide its actions. And perhaps he even believed it, for, as the shareholders savaged him, he seemed not to understand why. Writing in the *Sydney Morning Herald*, Robert Haupt wryly observed:

There was hurt on the face of the old salesman. He might still have had a shoeshine, but the smile had gone out.

The meeting didn't want Alan Bond and it didn't want his nominee. It didn't want his strategy and it didn't want his deals. It didn't want to sell the things that he wanted to sell, and didn't want to buy the things—breweries, optimism—he wanted it to buy. It didn't want his explanations. What did it want? It wanted its money back.

This, it also became clear, was the one thing that Alan Bond may not be able to give them.

Even as Bond spoke, 3000 kilometres away in Sydney the knife was being sharpened for the killer thrust: the NAB and its fellow bankers were deciding to apply for a receiver to Bond Brewing. Bell's shareholders had been told by their new chairman that a receiver for the breweries would spell disaster for them because it would snatch out of their hands any chance of a deal to save their $1200 million. But the banks had made up their minds. The 22 December deadline for repairing the breaches to the loan agreement had almost arrived and the default had not been mended. It was now just a matter of when they would demand their money. With Christmas coming, it might look uncharitable to plunge the blade in the season of good cheer; but they would call in the loans on 28 December, and go to the courts for a receiver in the New Year.

Eileen Bond told the newspapers defiantly that it would be a family Christmas as usual. They had seen good years and bad years, and perhaps this was the leanest, but she was sure they would pull through. Alan was handling it all very well, she said: he wasn't in the least upset. She would cook the turkey and do the decorating, and she had just spotted a love seat that she was going out to buy. They could face in opposite directions, she said: she could sit in the shade and Alan could sit in the sun.

Perhaps they could also saw it in half and Alan take his with him. Because on the other side of Australia Bond now went sailing. Having spent several days on Sydney Harbour at the height of the crisis thrashing the opposition in the Southern Cross Cup, on 26 December he lined up his new yacht *Drumbeat* for the classic Sydney to Hobart race. In front of huge crowds, and with his Nine Network helicopter among the hovering TV crews at the start, Bond was at the wheel of his magnificent $3 million ocean racer to wave cheerily at the cameras. With a hot, strong north-westerly roaring off the land, he now made his exit in style: in blazing sunshine the invincible *Drumbeat* raced down Sydney harbour at the head of the fleet with Bond at the helm. By Sydney Heads, with spinnaker flying, she was already a hundred metres clear of the pack. Then she turned south, with the wind set fair for a record-breaking run to Hobart. In typical Bond style, the last entrepreneur was leaving his troubles behind. Back on land his executives were still struggling to stitch a rescue together. But Alan was confident that the banks would never sink his ship. Sailing had saved him in 1974. He had every confidence that it would so again.

As *Drumbeat* roared past, some could still cheer "good on yer Bondy". Even his critics said grudgingly that you had to hand it to him. But the bankers watching from their office blocks on shore were not amused. As one had remarked fifteen years earlier to Western Australia's Premier Sir Charles Court: "It's our bloody money he's spending." Now, if they had any remaining doubts about driving home the blade, they were surely dispelled. With *Drumbeat* on her way to Hobart, the banks rapidly advanced their schedule. On 27 December they had warned Bond's top two executives, Peter Mitchell and Peter Beckwith, that they intended to apply for a receiver. And two days later, with the absolute minimum of notice, they did so. Having given Bond Corporation just half an hour to repay $800 million, the bankers marched into the Supreme Court of Victoria on the afternoon of Friday 29 December and persuaded Justice Beach to appoint a receiver to Bond Brewing and all its subsidiaries. By the time the Bond executives knew what was happening, it was a *fait accompli*—the court had closed for its New Year recess and the breweries had been seized.

On *Drumbeat*, meanwhile, Alan Bond was still sailing on in blissful ignorance. Determined to crack the record, he had no faxes, radio phones or carrier pigeons to keep him in touch with what was happening. Hours later, he stepped ashore in Hobart, first over the line but too late to break the record. At the dockside, he was told the bad tidings, and was visibly shaken. It was a poetic and pathetic finale, the parallels with 1974 inescapable. Then the banks had refrained from pulling the plug, but now they had no such qualms. Perhaps only Alan Bond was blind to the fact that he no longer carried the hopes of a nation, he no longer was a hero. He had torn the mantle that the Australian public had bestowed upon him. The Great Salesman had thought himself immortal; he had imagined he could walk on water, but arrogance and pride had brought him down. He had said after 1974: survival is the name of the game; we won't be making those mistakes again. But he had, and this time it was surely fatal.

Eileen Bond was no doubt also shocked by the news. But perhaps it was doubly bad for her because on the inside pages of several newspapers was a picture of Alan Bond on the quay at Hobart. Whispering in his ear, on tiptoe, perhaps telling him some titbit of the empire's collapse, was Tracey Tyler, his pretty young air hostess. Never before had Alan Bond taken so little trouble to hide his affairs from public view. To the gossips back in Perth, it seemed that it might not be just his business empire whose number was up.

CHAPTER 24

Going, Going, Going...

Alan Bond, if nothing else, was a master at the art of survival. Like that famous Russian holy man, Rasputin, it would take more than a blow to the heart or a bullet in the head to make Alan Bond lie down. Although the receivers were already in control at Bond Brewing, and the creditors of Bond's other companies were demanding instant repayment, the indestructible Mr Bond did not give up. Chastising the NAB for its "outrageous behaviour" (apparently with no sense of irony), Bond Corporation now challenged the receivership and prepared to beat off a mass of other legal actions. And not only did Bond's empire strike back, it also won a major victory. After two months of apparently hopeless legal battles, and a court decision which confirmed the receivers' appointment, the full court of the Supreme Court of Victoria dramatically put Bond back in business.

The troika of learned judges who upheld Bond's appeal concluded that the manner of the breweries' seizure had been unfair. It was, as the judges remarked, "perhaps the most momentous *ex parte* order ever made by an Australian court"—given that assets worth billions of dollars had been transferred, yet Bond Corporation had been given no opportunity to put its case. The decision to appoint receivers was also, in their view, a misguided one. In fact, in terms of principles, just about everything was wrong with it. There had been no "imperious necessity" that could justify Bond Corporation being denied its say; there had been no agreement to pay damages in the event of the receivers being removed; and there had been no limit to their tenure or their powers. But, most of all, the judges pointed out, receivership was the wrong remedy anyway, because the NAB was only an unsecured creditor. Having lent its millions on something similar to a Negative Pledge agreement, the syndicate had no right to have a receiver appointed unless there was no other course of action available. As it was, far less drastic measures would have given the banks protection.

After two months under sentence of death, the Bond Group was therefore reprieved, the receivers thrown out of the breweries, and the locks changed once again. And now, looking at the evidence, it became clear that the banks had deliberately denied Bond the chance to defend itself. Having originally intended to wait until the New Year, and having intended to give Bond proper notice, they had rushed into the Supreme Court of Victoria on 29 December, just ninety minutes before the court went into recess for the long weekend. By the time Bond's solicitors, Parker & Parker, had been warned that action to seize control of Bond's empire was afoot, the banks' case was already in full swing. As Justice Beach considered their "urgent" application, a fax was lying in a tray at Parker & Parker's offices, 2500 kilometres away in Perth, waiting to be read. Since it had been sent as the proceedings started, and had neither been marked urgent nor accompanied by a phone call to say that it was coming, it was hardly surprising that no one noticed it in time. But it seemed that this was the banks' intention: they did not want Bond to put up a fight. Why they had acted in such a hasty and underhand fashion was a mystery but it threatened to cost them dear, because Bond Corporation declared it would sue for damages.

The banks' defeat and Bond's victory, however, were unlikely to change the course of the war, for the Bond Group still had no money: its assets were still some $2000 million dollars short of its liabilities, and cash was pouring out at the rate of several hundred million dollars a year. There was also a mass of legal actions ranged against the companies, any one of which could send the empire crashing. The European creditors of Dallhold were closing in, so were two sets of US bondholders, and so was Bell Resources. There was another $385 million due to be repaid to the NAB (under a loan to Bond Media) at the end of March, for which court judgement had already been given; a further $200 million was due to Kerry Packer three days later. And after that, the NAB would be back in court on 1 May with proceedings it certainly could win which would make its $880 million loan to Bond Brewing immediately payable. In sum, the position looked hopeless. And Bond's lawyers seemed to know the odds:

they were demanding payment up front for their services.

But by this time, Alan Bond also had more than the collapse of his business empire to worry about. At the beginning of March 1990, a special investigator was appointed to the Bond Group of companies with a brief to examine whether civil or criminal action should be taken against any of the companies or their directors. No individual was mentioned by name but there was a very real possibility that Alan Bond and his team could now be made personally liable for some of the Bell Resources' $1500 million that had gone missing—or, in other words, made to pay it back from their own pockets. The special investigator's net was cast extremely wide—he was charged with searching out *any* offence that might have taken place—but his specific terms of reference made it clear that serious offences were to be considered.

The choice of an experienced corporate prosecutor, John Sulan, as special investigator also made it clear that the enquiry meant business. A former Corporate Affairs chief in South Australia, Sulan had once been headhunted by the Hong Kong Government to pursue the notorious George Tan and his failed Carrian Investments. Now he was anticipating at least a year chasing Alan Bond and his companies at an expected cost of $2 million. It was certain to be the biggest investigation in Australian corporate history—just as the demise of Bond would be the biggest corporate collapse.

Sulan's first task would be to discover whether there were grounds for winding up any of the Bond companies or for appointing a receiver to protect property. Next he would have to decide whether to seek court orders for repayment of any monies lost—notably Bell Resources' $1500 million. Here he would be investigating under Section 542 of the Australian Companies Code to see whether any person was guilty of "fraud, negligence, default, breach of trust or breach of duty in relation to a corporation". And after that he would examine whether any criminal offence had been committed. He had been guided towards Section 229 of the Code requiring directors to act honestly in the interests of all shareholders, where a breach of the Code could bring five years in jail plus a fine of $20,000; he had also been directed to Section 230, which prohibits directors making loans to themselves without proper authorisation, where a similar maximum of five years in jail and a $20,000 fine applied.

But his task did not end there: he was charged with looking for other specified offences in relation to Alan Bond and his team. And he was then required to investigate whether any of Bond's creditors had received preferred treatment. It was no secret that the Hong Kong Shanghai Bank had reduced its exposure to Bond by $500 million or more in the closing months, and that the new Bell board suspected that some of the money had come from their $1500 million "loan". He was also briefed to look at whether the various Bond and Bell accounts were true and fair, and whether the auditors had done their job. By the time he had finished, everyone would have come under scrutiny. If he did his job properly, the Augean stables would be thoroughly cleaned.

Whether action would be taken against Bond was obviously a matter for John Sulan and his investigators, after examining all the evidence. But the omens

for Alan and his men were not good. While the
learned justices of the Victorian Supreme Court had
thrown out the receivers from Bond Brewing, they
had not been too kind about Bond and his team.
They had approached the case on the assumption
that "in view of a number of matters", the previous
judge: "was entitled to think that those who
controlled the Bond Corporation Holdings Group
included persons in high positions who could not be
trusted".

As for Justice Beach, he had certainly been in no
doubt, declaring himself to have "little faith in the
business practices of Bond Corporation". He had
also predicted that the Bell "loan" and the Hilton
deal would be the subject of future court action.
And he had been most unhappy with the way that
Bond had conducted its defence. He had suggested,
in effect, that Bond had tried to conceal the true
state of affairs.

> The persons who were primarily responsible
> for the Bond Brewing Holdings Group's deal-
> ings with the banks were Bond, Oates,
> Beckwith, Farrell, Noonan, Friegard, Cronin
> and Creally. By deliberate decision of the
> directors of Bond Corporation Holdings
> and/or Bond Brewing Holdings, none of
> these persons was called to give evidence. I
> can only infer that that was done on the foot-
> ing that had any of those persons been called
> their evidence would not have advanced the
> case for the Bond Group. An extraordinary
> state of affairs if I may say so.

Nor was it just people Bond had kept back from the Court:

> Not only did the BBH Group fail to call witnesses who could give primary evidence in relation to many of the issues before the Court, in my opinion its case was conducted in a manner designed to exclude relevant material. I have the clearest impression that the case for the BBH Group was conducted on the basis of keeping away from the Court as much financial and accounting information concerning the Bond Group as possible.

If Justice Beach's impressions were correct, it did not augur well for Bond when the special investigator got down to business, for the Companies Code gave him extensive powers to seize documents and demand answers from witnesses. The NCSC had in fact considered seizing relevant paperwork from Bond Corporation on the very day that the enquiry was announced, but had dropped the idea on the grounds that raiding Bond's offices would look heavy-handed.

The NCSC had been pushing for this special investigation since late November 1989 but had been held up by squabbling over wider matters to do with corporate regulation. Then, in order to get things moving, the Federal Attorney-General had thrown his weight behind it. There was no question that the enquiry was long overdue. It was now more than a year since Bond had taken the $1200 million from the poor shareholders of Bell, nine months since it had all been made public and six months since the first investigations had started, yet Bell's money had not been repaid and precious little action had been taken. It was true that the NCSC had helped instal a new board at Bell Resources who might now seek civil remedy. But, in the meantime, the money had been poured into Bond's bottomless pit—and yet another $300 million had been taken by Bond after the alarm had been raised. The regulators had stood by, apparently powerless to act, as the money was lost.

But in a broader sense, the special investigation was years overdue. For two decades in Australia, Alan Bond's private companies had been allowed to deal freely with the Bond Corporation public empire, buying or selling assets or taking a share of the action, and Alan Bond had put millions into his pocket as a consequence. There was a clear conflict of interest in the way that the entrepreneur was often on both sides of multi-million dollar transactions—taking a gain for himself when he was meant to be acting in the interests of all shareholders. There was also a conflict when his private company Dallhold received multi-million dollar fees from the public companies for doing it was not clear what.

On the evidence available to the public and to the investigators at the NCSC, Bond seemed on several occasions to have taken money from shareholders to line his own pocket. Whatever the circumstances that had allowed Bond to get away with deals like the Palace Hotel, the very fact that he continued to do so seemed to make his behaviour increasingly scandalous. Alan Bond had never cared much for the rules in any walk of life, but after 1987 his business practices showed increasing contempt for propriety. Perhaps the moves had become more desperate in response to the problems that threatened his empire, but there had been nothing in the past to match the $1500 million that had been taken from Bell Resources and nothing that compared with the $74 million "profit" invented on the Rome property. Nor, when it came to downright immoral behaviour, had there been anything quite on a par with the "sale" of Perth's Emu Brewery.

The Emu Brewery saga went back to 1981 when Bond Corporation had bought the property for $12 million. Late in 1989 shareholders were being asked to buy it back again for $200 million, almost twenty times what they had paid for it in the first place. Meanwhile, they had already handed Alan Bond's private company, Dallhold, a fee of $30 million for presenting them with this extraordinary opportunity. It was a quite outrageous transaction, for not only did the "sale" give perks to Alan, it also created an entirely bogus "profit" for Bond Corporation to keep the bankers and shareholders happy.

The Emu Brewery site set off on its extraordinary trip to fame in 1986, when Bond Corporation sold it for $35 million to Inkberry, a $2 shelf company run by Alan's mate John Roberts, whose Multiplex Constructions put up most of Bond's buildings. The site was then sold again in June 1988 for $120 million, or more than three times as much, with the "profits" being split three ways between Inkberry, Bond Corporation and Alan Bond's private company Dallhold.

The "buyer" on this second occasion was another mate of Bond's, Larry Adler at FAI. But in fact the "sale" was nothing more than a sham. As with the Rome property deal six months earlier, put and call options were attached to the Emu "sale" which made the whole transaction reversible. And FAI apparently always intended to reverse the deal: the company did not believe it was buying the property at all; it was simply lending $120 million to Bond and taking the Emu site as its security.

Despite the fact that the transaction was in reality a loan, Bond Corporation nevertheless recorded a bogus $45 million "profit" on the "sale". Meanwhile, and perhaps more important, Alan Bond's private company Dallhold helped itself to $30 million of Bond Corporation shareholders' real money as commission. Naturally, Alan did not advertise the pay-off in the Bond accounts, nor did he send a circular to shareholders telling them of his triumph. Indeed, he kept very quiet about it—which was not surprising, since the only service Alan Bond had given for his family company's $30 million pay cheque was to mislead Bond Corporation sharehold-ers into thinking they were making genuine profits.

It had been left to the NCSC to bring this transac-tion to light, and to its credit, it had managed to put matters to rights. Having investigated the Emu deal for several months and questioned Bond executives, the NCSC had reached the opinion, late in 1989, that no sale had taken place. It had then threatened court action under Section 542 of the Companies Code to recover the money. Whereupon Alan Bond had agreed to repay the $30 million plus interest and to refund the costs of the NCSC's investigation.

Unfortunately, by the time Alan Bond finally got round to paying this money, he had persuaded the authorities that Bond Corporation shareholders should settle for an IOU instead of cash. So the $30 million was duly "repaid" to Bond Corporation without any real money changing hands. Dallhold effectively settled its debt by agreeing not to collect money that it was already owed. On paper this may have looked fair, but there was little prospect of Dallhold ever collecting its money anyway. The $50 million of Bond class B subordinated notes that Dallhold agreed to cancel were in fact worth little more than the paper they were written on. When the Bond Corporation scheme of arrangement was drawn up in 1991, the bonds proved to be worth only $2.55 million. None of this money would ever reach the minority shareholders from whom the cash had originally been taken. Meanwhile, the NCSC did not attempt to mount a criminal prosecution on the Emu deal, because it did not have the resources to investigate further.

Back in the 1960s when young Alan Bond was starting in business, his father Frank had always worried about the boy. He had often remarked to friends that Alan would either end up a millionaire or in jail. In some respects, Alan had come a long way from his troubled youth in the 1960s and his run-ins with the authorities. But perhaps in another sense he had not changed at all. He did what he wanted, when he wanted, whatever the world thought of him.

As to whether he had achieved what he wanted in life, it seemed unlikely. He had wanted his name to be in lights—but the lights were being taken down. He had wanted to build an empire—but it was now in ruins. He had wanted to be Sir Alan—but he was not. Above all, perhaps, he had wanted to be congratulated, to be appreciated, to be loved. And Australia was turning its back on him.

But whatever one thought of him, he could

certainly fight, and for that at least he would be remembered. As one adviser to his bankers remarked, marvelling at Alan's refusal to accept the inevitable: there would be three things left alive in the world after a nuclear holocaust—cockroaches, rubber plants and Alan Bond. Bond, he might have added, would no doubt be selling rubber to the cockroaches.

CHAPTER 25

Gone

As late as August 1991, eighteen months after most people had written off Alan Bond, the battling entrepreneur was still fighting hard. But by this time, the dismantling of Bond's business empire had proceeded to the point where personal bankruptcy appeared almost inevitable. A consortium of banks which had lent money to Dallhold Investments was holding a fistful of personal guarantees with a face value of some $250 million, and was behaving as though it intended to enforce them. Meanwhile, Alan Bond's corporate career was all but finished. He had been thrown off the board of Bond Corporation and all its satellite companies; he had been removed from the board of Bell Resources and all companies under its command; and finally on 5 July 1991 he had been forced to resign from the board of Dallhold Investments and all its subsidiaries. Two days later this citadel of his

private business empire was handed over to the
liquidators. Significantly, the assets of Dallhold that
were seized included some 171 million shares in
Bond Corporation, which constituted the bulk of
Alan Bond's holding. Also in the liquidators' hands
was a major stake in Mid-East Minerals, which
some incurable optimists were to the last minute
still touting as the likely stage for another Bond
Lazarus act.

The fight over the remains of the Bond Group
had meanwhile deteriorated into a squabble over
scraps. In May 1991, the creditors, bondholders and
shareholders of Bond Corporation Holdings, faced
with a company whose net deficiency was around
$2000 million, and whose most valuable assets were
tax losses and the hope of damages from the West
Australian Government, voted for a scheme of
arrangement that would keep their company out of
a formal liquidation. There was just enough to
tempt them into a scheme that would melt down
Bond Corporation's remaining assets over five
years, and leave a company with a stock exchange
listing that might be saleable sometime in the future.
For the unsecured creditors there was the promise
that, in five years time, they might get back one fifth
of what they were owed. For the shareholders, there
would be far less. As a group they would end up
with just ten per cent of this company; the other
ninety per cent of Bond Corporation would be
handed to the creditors and bondholders in lieu of
the millions of dollars that they were still owed. The
name of this company of doubtful value had not yet
been settled, but one thing was for sure—it would
no longer be Bond Corporation.

The ordinary people who had put their faith in

Alan Bond over the years thus found themselves holding shares that were practically worthless. They would probably get a better return by recycling their certificates or burning them to keep warm in winter. Then, as they sat in front of their fires, they could drink their beer and reflect that the fortunes of Tooheys and Castlemaine were already improving, now that they had been separated from their Bond parent company and renamed Australian Federated Breweries. Those breweries, placed in receivership in January 1990, had finally been sold in September of that year to the partnership that had been first in line to buy them. Against all the odds and all the omens, they had ended up in the hands of Lion Nathan and Bell Resources, which was itself now flying a new logo, Australian Consolidated Industries. And with another sign above the door and different management, the business had taken on a new lease of life. Market share had risen again, new beers had been launched in spruced-up packaging, and the old success had returned. Bell Resources' shareholders had even recovered a small part of their $1500 million that Bond Corporation had earlier swallowed. If it was true that their share in the brewery came with plenty of Bond debts attached, giving them little equity, there was at least the prospect of creating some value; the improvement in the breweries' fortunes in NSW in particular suggested that it would not take long.

But the story of Alan Bond was now leading away from the breweries and the public companies, to the citadels of Bond's private business empire, and ultimately, perhaps, to his own private wealth. The first castle to be stormed by the creditors was

Dallhold Investments. After that, the banks with their personal guarantees from Bond could be expected to move in on the king himself.

Once upon a time, Dallhold had been an extremely wealthy company, or had at least appeared so, with large tracts of West Australian farming property, a fabulous art collection, a large portion of Kalgoorlie's Golden Mile, a nickel mine in Queensland, and the Cotswold estate of Glympton. But like almost everything associated with Bond the company was now completely bust. Not only had it borrowed several hundred million dollars in its own right, it had also in 1990 been required to guarantee several hundred million dollars more of old Bond Corporation loans because there was nothing left in the Bond Group that wasn't either hocked to the hilt or worthless. Dallhold had taken on this huge extra commitment when it was already in the hands of receivers back in January 1990, simply because it was the only way to get those receivers out the door and pay back $50 million to Standard Chartered, the bank which had appointed them. But in exchange for Dallhold's survival, Alan Bond had been made to pay dearly. The trio of banks who came to Dallhold's rescue, the Hong Kong Shanghai Bank, Tricontinental and the Bank of New Zealand, had driven a hard bargain. Not only had they loaded Dallhold with a huge additional burden of Bond Group debts, previously secured on a sheaf of worthless Bond Media shares, they had also extracted personal guarantees. If Dallhold ended up being unable to repay the banks, they had the right to go knocking on Alan's door for the balance of the cash.

By mid-1991, the bulk of Dallhold loans, both old

and new, were pledged against the group's share of the Greenvale nickel project in Northern Queensland, which was the only asset of significant value left in the Dallhold empire, and there did not appear to be sufficient security to cover them. At its peak in 1988, Dallhold's shares in Greenvale had been valued by the company's directors at $1300 million, which would have been more than enough to send the bankers home happy. But as with so many of Alan Bond's valuations there was more than a little hope in this figure. The 1989 Dallhold accounts had written down the $1300 million to nearer half that figure, and since then the value had more than halved again.

The purchase of Greenvale had been Bond's "best deal ever", or so said Alan Bond—a fantastic bargain for the $18 million of real money that he reckoned he had spent. But in another way it represented an opportunity gone to waste. He had come by a half–share in the project in 1984 through purchase of a controlling interest in the quoted mining company, Mid East Minerals. He had then bought out Greenvale's joint venture partner for just US$15 million. And finally he had persuaded the banks who had funded the original project to the tune of $1000 million to settle for just ten cents in the dollar. This he had borrowed from Standard Chartered, and failed to repay until the new banks came along. Meanwhile, Greenvale's cash had been used for other schemes that took his fancy. And here was where the chances had been missed. When Bond had taken over in 1987, Greenvale needed secure long-term supplies of ore to stay in business, since its own mine was almost exhausted. But by 1991, there were still no long-term contracts in place

because plans had not been properly pursued. There
was no port big enough to take the ore in the quan-
tities needed, and plans to build a vast unloading
facility in the Great Barrier Reef Marine Park had,
not surprisingly, been turned down by the Federal
Government. The ore was set to run out and
Greenvale's future was looking shaky. Meanwhile,
with a falling nickel price, the project was not earning enough cash to pay the interest on its debt.

By late April 1991, Dallhold had missed two
interest payments in a row, and the banking trio that
had saved Alan Bond and his company in early 1990
lost its patience. Repayment of the full US$390
million debt to these three banks was promptly
demanded, and six weeks later, on 5 July 1991, a
NSW court delivered the Greenvale project, or the
shares in the companies that owned it, into the
hands of the receiver. Two days after that, the rest of
Dallhold Investments came crashing down as a
different NSW court was persuaded that the
company was "hopelessly insolvent". Last minute
efforts by Bond's lawyers to strike a deal with the
banks were to no avail—neither Mercantile Credit,
the small creditor petitioning to wind up Dallhold
for a debt of just $640,000, nor the judge hearing the
case, was prepared to play. Waving talk of deals
aside, Justice Lockhart said "the company in view of
its parlous position is one that should be in the
hands of the liquidator". And with that, the death
warrant was signed. Sydney's *Sun-Herald* dusted
down the type that had been sitting on the shelf for
months and ran the headline "Bond Finished",
adding for good measure "See page 15".

Alan Bond was not in Sydney that day to receive
the snub of being relegated to the inside pages. Nor

had he been in court on the Friday to hear the judgement. He was in Perth at Dallhold's offices, or was on his way to them, to prepare for the liquidator's arrival. He had left his Mercedes in the underground car park while boxes of papers were being ferried to and fro in the offices above. Later that afternoon he was to be discovered standing alone in the foyer, in no mood to talk to wandering journalists. One financial writer was dismissed with an abrupt "Who are you?" followed by the advice that he was on private property and should leave at once. Bond's right-hand man at Dallhold, managing director Michael Cross, told those who enquired that night that Alan was "very disappointed that it has got to this stage". Just two days earlier, he had been brushing aside any talk of problems for Dallhold Investments and its owner. Now he was admitting that the banks had the power to make Alan Bond bankrupt if they wanted to.

Certainly there was nothing much inside Dallhold to hold up the advance on Alan Bond himself. The company's liabilities, the court had been told, were more than $1000 million, while its assets were agreed to be worth $17 million in a firesale, or $40 million with luck and time. There was undoubtedly more value in the Greenvale shares, which were now separately in the hands of the banks. And Dallhold's managing director was probably right in saying that the $1000 million involved a large amount of double counting. But there wasn't anywhere near enough. The banking trio alone were in for US$390 million and Greenvale was worth less than half that amount. There would therefore be a shortfall of some $200 million to send them knocking on Alan Bond's door, guarantees in hand. What they found there might well disappoint them, however, for Dallhold's managing director Michael Cross had indicated to the court that his old boss would be presenting an affidavit to the effect that Alan Bond's net worth was "negligible". In common parlance, he would be claiming to be skint.

Once the Dallhold liquidators had been appointed, the insolvency team from the accountants Duesburys moved as fast as they could to freeze bank accounts, secure assets and preserve the records so that they could later investigate where monies had gone—a task in which the new Australian Securities Commission immediately promised to help. They did not, however, immediately seize what remained of the private art collection, valued at some $10 million, which had been bought in Dallhold's name. Renoir's *Femme a la guitare* and a variety of works by Rupert Bunny, Arthur Boyd and others continued to reside in the special, secure air-conditioned environment that the insurers had demanded; that is, in Alan Bond's riverside mansion on the banks of the Swan. The said paintings and sculptures were mortgaged to the National Australia Bank as security for an $8.5 million debt, but the liquidators soon claimed them on behalf of all Dallhold's creditors, on the basis that the mortgage had been registered less than six months before the liquidation. Once again, there was the prospect of a legal battle to decide who would pocket the cash.

More serious legal action, meanwhile, threatened Alan Bond himself. Not only was he one of the largest debtors to Dallhold, owing the company $23.4 million, which the liquidator might seek to collect. But there was also the small matter of the personal guarantees. If either the liquidator or the banks came after him, the America's Cup hero and former corporate colossus would soon be in the bankruptcy courts, with every possibility he would emerge a bankrupt. If that indeed was the future for Alan Bond (and the banks had started legal action to recover their money), then he would be unable to act as a director, promoter or manager of any company in Australia (and several other countries including the UK) until he had been discharged. Even worse, given his love of borrowing, he would be unable to run up credit. But bankrupt in law would not necessarily mean that Alan Bond or his family would be broke in practice. As he had told many an interviewer over the preceding years, he was "personally secure". He was not going to be short of a bob or two—or even the odd million.

His personal wealth included the family house in Dalkeith, a vast pillared mansion on five levels, built on the banks of the Swan River, and including an acre of land. That alone, probably worth $10 million, was far from the reach of any corporate liquidator or action in bankruptcy. It was registered in the name of Armoy Pty Ltd, in its capacity as trustee for the Alan Bond No 1 and No 2 Family Trusts, and it had been in that ownership for fifteen years. There was also plenty more. It was true that by mid-1991 the Admiral's Cup yacht was up for sale, Glympton had gone, *Southern Cross III* had been sold, *Irises* repossessed, and Manet's *La Promenade* put to auction to meet some of the deficit. But there remained a fair number of properties in and around Perth that were identifiably part of the Bond family fortune. To begin, the three Fairlanes bowling alleys, plying a good trade and worth a few

million dollars, were safely in the hands of Armoy
Pty Ltd. Then there were the farming properties
ninety minutes north of Perth, held jointly by
Armoy and Yathroo Estates Pty Ltd; with their
42,000 sheep and 4500 cattle, these were worth $10
million or more. They had originally been bought
by Dallhold in 1987, but had been passed over to the
family trusts in late 1989 for a fraction more than the
original purchase price. As the transaction had been
stamped through the Titles office only two days
before the Dallhold collapse, the liquidator might
take an interest in whether the price was fair,
but would be unlikely to strike the transaction
altogether.

Back in Perth, and worth another few million
dollars, was a large block of land in the suburb of
Mosman Park. Registered in the joint names of
Susanne Bond and her mother Eileen, it amounted
to 14,900 square metres in a built-up area of the city
and was also utterly secure from the liquidator's
grasp, since it had been in the family for sixteen
years. Also in Perth, in the university suburb of
Nedlands, Susanne and Eileen had joint title to
seven strata units which had been in the Bond
family for a decade and might well be worth
another million dollars. There was also some land
up at Yanchep, registered in the name of Shield
Enterprises, another Bond family company, where
Alan personally owned the shares. And there was
an $850,000 unit in Perth that Alan had given to
Susanne in December 1990, although both of these
might be harder for the Bonds to hang on to.

As to what else there was, it was impossible to
say, because the law does not permit investigation
of private trusts. But it was a fair guess that the

Bond family had assets worth $50 million or more, with only a small proportion mortgaged. On top of that, there were one or two properties whose ownership was hard to establish: Upp Hall, the moated manor house in Hertfordshire, England, was not recorded in either the Bond Group or the Dallhold lists of assets, but this beautiful English estate had been used by Alan Bond as a weekend retreat, and had once been the centre of Susanne Bond's equestrian activities. With ten bedrooms and 1000 acres of prime farmland close to London, it was thought to be worth some $10 million. Until 1987 the house and land had been owned by the Wydgee Pastoral Company Pty Ltd, a subsidiary of Bond Corporation, but the estate had then been transferred to a company called Lindsey Trading Properties Inc, which was registered in Panama. Its backers remained a mystery. Meanwhile, the agent who had run the place for Bond continued to live there, Alan Bond and his executives had continued to go there, and even in 1991 it was still farmed by a Dallhold subsidiary. Finding out who was behind the Panamanian company would be a task for the Dallhold liquidators. They might also be interested in the ownership of a five-bedroomed, six-bathroomed lodge in Vail, Colorado, USA, which the Bond family used for skiing holidays in the season. Alan Bond was reported by local real estate agents to have bought the property in 1985 for half the asking price. It was on the market in mid–1991 for US$5 million. Whatever place this property and Upp Hall now held in the Bond portfolio, there was clearly no shortage of wealth in the family, regardless of any affidavits declaring Alan's net worth to be negligible.

Nor did Alan Bond behave like a man on his uppers. As one friend put it, he was still dining at the best restaurants and drinking wines off the top shelf. In mid–1991, as Dallhold collapsed around him, the gossip columns reported him as a recent visitor to Sardi's, one of New York's best eating spots, picking up the tab for forty people at the launch of his old friend Di Bliss's production of *Our Country's Good*.

Eileen Bond, for her part, was also reported to be enjoying herself and clearly still in funds. In July 1991 she was telling Perth's *Sunday Times* about her thirty-six hour dash to Bermuda to appear at Robert Stigwood's birthday party. As she told the tale, she had been smuggled into the Stigwood home, wrapped up in a brown paper bag and then presented to the music millionaire as his birthday surprise. On opening the bag, said Eileen, Mr Stigwood had fallen to the ground, unable to speak. Indeed, who could blame him? According to Eileen it then took him so long to recover that she thought she had "done Robert in".

Sadly, almost a year earlier, the more serious strains at Bond Corporation had helped do in Bond's former managing director and right hand man, Peter Beckwith, who had died of an inoperable brain tumour. He had suffered heart attacks in late 1988 and then became progressively weaker through 1989, though working almost to the end. Beckwith's importance to the Bond Group had been acknowledged in 1988 through the $10 million so-called Golden Handcuff payment, designed to keep him from going elsewhere. And unlike some of Bond's creditors, he had actually been paid his money. It was therefore a surprise when his estate was declared bankrupt shortly after his death in July 1990, not least because the $15 million house on Jutland Parade still stood as a living monument to his wealth. The magnificent mansion, it soon turned out, had not been a part of the estate. Up to Beckwith's death it had been owned by Peter and his wife Valerie as joint tenants in common, but it had then been transferred to Valerie alone. The valuable antiques contained therein were also unavailable to meet his debts. There were shares, land and an interest in a $600,000 motor launch, but there was still a deficiency of $3.5 million. In June 1991 it was reported that the Australian Taxation Office was seeking a further $5 million for unpaid taxes. The trustee, meanwhile, was contemplating legal action to grab hold of the Beckwith mansion.

There were fights looming on other fronts which threatened the financial health of the key Bond Corporation directors who were still alive. Peter Mitchell and Tony Oates were being sued along with Alan Bond for their part in the loss of some $285 million by JN Taylor Holdings Ltd, once a cash-rich part of Holmes à Court's Bell Group. In January 1991 the preference shareholders in JN Taylor, a group of large, conservative Australian institutions, had persuaded a court that the remains of their company should be taken to the corporate undertaker, for a thorough post-mortem and a decent burial, and within months, those shareholders were being offered the possibility of some future reward. The demise of JN Taylor Holdings had undeniably been due to the lending practices of its former directors, Alan Bond, Peter Beckwith, Tony Oates and Peter Mitchell who, in late 1989 and early 1990, had voted to lend almost all of JN Taylor's funds to Bond Corporation Finance and Dallhold Investments. At the time, both of these companies were in dire financial difficulty and needless to say, they had not repaid the money. But rather than wave goodbye to the $285 million, as so many Bond creditors had been prepared to do, the JN Taylor liquidator was suing Messrs Bond, Mitchell and Oates for damages. As a result Alan Bond's closest lieutenants now clearly faced the threat of bankruptcy too. And it was a bad omen for them that the new Australian Securities Commission had weighed in on the liquidator's side.

Alan Bond was also facing criminal proceedings which could do rather more than rattle the walls of his supposedly destitute estate. In December 1990 he had been summonsed to Perth police headquarters to be charged with fraudulently inducing persons to deal in securities, under Section 126 of the Securities Industry (WA) Code, an offence which carried a penalty of $20,000 or five years in jail, or both. According to the charges, Bond had persuaded Brian Coppin, one of his oldest friends and a wealthy WA businessman, to put money into the October 1987 rescue of Rothwells, while dishonestly concealing the material fact that Bond Corporation was receiving a $16 million fee. This fee, according to the report tabled in parliament by the Rothwell's Special Investigator, Malcolm McCusker QC, had been demanded by Bond as a condition for taking part in the rescue. Brian Coppin had told McCusker that he would not have invested his money (and lost it) had he known about the fee that Bond was getting. Bond had emerged that day from police headquarters, having put up bail of $100,000, to be met by a swarm of journalists.

Making no comment, he had been driven away, head bowed, in the back of his blue Mercedes. Later, he issued a statement denying that he or Bond Corporation had received the fee, denying that he had misled Coppin, and saying that he would strenuously defend the charge. He also declared himself "absolutely innocent of any wrongdoing".

But this charge, which was set down for preliminary hearing in September 1991 (and likely to come to trial in early 1992, if it passed the committal stage) was perhaps not the greatest of Bond's worries. Things were coming to a head elsewhere. Almost eighteen months after the appointment of John Sulan to investigate Bond's business affairs, there was still no official word of any outcome—except to say that action, or a decision to take none, was now close at hand. John Sulan had, however, reported to the new Australian Securities Commission, and they in turn had set up a task force in Perth and another in Adelaide to prepare briefs of evidence for the Director of Public Prosecutions (DPP). Their main focus appeared to be on the cash-strip of $1500 million from Bell Resources, and on the accounting treatment of the Rome land deal. More news was expected after October 1991, but the DPP's decision whether to proceed would clearly depend on what evidence had been mustered. All one could say was that the new Australian Securities Commission seemed keen for charges to be brought. When asked by journalists whether he expected the Sulan report to be published, the Australian Securities Commission's chairman, Tony Hartnell, had replied that he thought the Attorney-General, Michael Duffy, would want to keep the report under wraps "if there are trials pending". He then added, "So if all occurs as I believe it should, we aren't likely to see that report for some time."

Alan Bond's likely answer to any charges was that he was entirely blameless. Indeed, he had already made it clear that he believed his only crime was to take too little interest in how others were running the group. In a remarkable Bruce Stannard "Exclusive" in the *Bulletin* magazine in December 1990, foreshadowing Bond's "corporate comeback" Alan had been allowed to explain that it was his closest friend and colleague, Peter Beckwith, the former Bond Group managing director, who had steered the ship onto the rocks. At the time of Beckwith's death, Alan Bond had declared himself "desperately sad" to lose such a loyal friend, but now the great entrepreneur had recovered his composure sufficiently to tell the world that the critics had got it all wrong. The collapse of the Bond empire had been almost nothing to do with Alan Bond; it had been the fault of the media who had attacked him relentlessly, the fault of the banks who had lost their nerve, and was above all due to the errors and incompetence of Peter Beckwith.

> It's not entirely true that I was driving the company full throttle. Certainly, that is the public's perception. But in fact I was not at the helm for much of the time. Peter Beckwith drove the company. He drove it as if it were his own business. If I made any mistake at all it was to give him too much responsibility, too much autonomy. I was busy doing Bond International Gold, Queensland Nickel, Chile

and Hong Kong. I took my eye off the ball with Bond Corporation because I thought I had a competent man there. Now, Peter was ill for quite a lot of that time and maybe his judgements were out. People think I made all those business judgement calls myself. I didn't. I was in overall charge, I don't deny that at all. But I did leave the running of the business to Peter Beckwith and, as it turned out, that was the critical factor in the downturn. The company had too many balls in the air, and I was too busy elsewhere. The things I was personally responsible for we didn't have any problems with. While I was away overseas I thought the backyard was being looked after whereas it had grown too quickly... I know now that I passed on too much responsibility for running such a large concern. I very much regret that now.

There was no mention in the article of the disastrous purchase of New York's St Moritz hotel, where Alan had personally handed Donald Trump a US$110 million profit within half-an-hour of walking through the door (according to Trump). There was no recalling of the $800 million loss on Channel Nine, where Alan Bond's generosity in negotiation had turned Kerry Packer into an instant billionaire. ("You only get one Alan Bond in your life", Packer had said.) Nor was there any reference to the fact that the suicidal Lonrho venture had been Alan Bond's personal scheme, set on its way while Peter Beckwith was laid low with a heart attack. There was not even a hint that Beckwith had on several occasions almost resigned because of the deals that Alan Bond had struck on his way round the world. But in the aftermath of that article, all of these things and more were said. And while Peter Beckwith was no longer alive to defend himself, his wife Valerie certainly was. Her reply came the next day:

> It is despicable that after all the loyalty Peter showed to Alan and the company over twenty years, and after all he did to save Alan from his own self-destruction, Alan should blame Peter for the downfall of the company. Alan knows perfectly well that Peter worked himself to death for Bond Corp while Alan floated round the world.
>
> I suppose this is only the start, and as Alan's problems get worse he will heap further blame on a dead man. For a man who claims to be Peter's friend, he has treated Peter's family and his memory cruelly.

It was a suitable finale for Alan Bond's dazzling corporate career. Having lost $5000 million of other people's money—while his own family held on to a fortune—he was more than ready to blame the man who had helped him build the corporation, who had been by his side for twenty years, whom even he described as his closest friend.

Epilogue

There are times in the life of every nation when the financial system goes crazy: Britain in the property boom of the early 1970s was a notorious example, New Zealand was another ten years later. But Australia in the 1980s was probably in a class of its own. We were persuaded for a time that the boring trappings of accumulating wealth—like having to grow wheat, or dig coal, or manufacture things that people wanted to buy—could be bypassed or forgotten. We were told we could all just make *money* instead. The prophets of the new creed said that greed was good. And we oohed and aahed as they dazzled us with their tricks. It was not just in Australia that this mentality took hold—in the USA there were Boesky and Milken; in the UK there were the cohorts of Thatcherism with their me-and-money values. But nowhere were its champions more admired than they were Down Under.

Entrepreneurs like Bond, Connell and Skase
became Australia's heroes—its movers and shakers,
tripping twixt limo and ballroom under the adoring
glare of the TV lights. They were the idols whom so
many looked up to and wanted to be like, role
models for young Australians starting their working
lives. And their collective insanity became our new
religion. The worship of serious money. We saw
them glorified in the weekend colour supplements
and the glossy business magazines. We flew with
them on their Falcon jets, swam with them in their
palm-fringed pools, listened as they talked about
their vintage cars, racehorses, paintings and ocean
racers. We scrutinised their brilliantly clever deals,
which none of us could understand, and we
believed in what we thought we saw: here was an
answer for Australia and for all of us. The dull and
lacklustre past was over: in the future which these
men were creating, we could all get rich.

And then came the stockmarket crash. Not only
did their empires fall apart, but we saw for the first
time how their money machines worked: it was
ours and the banks' money they had been playing
with to make their fortunes; ours and the banks'
money they had now lost. And as the investigators
moved in among the wreckage, lighting up the dark
corners as they went, it became clear that these
entrepreneurial heroes had never been magicians or
messiahs: they had been tricksters, jugglers, and
gamblers, riding their luck on a rising market—and
taking us all for fools. When their party ended there
was nothing left but broken glass and the stale smell
of revelry: it was hard to believe we could have
loved them so much.

As far as their personal fortunes were concerned,

the entrepreneurs had often swelled their millions
by the simple device of paying our money to themselves—either in huge fees or by selling assets to
their shareholders for more than they were worth.
And as for the "profits" of their businesses, that was
even simpler: these had often been no more than a
lie. Their businesses didn't so much generate
money, as borrow it in increasingly large amounts.
When one deal went wrong, money was hauled in
on an even larger scale to cover the problem. They
appeared to grow fast because they had to, because
their losses demanded they do so. They grew to keep
the cash flowing in. Once the cash stopped coming,
there would be no more money to fill the empty
vault where the last tranche was supposed to be.

It was fitting in the great crash of the
entrepreneurs that Laurie Connell should be the
first to fall because, on a scale of one to ten in the
world of financial fantasy, Laurie was a ten. Even
ignoring Connell's close friendship with the
Western Australian Premier, Brian Burke, and the
Labor Government's three attempts to rescue
Rothwells at the taxpayers' expense, the story of
how Alan Bond's great mate Laurie lost hundreds of
millions of dollars of the public's money remains an
absolute scandal. But by early 1990 it was looking as
though Alan Bond's behaviour was almost on a par.

Typically, it was the chairman of the NCSC,
Henry Bosch, who went furthest in saying about
Australia's "entrepreneurs" what others were thinking. Without naming names, he said they were
"scum on the broad river of industry" and scum
that should be swept aside. It was time, he went on,
for others in business to declare the conduct of these
people unacceptable. They had inflated the value of

their profits to mislead shareholders, had siphoned off huge fees to make themselves rich and had sold private assets to their public companies to make large personal gains at their shareholders' expense.

Aptly, Bosch chose to make his remarks to Brisbane's Castlemaine Club, which shared its name with the brewery that Bond Corporation had taken over in 1985. Alan Bond was clearly one of the individuals Bosch had in mind, as he, perhaps alone of all the entrepreneurs, fitted the bill on all three counts. His own and his companies' history was a catalogue of unacceptable and immoral corporate behaviour. It was a particular disgrace to Australia because Bond Corporation was one of the nation's largest companies and Alan himself had the highest profile of all the entrepreneurs. Not only was he Australia's best-known businessman, he was the winner of the America's Cup, a sporting hero and the Prime Minister's friend. When criticism had begun to be directed against Alan Bond in the late 1980s, Bob Hawke had gone out of his way to give him his backing. Speaking in late 1987 at the launch of the Bond Corporation's *Endeavour* project, Hawke had dismissed the critics of Bond's business practices as out of order, saying:

> There's a lot of sloppy talk going around this country at the moment that somehow there should be no place in the concerns of a Federal Labor Government for the Alan Bonds of this world. Now I want to repudiate that nonsense unequivocally. It would be an entirely perverse concept if we didn't recognise the enormous contribution of the

> Alan Bonds and the other great entrepreneurs and risk-takers of our country.

A year later, Bob Hawke had done an about-face. Advised by his minders that he was losing votes because he was seen to be "mates" with rich tax-avoiders and bloated borrowers like Bond, he no longer made himself available to launch Bond's projects. He turned down an invitation to open Bond University because of "prior commitments", even though he had been asked several months in advance. He sought now to distance himself from Bond and all Bond stood for. It would have been entirely perverse if he had not. More than any other single person, Alan Bond had brought Australian companies and Australian entrepreneurs to the notice of the world. And if both were now held in disrepute, which they were, there was one man above all who could be blamed.

But Australia also had itself to blame for what certain businessmen had been allowed to get away with, because its system of corporate regulation in the 1980s was pathetically inadequate. Leaving aside the individual case for a moment, it is worth considering the difficulties that face any society in combating or preventing corporate crime. It is probably true of almost anywhere that it is easier to steal $10 million from the shareholders of a public company than it is to take $1000 from a company's Christmas Club. It is probably also true of any country that the white-collar criminal is far less likely to be convicted and sent to jail than the petty thief. But it is certainly true of Australia. The way we treat the two offenders is salutary: if someone robs the

Christmas Club and cannot pay the money back, the police will be called, the culprit will be taken away to be questioned, perhaps even put in the cells overnight. Prosecution and public disgrace will follow. The offender will almost certainly end up in jail and emerge to find his job has gone. But when a company director steals $10 million from his shareholders, if the corporate regulators find out about it at all, Mr Bigshot will be interviewed in his office, flanked by lawyers who are outraged on his behalf at the slur being cast on his name. He will probably say nothing, but his advisers will assure the investigators that the transactions are perfectly legal and have been approved by the top law firm in the country. It will then be the investigators' thankless task to prove them wrong. Even if they can gather the documentary evidence, they will be lucky to find a jury that can understand it and will convict. That is true almost anywhere in the world—corporate structures, clever lawyers and sheer complexity both protect and sanitise unacceptable conduct. Compounding matters in Australia is the fact that there simply have not been enough investigators to do the job.

Australia's small band of corporate regulators in the 1980s dealt with the problem in two ways: one by consigning important cases to the too-hard basket; the other by seeking "commercial" settlements. The NCSC in particular used the threat of civil action to get monies repaid. But while this solved a part of the problem, it could not deter corporate criminals from trying again. The message of commercial settlements is that stealing money is a game and a lucrative one at that. If you win you make $10 million or maybe more; if you lose you just pay it back, with at most $1 million on top. Since only one success is needed to fund an awful lot of failures, it is almost an encouragement to continue. The contrast with the SEC in America, where suspected offenders are taken away in handcuffs, or even with the UK, where the Guinness "conspirators" faced criminal charges amid great publicity, could hardly be greater.

The difference, though, between Australia and the United States (and to a lesser extent between Australia and the United Kingdom) has been that the United States takes corporate regulation seriously. Not only does it have extremely tough accounting and reporting standards but, in the Securities & Exchange Commission, it has several hundred highly paid and highly professional corporate policemen, with a budget of more than $200 million a year to back them up. Australia's NCSC, by comparison, had an annual budget in the late 1980s of $6.5 million. This was less money, in fact, than it costs to subsidise the buses for Canberra's schoolchildren. And even that gives an unreal idea of the scope it had for manoeuvre: after rent, running costs, and staff were paid for, there was a discretionary budget of just $200,000 to cover almost everything else. On this budget, the NCSC attempted to run ninety investigations at any one time, each of which would ideally employ a task force of twenty investigators. Yet its total investigation staff amounted to just a dozen people. For investigations to proceed at all, staff had to be persuaded not to claim allowances to which they were entitled. It is little wonder that the NCSC was forced to seek quick and easy commercial solutions, funding itself by winning battles and getting the losers to finance its next campaign.

But the problem did not start with the NCSC. In Australia, for decades now, the policing of companies has been absurdly weak. The expertise, the resources, and the commitment to attack corporate malpractice and fraud have not existed. These have been lacking in Australia because the Federal system left regulation to the states, where budgets were tight and the bandits were often too big to tackle; and because the public service will always lose its best people to the private sector (where they are paid four times as much to circumvent the rules than they have been to police them). But partly, too, it is because the pursuit of fraud has just not been given the priority it should be given in a civilised society. A notorious example of this is the 1974 collapse of Cambridge Credit; it took fourteen years before the matter finally came to trial when, not surprisingly, the charges were thrown out of court for being so late.

One can only hope that in the 1990s the problem of immoral and unacceptable corporate behaviour will at last be attacked. Special investigations into Laurie Connell's Rothwells and Brian Yuill's Spedley Securities have already produced a number of criminal charges. There is also a new and more powerful regulator in the form of the Australian Securities Commission, with far greater manpower and money at its disposal, which has aquitted itself well to date. There are moves afoot to tighten accounting standards, to monitor auditors' performance; Stock Exchange surveillance of companies has strengthened considerably. And perhaps, too, there has been a change in the moral climate. It may be too much to hope, but the highly paid lawyers and merchant bankers, with their Porsches and waterfront houses, who facilitate illegal and immoral transactions, may even notice the change and mend their ways. Certainly with the end of the 1980s an era has passed. One can only hope that in the 1990s a new one has begun.

Acknowledgements

There are several people without whose help this book would never have been written. Foremost among them is Kate McClymont, who did some of the most important and productive research. For their courtesy and help beyond the call of duty, thanks are also due to: Kate Owen and Adelaide Beavis at the *Four Corners* library whose assistance was invaluable; Julie Martin and others at the Battye Library in Perth, and Dan Midalia and his colleagues at Australian Archives. I would like to thank, too, those who knew the young Alan Bond or did business with him over the years, and shared their memories—I hope I have done them justice. I am indebted to the many journalists whose work on Bond I have drawn on constantly, and to the help that they have given, particularly Martin Saxon and Hugh Schmitt. Credit should also go to Richard Hamilton-Jones in England and Vicky Laurie in Perth, who did useful research; and to Caradoc King in London, Michael Sexton and Bruce Donald in Sydney, who each took some of the strain off me.

A special thank you to all the staff at *Four Corners*, but most of all to Sue Spencer, Peter Manning, Alec Cullen and Ian Macintosh, and to all at Transworld Publishing, but especially Angelo Loukakis, Judith Curr and Jacquie Kent. Last but not least, to my family, who encouraged me, kept me going and, most of all, put up with me both when I was home and when I was absent.